Electrifying

Calgary

Electrifying Calgary

a century of **P**ublic & **P**rivate **P**ower

W.E. Hawkins

The University of Calgary Press

ISBN 0-919813-43-7

The University of Calgary Press
2500 University Drive N.W.
Calgary, Alberta, Canada T2N 1N4

Canadian Cataloguing in Publication Data

  Hawkins, William, 1922-
    Electrifying Calgary

    Bibliography: p.
    Includes index.
    ISBN 0-919813-43-7

    1. Electric utilities - Alberta - Calgary -
  History. 2. Electrification - Alberta -
  Calgary - History. 3. Calgary (Alta.) -
  History. I. Title.
  HD9685.C23C34   1987   363.6'2'0971233   C87-091141-4

Funding for research and publication of this book was provided by The City of
Calgary. However, The City of Calgary has taken no official position and assumes
no responsibility regarding the content of the volume. The content of the volume
and any opinions or conclusions contained therein are the sole responsibility of
the author.

Cover photo credit: Bilodeau/Preston Commercial Photographers

Printed in Canada

CONTENTS

ACKNOWLEDGEMENTS

My interest in the historical background of electricity supply in the city of Calgary did not take root until the last years of my tenure as general manager of the City of Calgary Electric System, a synonym for the Calgary Electric Light, Heat and Power Department. Much of the record previously written, such as Robert Mackay's brief 1936 historical account, was very sketchy and anecdotal in character but nevertheless worthwhile. My only regret is not having exploited the memories of many "old-time" employees of the Electric Light Department who were still working in 1949 when I joined that organization as a graduate engineer. Many of these "old-timers" had tenure which extended back to the first decade of this century but their first-hand recollections are lost forever. The value of history is, with rare exceptions, not an endemic quality of youth and with no small degree of contrition, I dedicate this book to their memory.

When I first spoke to George Cornish and Alan Womack, commissioners of the city of Calgary, about my desire to write this account, I received their immediate encouragement and that support did not diminish over the three years of its preparation, for which I sincerely thank them.

Posthumously, I must thank the late Harry Sales, who, during his career as city clerk, zealously guarded the remaining old files of his office, which extended back to the time of Calgary's incorporation as a town in 1884. More than once Harry mentioned his concern to me about the preservation of these important early files during times when no one seemed to care whether they survived or not. Today they rest secure in the Glenbow Museum Archives and have been an invaluable source of material from which this account was prepared. Without the full support and help of the staff of the City Clerk's Record Division, my task at times would have been intolerable. Their patience in assisting me to locate old records is deeply appreciated. I single out Neil Watson, the young and talented staff archivist, for special thanks. His coordinating function between the Clerk's Record Office and the Glenbow Museum lent itself ideally to my need for information while I was writing most of this account in Delta, British Columbia.

Special acknowledgment is due to my retired contemporaries, Albert Bishop, Don Little and Edward Walker, who helped me to recall earlier events and keep them honest. Gavin Hanslip, the operations manager of the Electric System is a compulsive collector of older and more contemporary memorabilia, and I thank him for searching out material from his collections which was apropos to my needs. Eric Cameron, the public affairs coordinator for the Electric System, contributed freely from all his journalistic experience in helping me edit the manuscript. My personal secretary, Miss Joan Thomson, who has served me so faithfully over past years, simply picked up where she left off during those times when I returned to Calgary. Charles Dyson, a retired long-service tradesman with the Electric System, deserves special recognition for allowing me access to his thirty-year diary thus helping me greatly in the preparation of the manuscript.

This account was so closely tied to much of the early history of TransAlta Utilities Corporation (formerly Calgary Power Company, Limited) that regular consultation with that organization was required and this was provided freely and enthusiastically by Tim Finnis, advertising supervisor, and W.L. "Bill" Fraser, senior vice-president of Resource Planning. I also spent a very pleasant morning with D.A. "Happy" Hansen, now retired as the general sales manager with Calgary Power Limited, who had started with that company in the 1930s. His memories of earlier days were most helpful and appreciated.

Professors V. Nelles and C. Armstrong of the Department of History, York University, Toronto, were both very supportive of my project, and provided me with invaluable information relating to the early attempts of Max Aitkin to gain control of the Bow River for hydro-power development. Their help provided the door through which I was able to document the early negotiations between Max Aitken and R.B. Bennett and the city of Calgary for a wholesale power supply. My son, Richard, who fortuitously happened to be in Britain at that time, did the necessary research for me in the House of Lords Registry Office where the Lord Beaverbrook papers are maintained. I sincerely thank him for this as well as for his advice and help in the preparation of my manuscript.

The time spent with Marion Nichol, now deceased, one of Calgary's notable artists and the daughter of Robert Mackay, superintendent of the Electric Light Department up to 1948, was most rewarding and informative, as were the interviews held with Mrs. Tom Pinder, daughter of J. Harvey Wilson, the superintendent who succeeded Mackay. Graham McIvor, the long-time personal secretary to R.A. "Bob" Brown while he was with the city of Calgary, and later Home Oil, provided me with first-hand recollections of the man who became a legend in Alberta's oil industry.

Jack Sexton, a senior consulting engineer and executive with the Montreal Engineering Company, and now retired, provided me with many fascinating accounts of his early days with Calgary Power Company, Limited. His own recently published book on the history of Montreal Engineering, in which he traced the early days of Max Aitken's financial and corporate exploits in the Maritimes and Quebec, was very useful.

Finally, the person who assisted me most and who, in a very real sense, became the project manager was my wife, Dorothy. She typed and proof-read all of the manuscript material, made suggestions for improvements and, above all, tolerated my frustrations with extreme patience. Dorothy shared equally in the joy we experienced as we prepared this record.

The source material, both written and photographic, has come from the follow-ing principle collections and has been acknowledged and used with permission in the manuscript:

Source Material

1. Glenbow-Alberta Institute, Calgary, Alberta.
   Calgary Power Collection BB.2 C151P. (papers)
   City Clerk's Collection BE. 33 C151P. (papers)
   City Commissioners Collection

2. Public Archives of Alberta, Edmonton, Alberta.

3. Public Archives of Canada, Ottawa, Ontario.

4. House of Lords Registry Office, London, U.K.
   (Beaverbrook Papers)

5. Calgary City Hall, City Clerk's Record Division.
   (Council Minutes)

6. City of Calgary. Electric System Archives.

7. TransAlta Utilities Corporation Archives, Calgary, Alberta.

8. Records of Calgary newspapers from the collections of the Calgary Public Library, the Glenbow-Alberta Institute and the University of British Columbia.

The subject matter of this book, I concede, is rather esoteric and as such may not appeal to a wide spectrum of readers. I have tried to keep technical matters to a minimum although at times I could not escape their trap since they were essential to the story. The rest I leave to the reader's judgment.

Bibliography

Cashman, T. *Singing Wires*. Edmonton: AGT, 1972.

Foran, M. *Calgary, Canada's Frontier Metropolis*. Windsor Publications (Canada) Limited, 1982.

Gray, James H. *Troublemaker*. Toronto: Macmillan, 1978.

Hatcher, C.K. *Stampede Streetcars*. Montreal: Railfare Enterprises Limited, 1975.

Klassen, H.C. *The Canadian West*. Calgary: University of Calgary, 1977.

Murray C. Hendry, *Water Resources Paper No. 2: Bow River Power and Storage Investigations*, Ottawa: Dominion Water Power Branch, Department of Interior, 1914. [Trans-Alta Utilities Corporation Archives.]

Sexton, J. *Monenco, The First 75 Years*. Montreal: Montreal Engineering Company Limited, 1982.

Taylor, A.P.J. *Beaverbrook*. New York: Simon and Schuster, 1972.

Ward, T. *Cowtown*. Toronto: McClelland and Stewart West, 1975.

INTRODUCTION

The technology which allowed the development of electricity into a major source of man's energy needs in the late nineteenth and twentieth centuries is only slightly older than the City of Calgary. It is not unusual then that electricity would be a part of Calgary's development from its very beginning although it is surprising that this new technology found roots so soon in a frontier settlement spawned by a troop of North-West Mounted Police and, a few years later, the Canadian Pacific Railway. The application of electricity as a source for lighting the town's rough dirt streets sparked the first interest, and the town fathers were quite happy to welcome the first primitive electrical supply from a group of private entrepreneurs who included George Clift King, Calgary's second mayor. Once a supply of electricity was available it did not take long before the citizens of the frontier town saw the advantages of having the new energy source piped into their homes for lighting in place of oil lamps and candles.

The early town fathers were soundly committed to the principles of free enterprise and a free competitive market place as a reflection of their predominantly Anglo-Saxon origins. The pre-CPR era, during which their economic survival depended to a large extent on established trade routes into the northwest United States, undoubtedly contributed to the strong spirit of entrepreneurship. How then can we account for the fact that eighteen years after the introduction of electricity to frontier Calgary, the city was involved in the ownership and operation of an electrical utility which, on the surface, appears to be a contradiction of the earliest philosophical principles of its citizens, and certainly those of the town fathers?

The new frontier town urgently required building material in the form of lumber and lumbering promoters soon arrived from Wisconsin to evaluate the timber stands of the Kananaskis. It was not long before the pioneer Eau Claire Lumber Company was established by Peter Prince and his Wisconsin backers. Probably Calgary's most aggressive early industrialist, Prince saw the potential of his steam-powered sawmill for producing electricity as a by-product. Hence began the fierce competition between Prince and his early rival to supply the Town of Calgary with competing electricity service. Prince won the day for the reasons detailed in this narrative but he too became a victim of another private syndicate which sought to develop a hydro power source at Horseshoe Falls, about fifty miles upstream on the Bow River. For over a decade Prince ran his Calgary Water Power Company, Limited as a monopoly, having eliminated his competition. This state of affairs was a constant source of irritation to the free competitive market orientation of the mayors and aldermen of the early twentieth century. They were frustrated by Prince's obstinate position in his refusal to modify his terms for an extended streetlighting service so the new city council, with the overwhelming support of the citizens, finally decided to provide the service using its own resources. With excess generating capacity at its disposal, it was not long before the city was in full-blown competition with Prince and, in the years that followed, even the city took unfair advantage of its competitive edge. The increased pressure on Prince's company became a factor in its demise.

During the first decade of this century intense battles developed between private syndicates and the city of Calgary for water rights on both the Bow and Elbow rivers for the development of hydro power plants. In the end only one was successful, that of an eastern syndicate spawned by Maxwell Aitken, later Lord Beaverbrook, and his mentor from New Brunswick, R.B. Bennett. The success of this syndicate took concrete form in a Montreal-based company, the Calgary Power Company, Limited, whose immediate target was to corner the electrical needs of the then booming City of Calgary. The initial tenuous agreements between the company and the city were far from cordial but they have persisted to the present day. In fact, except for the naming of a Calgary High School after Bennett resigned from federal politics to return to England to live out his days as a peer, the present contractual agreement between the City of Calgary and TransAlta Utilities Corporation (Calgary Power Company, Limited) remains as one of the few substantive reminders of the legacy left to Calgary by R.B. Bennett.

Electrical power and politics have always gone hand-in-hand in Canada and we are reminded of this fact because most provinces in Canada, except Alberta, Prince Edward Island and Newfoundland, own and operate integrated province-wide power systems. Alberta still remains aloof from this pattern and two of the private electrical utilities remaining in Canada have their residence in this province. In fact TransAlta Utilities Corporation has the distinction of being the largest private power company in Canada. The electrical utility owned by Calgary is today a distribution authority only and it has learned to live with its electricity supplier in a relationship which, prior to 1971, had been of genuine economic advantage to the city. The municipal utility patterned its own financial policies to parallel, in most respects, those of its contractual partner. Since 1972 the varied regulatory processes of the provincial government have all but destroyed the earlier economic advantages enjoyed by the city by virtue of its strong bargaining position with the company. It is not without significance that the most recent contract between TransAlta and the city contains no reference to price since that is now determined by the provincial government and its agencies. In effect the province, by its regulatory authority and more recently its Electric Energy Marketing Agency, has succeeded in uniting the private utilities into a monolithic economic unit even though the two private companies remain as separate corporate entities. The city of Medicine Hat has, because of its remote location in the province, retained its autonomy with little senior government interference and the citizens of that fair city still reap the entire economic benefit of their municipally-owned power plant and distribution system with the lowest power rates in Alberta.

The City of Calgary Electric Light, Heat and Power Department was not without its array of interesting and distinguished characters. R.A. Brown, having devoted a quarter century of his life to the electrical and street railway departments of Calgary, stands out from all of them. His parallel interests in early petroleum developments in Alberta led to the discovery of the first crude oil well in Turner Valley, ushering Alberta into the modern world of oil.

In the electrical utility business it is axiomatic that the public takes electrical service for granted until it is no longer there when the switch is turned on, or until the regular bill for payment of service arrives. If this treatise serves to underline the political, social, and economic factors which have interacted over almost a century to provide electricity for Calgary, it will have accomplished its purpose.

W.E. Hawkins

Chapter 1

"CALGARY, CITY OF LIGHTS"

It is no accident that the present extensive municipally-owned electrical distribution network had its beginnings in the basic need, expressed by the earliest local government of the frontier settlement, for some method of providing nighttime illumination on its primitive streets for the protection and enjoyment of its citizens. The present public streetlighting system in Calgary ranks as one of the world's finest, not necessarily in the ornateness of the physical plant such as one would experience in parts of Victorian London, but by the measure of the quality and quantity of light distributed on every public road and walkway. As one of Calgary's earliest public amenities, the streetlighting system bears witness not only to past events but to the continuing achievements of one of Canada's most dynamic cities.

Some years ago when a local radio and television broadcasting company located its facilities on the high escarpment running parallel to the western limits of the city, it became known as "Broadcast Hill" and was a favourite place from which Calgarians could show off their city to visitors. The spread of lights viewed from that vantage point defined, as nothing else could, the extent of the city from Bowness on the west, sweeping northward, eastward and south to artificial horizons defined by a single continuous bright line against the black background. How did it all start?

A common story from early Calgary folklore holds that Peter Anthony Prince, one of Calgary's early industrialists, tripped over a broken plank in the wooden sidewalk while walking to his home one night. He is said to have vowed on the spot to seek means to provide street lighting for the citizens of the frontier town. However, Prince did not become a major player in the supply of electricity to the Town of Calgary until 1889. By 1887, Calgary was already enjoying some benefit from a streetlighting installation made under the auspices of the town's earliest electrical utility enterprise known as The Calgary Electric Lighting Company,

1

Limited. Mr. Prince's nighttime accident may well have provided the incentive for his decision to provide better, but certainly not the first, lighting for his fellow citizens.

Prior to 1879, lighting was still being provided by flickering candles, oil lamps or gas mantle lamps. Electricity, which was regarded as a novelty during the eighteenth and early nineteenth centuries, suddenly became the basis of a technological revolution with the invention of the incandescent electric lamp. Both Thomas Edison in America and Sir Joseph Swann in England had experimented with the production of light using an electrically-heated filament supported in an evacuated glass bulb. Both men achieved success independently with Swann's commercial debut taking place in Newcastle in 1880, just one year after Edison's success. At once all previous forms of lighting were rendered obsolete and the use of electric lighting in its new practical form swept the western world like wildfire. The "gaslight" era did persist into the twentieth century but by the end of the first decade it was also becoming a novelty as the primitive incandescent lamp of Edison's day rapidly improved in light output, efficiency and cost reduction. However, parallel with the development of the incandescent light source came substantial improvements in electric arc-lighting and these improvements played a large role in providing the "great white way" lighting of North American cities, including Calgary, well into the fourth decade of this century.

Before its incorporation as a town on 17 November 1884, Calgary had existed as a frontier community fostered by the arrival of the North-West Mounted Police nearly ten years earlier. At one of its first meetings after incorporation, the new town council, on 17 December 1884, appointed five standing committees for the following year.[1] One of these was the "Fire, Water and Light Committee" composed of Mayor George Murdoch as chairman and Councillors S.J. Clarke and J.H. Millward. It is understandable that during its early years this committee devoted most of its attention to matters relating to water supply and fire protection, matters of great importance to the infant town. While "light" may have been an essential part of the committee's mandate, without a supply of electricity few alternatives were available other than the existing oil lamps. In fact, the earliest record of any public interest in streetlighting was speculation about using oil as a source of energy, and appeared in the *Calgary Herald* on 16 January 1884: "The promoters of the City of Calgary are certainly enterprising men. We are glad to be able to state that they are in negotiations with the Naptha Lighting Company for the purpose of placing lamps on the main street and in front of the hotels on business squares." The Naptha Lighting Company left no trace of its existence but an 1885 photograph of the Beaudin and Clarke Saloon on the southeast corner of Stephen (8th) Avenue and Drinkwater (2nd St. E.) Street, clearly shows a cage-like lantern object suspended from a pole and this may have been one of the lamps referred to in the *Herald's* news item.

Beaudin and Clark Saloon, 8th Ave. and 2nd St. E.
The "Lantern" may have been one of Calgary's earliest street lights in 1885
before electricity was available.
Source: Glenbow Archives

Electricity arrived in Calgary in August 1887 when the Calgary Electric Lighting Company, Limited, of which we will hear more in succeeding chapters, opened the first central electrical power generating station. The *Calgary Herald* immediately championed the cause of public street lights:

> The question of street lighting has occupied the attention of the present council on one or more occasions but nothing definite was decided upon. There can be no question as to the desirability of having the streets lighted, especially during the long winter nights and we think the Council would be justified in incurring the necessary expenditure for that purpose. The kind of light that will best suit the purpose is a question for practical men to decide and the matter should be taken up without delay. The company which is now putting in the electric light for stores and houses would perhaps give favorable terms to the council for a number of street lights. There can be no harm in opening negotiations with the company and learning their terms so as to get an idea of what it will cost. We hope the Council will give this matter their attention at the next meeting.[2]

In a direct response to the editorial, the Calgary Electric Lighting Company made a submission to the town council for the installation of twelve street lights.

The *Herald* duly reported the proceedings:

> Mr. W.T.Ramsey, for the Electric Light Co. made a proposition to the council last
> night to furnish 12 lights of 32 candle power for $4.50 each per month. Coun.
> Martin strongly objected to such extravagance and said that 11 lights would be
> enough. It was, however, decided to take the whole 12 but there was a unanimous
> kick against paying the sum of $84, for lamp material and putting in (sic). Mr. Martin
> thought that it was preposterous to have to pay for the lamps and then pay for the
> light as well. Coun. Shelton was instructed to try and beat down the company on
> that item and report at a special meeting to be held tonight.[3]

The proposal from the Calgary Electric Lighting Company was referred to the
Fire, Water and Light Committee, which in turn recommended a one-year contract with the company for the provision of ten, 32 candlepower lights at a
monthly cost of $6.00 for each light. The lights would be turned on all night,
with the council retaining the right to turn them off early. The company, however,
objected to the counter proposal with the Herald again reporting in detail on the
conflict:

> It seems that the street lighting matter has not been settled yet notwithstanding that
> the council accepted a proposition from the company to light the streets all night for
> $6 a light. The company found that they would be unable to do that and accordingly
> wrote to the council last night making a new offer viz: to light the town till 4
> o'clock a.m. for $5 a light per month for ten lights or upwards. Councillor Shelton
> expressed his disgust at the way the company had acted and was mad enough to
> refuse to take the light at any price but his good nature soon reasserted itself and he
> agreed to rescind the motion accepting the first bargain and will enter into new
> negotiations with the company.[4]

It appears that the company's main objection to burning the lights during all of
the night hours was having to mount a further working shift to keep the generators running for that purpose alone. Happily for both parties the conflict came to
an end on 31 October 1887 when the council agreed unanimously that Mayor
King should enter into a contract to light the streets of the town. The contract
provided for the lights to burn until 4 a.m. each morning at a cost of $5.00 per
lamp each month. On 9 September 1887 the locations of the ten original lights
were listed in the *Calgary Tribune*:

1. Power's Corner.
2. The Tribune Office
3. Royal Corner
4. One in the middle of that block
5. Exchange Corner
6. Parrish's Corner
7. Presbyterian Church Corner
8. Methodist Church Corner
9. Corner Scarth and Atlantic
10. One at the Fire Hall

8th Ave. and 1st St. W., c. 1888.
One of the original eleven street lights can be seen attached to the pole on the right.
Its light output was the equivalent of a modern 40 watt incandescent lamp.
Source: Provincial Archives of Alberta

Unfortunately, the locations are addressed in such a manner that they cannot all be related exactly to present day locations. It is safe to say, however, that the original lights favoured Atlantic, Stephen, and McIntyre avenues between Scarth and Drinkwater streets, and early photographs of the period show that the roadway intersections received the most attention.

The first electric lights were incandescent and their rated light output of 32 candlepower was equivalent to a modern 40 watt incandescent lamp. By today's standards the light could hardly be described as spectacular but in 1888 it was sufficient to evoke a response from Robert H. Moody, a real estate agent with offices on West Stephen Avenue, that was akin to the "boosterism" of twenty years later:

> The Town, now only four years old, has a population of 3,000. In it are solid business blocks built of native free stone. There are also churches, schools, hotels in everyway first class for the age of the place. There are two daily newspapers and the town is lighted with electricity. In fact it possesses all the evidence of steady growth and increasing wealth.[5]

There are no records left to tell us of the exact day when the original ten streetlights were placed in operation but we can rest assured that it was a gala occasion if for no other reason than the novelty of the event.

Any prestige enjoyed by the Calgary Electric Lighting Company by virtue of being the first to provide the town with streetlights was threatened in 1889 when the proposal of Peter Prince to supply additional streetlights at discounts of up to 33 percent was presented to the town council. The events which followed are described in the next chapter but suffice to say that, the fortunes of the Calgary Electric Lighting Company were seriously impeded by Prince's enterprise which obtained a franchise from the town in September 1889, and was incorporated in November 1889 as "The Calgary Water Power Company Limited." As the town continued to flourish and grow, the town council, in late 1889, considered the need for extended streetlighting facilities and instructed the Fire, Water and Light Committee to call for public bids from both companies for additional lights up to a maximum of forty but not less than thirty including their regular maintenance. The tender documents gave the bidding companies an indication of the extreme limits for the new lights. They were given as the Bow Marsh (present Hillhurst) Bridge on the west and the Langevin and Elbow bridges on the east. Surprisingly, in view of Peter Prince's threat to undercut the prices, the lowest bid came from the Calgary Electric Lighting Company to whom the contract was awarded on 14 November 1889 with the Fire, Water and Light Committee finally confirming with the company "that the numbers of street lights to be taken on new contract be 40, and that the Company be instructed where to place lights by (the) Committee."[6] The forty lights were inclusive of the original ten installed in 1887.

The town council proved to be very impatient and less than one week after the contract was awarded it began complaining that the company was dragging its feet. A certain Mr. Watson, the manager of the Calgary Electric Lighting Company, appeared before the council on 23 January 1890 to defend his company and he produced letters and data showing that preparations had been underway immediately upon the awarding of the contract. All the material, he reported, was on hand and only the severe weather had delayed the placing of poles and the stringing of wires. The councillors then debated amongst themselves over the location of the new lights and whether the original map showing the locations of the new lights was correct. Some councillors thought that there were too many lights while others argued for more lighting in other public places and at the entrances to the bridges. However, the councillors finally agreed on the locations as shown on the original plan but made a surprising move by changing all of the 32 candlepower lamps to 50 candlepower, provided the company would agree to a rate of $2.00 per month for all of the lamps. The company agreed and the contract was amended to continue the lighting service commencing 1 March 1890. The *Calgary Herald* was obviously well satisfied with the ending of its campaign championing town streetlighting:

> Lamps will be extended to Bow Marsh bridge, to Elbow bridge and Langevin bridge. There are to be two lights each on Osler and Scarth Sts., south of the railway. When the bargain was completed all present expressed themselves well satisfied, and so will the taxpayers be pleased when the first of March comes and

the lights are turned on. Calgary will then be not only the best lighted but the cheapest lighted town in Canada.[7]

The *Herald's* opposition, the *Calgary Tribune*, was hardly as enthusiastic but did report a detailed location of all the newly acquired lights.[8]

A further extension which would have added ten more lights was requested by the Fire, Water and Light Committee on 25 August 1890 and after debate it was decided to delay the request because a new civic election was in the offing. The matter was referred back to the committee and in February 1891 the new town council accepted an offer from the Calgary Electric Lighting Company to add an additional eleven 50 candlepower and thirty 32 candlepower lights with the locations to be determined by the committee. The new additions were never made because the Calgary Electric Lighting Company was now in financial difficulty due to competition from the Calgary Water Power Company Limited in which its Managing Director, Peter Prince, still retained a financial interest. The town council wasted no time in asking Prince to continue to supply the lighting service. His initial terms were $1.25 per month for each 16 candlepower lamp installed with the town to pay for the installation costs and repairs. Prince's offer to continue the lighting service using lamps of only one-third to one-half of the light output of the existing lamps was a clear indication that he did not take the overtures of the town council very seriously and, in fact, all of his subsequent dealings with the Calgary council were marred by mutual distrust.

The town council struck a special committee to discuss with the now troubled Calgary Electric Lighting Company its ability to continue with the contract to light the town streets. All of the council's efforts during the remainder of 1892 to keep the old company in operation failed and by November the company was in receivership. The recently acquired streetlights now faced the bleak prospect of being rendered inoperative and the council, having no alternative, directed the Fire, Water and Light Committee to determine from Prince his best terms for lighting the streets of the town.

For a brief period during 1893 the town council gave consideration to acquiring the assets of the defunct Calgary Electric Lighting Company but soon gave up the idea. They did, however, decide that an arc lighting system was preferable to the incandescent lights which were in place. The question now facing the town council was whether it should install a town-owned plant or contract with Prince's company for new streetlighting. To further complicate the question, Councillor E. Watson had a brother who proposed that the town investigate the use of gasoline lamps. He offered to provide 100 lamps of 25 candlepower and to "take care of them for $1,000 per year."[9] Watson argued that the gas lamps he was proposing were being used in St. Paul, Minnesota, but his offer fell on deaf ears. The debate carried on throughout the spring and summer of 1893.

Everyone was in favour of having the streetlighting restored with many of the councillors adamant that the town should own its plant rather than contract with

Prince. The Fire, Water and Light Committee recommended a contract with Prince at a council meeting which, consistent with any matter before council in which Prince was involved, gave "rise to considerable discussion, which, at times, was rather acrimonious."[10] As if this were not enough, another new aspiring private enterprise calling itself "The Calgary Electric Light, Power and Heating Company" threw its hat into the ring. As the town had done earlier, this company had given consideration to buying the assets of the original Calgary Electric Lighting Company but according to its representative, Mr. Peter McCarthy Q.C., had decided instead on the option of a new plant to supply power for both public and private use in direct competition with Prince's company. According to McCarthy, his company had the backing of "men of capital...perfectly reliable and capable to carry out any contract they entered into."[11] On 31 May 1893 the council received a petition from McCarthy requesting that no decision on streetlighting take place without a public tender first having been called, despite the recommendation already tabled from the Fire, Water and Light Committee for a new contract with Prince's company. The council agreed and a public tender was called on 13 June 1893. The only bid received was from McCarthy's company. Peter Prince, obviously holding this potential competitor in contempt, did not even bother to submit a proposal.

McCarthy's company was awarded the contract on 3 August 1893 for a period of ten years. The contract, at best, was very tentative since the new company had not even made a start on its proposed power plant and so not wanting to be without any streetlighting during the oncoming winter months, the council requested the Calgary Water Power Company to provide "about 24 street lights for the coming season (of) about 4 or 5 months."[12] Prince, however, was not about to agree to this request for temporary lighting, claiming that the only way he could afford to add the additional machinery was if he had a five-year contract. The *Herald* was not the slightest bit happy over the turn of events: "the unwillingness of the council to enter into a long term contract with anyone now that their period of public service is drawing to a close...makes the probability almost a certainty that we will be without street lights for some time to come."[13]

And so the streets of Calgary went unlighted during the winter of 1893-94. To make affairs even worse, McCarthy's company which now held the contract for streetlighting was unable to find a location for its proposed electricity generating plant and the company quietly died.

The City of Calgary, having been incorporated by the Legislative Assembly of the North-West Territories on 16 September 1893, was now left with two alternatives: either to build its own plant or to negotiate a contract with the Calgary Water Power Company. Both of the options were considered. In May 1894 city council decided to raise $35,000 "for the establishment of an electric light plant by the Corporation."[14] Just what precipitated this move is not exactly known but it was without doubt assisted by several lobbies from electrical equipment manufacturers all of whom painted glowing reports to council of the profits which were available to it under municipal ownership. By-Law 230 was prepared for this purpose and given its first reading on 1 May 1894. Neither of the two local newspapers were very warm to the idea of a city-owned lighting plant with the *Herald* arguing, on 11 May, that any experimentation was better left to private enterprise provided the service could be obtained in a satisfactory manner. The *Calgary Tribune*, which had been a staunch supporter of Prince's company since its inception, postulated that the city was far too young to have enough experience to operate a civic plant at a profit and that Mr. Prince should be given the contract unconditionally.[15] All subsequent readings of the by-law were abandoned and the way was cleared for the Calgary Water Power Company to be awarded the streetlighting contract.

The city council entertained a detailed hand-written proposal from Prince and on 5 June 1894 entered into a contract with the Calgary Water Power Company. The contract provided for twenty-five or more 1,200 candlepower arc lights to burn all night at a cost of $7.00 per month for each light. A novel feature of the contract was its provision for "moonlight" service whereby the lights would operate "from dark to one-half hour after the moon rises"[16] for which an allowance of $5.00 per month per lamp could be achieved. The agreement was for a

8th Ave. S. at Centre St., c. 1900.
One of Peter Prince's 1200 candlepower arc lights.
Source: Provincial Archives of Alberta

five-year period during which the company would add lights at the city's request. The limits of the area to be lighted were specified on the east by the Elbow River, on the south by the Corporation Line (present 17th Avenue), on the west by present 7th Street and on the north by the Bow River. Calgary had its public streetlighting again after almost two years of darkness. The new arc lights were to be in operation by 1 September 1894 but the company was granted an extension because of damage to the new dynamo suffered while it was in transit. Even with a new contract which ensured that the streets would again be lighted, bad feelings persisted between the council and Prince.

The first lights started to appear shortly after 30 October 1894 and immediately the council disputed the payment of the company's first account because it felt that the lights were not being turned on early enough and often were not burning brightly enough. Prince responded in an equally autocratic manner: "If the city refuses to pay our accounts under such a pretext we have no fear of applying to the court to decide in the matter."[17] The city solicitor, Arthur L. Sifton, advised the council that since the city had received some benefit outside of the contract period while Prince was experimenting with the lights during their installation, the matter should be dropped, which it was. Apart from a defeated motion in January 1895 to terminate the contract with the company, nothing of any significance transpired until after the expiration of the contract at the end of September 1899 when the city clerk advised Prince that Calgary would no longer be responsible for the lighting of public buildings and streets. Prince replied curtly that at the end of September "we shall discontinue them, unless satisfactory arrangements are made in the meantime."[18] Satisfactory arrangements between the parties were made when the city agreed to take the streetlighting service on a temporary month-to-month basis at $6.25 per month for each lamp with either party reserving the right to terminate upon one month's notice. At least the lights did not go out and this arrangement continued until the early summer of 1900 when the city proposed a new contract to the Calgary Water Power Company. The contract contained an option clause allowing the city to purchase the plant that was being used to supply the city streetlights.

The company submitted a new offer which provided for new enclosed 1200 candlepower arc lights to replace those installed under the 1894 contract, and a five-year contract at $65.00 per light per annum with any additional lights requested by the city beyond the extent of the company's power lines requiring an extra charge for installation. In response to the city's proposal the company offered an alternative option to sell the existing streetlighting plant to the city at 10 percent below cost. The city could then run its lines on company poles in return for payment of one-half of the cost of all the poles required to light the streets. The electrical power to operate the streetlights would be supplied by the company at $35.00 per horsepower per annum on a "moonlight schedule" with additional charges to cover line losses and with the company undertaking repairs at a reasonable charge to the city. The company's proposals were not seriously considered by the council since by now several councillors believed that the city should own and operate its own streetlighting plant. Simultaneously another offer was made to the city by the E.S. Harrison Company Ltd. of Winnipeg, who billed themselves as electrical engineers, to install a lighting plant in Calgary if the city would grant them a franchise similar to the one held by the Calgary Water Power Company.[19] Prince, as the managing director of the Calgary Water Power Company, smartly countered the Harrison offer by meeting their rates and further proposing the addition of a new auxiliary steam plant "so that there will be no break in the light service to either the City or public."[20] The Harrison proposal was quickly dropped although a by-law had been drafted which would have granted the franchise. The undercurrent of opinion in the city council suddenly surfaced in August 1903 with the approval of a money by-law to raise $30,000 for the purpose of establishing an electric lighting plant, only to have it rejected by the electors on 7 September 1903. A second attempt to revive the by-law was made a month later but was abandoned after second reading when it was discovered that one of the councillors who had voted for the by-law was not qualified because his seat had previously "been declared vacant owing to absence."[21]

Getting nowhere with its plan for a municipally-owned plant, the council again approached the Calgary Water Power Company for a new contract of five or ten-years duration including an option, at the end of five years, to purchase that part of the company's power plant which was used to supply municipal streetlighting. The Fire, Water and Light Committee recommended a contract for at least sixty-five 1,200 candlepower arc lights but some of the councillors wanted to delay the decision because, with the recent discovery of natural gas in the Calgary area, there was the possibility of using gas lights. Despite this objection a public tender was issued and the Calgary Water Power Company, along with the major electrical equipment manufacturers, were invited to submit proposals for lighting the streets of Calgary. In a letter written by City Engineer F.W. Thorold to one of the manufacturers, Thorold confirmed that in 1904 there were only twenty-five arc lights operating in the city and this was exactly the same number provided under Prince's 1894 contract. Thorold went on to say that, "There is great disappointment with the amount and quality and price of the light supplied and...we cannot make any satisfactory terms with the Company now supplying light."[22] However, the only bid received was from Prince's Calgary Water Power Company for eighty-five 1,200 candlepower arc lights at $85.00 each per year, a ten-year contract and an option for the city to purchase the streetlighting plant at an arbitrated value at the end of the contract.

The Fire, Water and Light Committee recommended acceptance of Prince's offer arguing that the city did not have an alternative because it had rejected Harrison's previous offer. Although the committee was concerned about some of the terms of the proposed contract, it felt that the conditions were the best that the city could hope to negotiate with Prince. Prince was invited to the next council meeting to discuss his contract with the councillors. At that meeting the council was successful in negotiating a five-year contract at a price of $80.00 per light per annum with the option to purchase the company's streetlighting plant at the expiry of the contract at cost. A new contract was quickly drafted but both company and city solicitors drew attention to the fact that continuation of the contract beyond the five-year term as an additional option desired by both parties would require approval of the ratepayers.[23] Both the company and city council were now backed into a corner since neither party wished to take the matter to the electorate for approval and this almost innocuous issue finally caused the city to break with Prince's company. The council expressed the fear that negotiations with Prince were nearing an end and "the labours of the entire summer had gone for nothing."[24] The following day, on 29 October 1904, Prince confirmed his position in a newspaper release published in the *Calgary Herald* advising his readers that his proposal could not entertain a termination of contract at the end of five years because he would have to "throw $5,000 worth of machinery etc., on the scrap iron heap," and he now preferred a referendum of the ratepayers to settle the matter. Prince seems to have made his point because on 10 November the council agreed to a ten-year contract with the options which would be submitted to the ratepayers for their final decision. However, a new concern reared its head in council. How was the purchase price of Prince's plant to be determined at the end of five years?

Council decided that it wanted the terms of arbitration for the purchase price clearly spelled out in advance in the contract and in the event that negotiations with Prince failed altogether, Councillor O.H. Bott gave notice of his intention to "introduce a by-law providing for a Municipal Electric Light Plant."[25] That the motion was carried at the next council meeting is sufficient evidence of the undercurrent of suspicion that the council held towards a new contract with the Calgary Water Power Company. On 24 November 1904 the council gave first and second readings to By-law 562 authorizing the city to raise the sum of $60,000 for an electric light plant. For the first time the council and Prince, along with his solicitor, R.B. Bennett, were faced with the presence of a large crowd of citizens who were vitally interested in the outcome of the debate. The *Calgary Herald* reported that the decision by the council to proceed with a municipal lighting plant "was greeted with cheers of the crowd present."[26] Prince wrote to the city clerk stating that he could not entertain a contract with the city since there was now no guarantee of acceptance of any contract submitted to the ratepayers for approval. The show of public support for a municipally-owned lighting plant had given him understandable cause for concern.

On 16 March 1905 just when it appeared that any further discussions between Prince and the city were impossible, Councillor R.C.Thomas presented a new offer which he had quietly negotiated. Thomas announced that he had "lately felt grieved that the city council and Mr. Prince were not better friends."[27] Prince's new offer proposed a reduction of $5.00 monthly from his previous offer and some minor reductions on the cost of private domestic lighting which was aimed at regaining public support. Much discussion followed the Thomas proposal and the matter was referred to a special committee for a recommendation. Coincidentally with this decision to review a new proposal from Prince, the quotations for prices on the city-owned plant, which had received the approval of the ratepayers on 20 December 1904, were beginning to arrive and they were very favourable. The city solicitor, J.B. Smith Q.C., cleared the last hurdle by giving his opinion that there was nothing in Prince's original 1894 contract which prevented the city from installing and operating an electric lighting plant for the provision of domestic lighting to the citizens of Calgary. On 27 March 1905 the council rejected any final effort at a compromise with the Calgary Water Power Company by a vote of six to four. The City of Calgary now assumed sole responsibility for lighting its streets.

Considering all of the delays and debates of the previous five years it was remarkable that the city managed to proceed with such dispatch to get its own streetlighting system in place. The specifications for the new municipal plant consisted of five sections, of which the last one covered all of the material required to install the streetlighting system. The *Calgary Herald*, a staunch supporter of the new municipal project, announced that "gangs of men are at work day and night...(and) there are strong hopes that the lights may be turned on for street service by the middle of the month."[28] The original number of city-owned streetlights was ninety of which forty were located in the central city core between 7th and 11th avenues from 4th Street W. to 4th Street E. The remainder reached into the surrounding residential areas. The lights were first illuminated for testing purposes on Saturday morning, 2 December 1905, and by that evening eighty of the new arc lights were shining brightly. The first city lights were enclosed alternating current arc lamps of 1,200 candlepower each. Unfortunately, none of these original lamps have survived nor do surviving records provide any information regarding the identity of the manufacturer. Electrical service to operate the new lights was provided by means of three series electrical circuits originating from the new Atlantic Avenue power plant located on the northeast corner of present 9th Avenue and 5th Street W. James F. McCall, chief engineer of the new plant, left a handwritten record of the areas serviced by the new arc circuits.[29] Number 1 circuit extended north of 8th Avenue, number 2 circuit serviced the area south of the CPR tracks, while number 3 circuit operated the lights along 8th and 9th avenues. It did not take long before petitions were being received by the council for the extension of streetlighting services, the first coming from ten citizens who wanted the service extended along 8th, 9th, and 10th Streets West to benefit their properties.

An interesting and little known aspect of Calgary's streetlighting is that between 1910 and 1918 gas lighting was used in East Calgary from the Elbow River Bridge to near 15th Street E. extending on both sides of 9th Avenue. The local Calgary Natural Gas Company, of which A.W. Dingman was the managing director, had installed the earliest gas lights in 1907 when five 500 candlepower

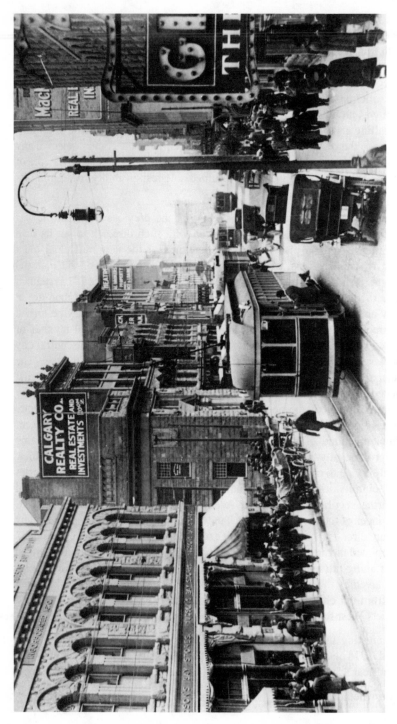

8th Ave. at Centre St., c. 1910.
Showing the original city-owned 1200 candlepower arc lights.
Source: Glenbow Archives

gas lights were placed on 1st Street W. outside the company's offices. In August 1910 city council gave approval for the Calgary Natural Gas Company to install gas lighting in the east Calgary location, consisting of twenty-five 700 candle-power lights along 9th Avenue. The original plan was altered to 1400 candle-power lights and on 10 May 1911 the *Calgary Albertan* reported that gas lamps were illuminated on 9 Avenue east of the Elbow River, along Pearce Avenue and in the Walkerville district:

> The gas was first lighted on Monday night and has made a wonderful transformation in the appearance of that part of the city east. The light is much clearer and steadier and more mellow than the electric arc lights. Its superiority over the electric lights is very apparent where the two lights are close together, and there is little doubt that it will be favored as soon as the proposed supply is piped to the city.[30]

Only a month after the glowing report, the extension of gas lighting to all of east Calgary north and east of the CPR tracks was turned down because the annual cost of $80.00 per light was considered too expensive. The city commissioners, who by this time had taken over all of the previous responsibilities of the old Fire, Water and Light Committee, recommended that the gas lighting be replaced by electric lights in the following year and so Calgary's brief fling with the "gas light" era ended abruptly. It is unfortunate that so little information about Calgary's gas lights has survived.[31]

The early lights installed by both Peter Prince and the city depended on a electric arc sustained between two carbon rods. The light produced was largely from the glowing ends of the heated carbon rods rather than from the electric arc itself. The number of alternating current arc lights of the type originally installed by the city never exceeded 260 and unfortunately none of them have survived. Between 1913 and 1920 they were converted to 200 watt tungsten filament incandescent lamps but still operated in series circuits. Some time prior to 1910, a brighter and more efficient arc lighting source was introduced for lighting streets. It was variously known as a "luminous" or "flaming" arc light under a trade name such as "Magnetite." It depended upon direct current as a power source and utilized a single adjustable carbon electrode and a fixed copper electrode between which an electrical arc was drawn. The carbon rod contained chemicals which, when vapourized by the heat of the electrical arc, produced an intensely bright arc flame. City Commissioner A.G. Graves had seen some of these lamps in operation during his travels and, on 15 August 1910, recommended to the council that fifty of these new arc lights be ordered to replace the original lights installed along 9th Avenue in 1905. "These lamps," said Graves, "will produce a brilliant illumination in the business section of the City and will consume less current than our present arcs, and maintenance expenses will be considerably reduced."[32] Public reaction to the experimental installation would determine whether the use of the new lights would be extended. In a lengthy

Pedestal-mounted "Flaming Arc" lights on 7th Ave. c., 1915.
Source: Electric System Archives

article under the headline, "Our Great White Way," dated 9 November 1910, the *Calgary Herald* extolled the new lights, expecting them to be "aglow by Christmastide":

> When the ornamental street lights are installed, and there are several petitions for these lights now on certain streets, the city will fairly bask in electrical rays. In Edmonton the people will think a huge gas well has been struck down south, or a new comet is appearing on the southern horizon.

The new flaming arc lights received instant public acceptance. Consequently an earlier scheme to relight downtown streets using 100 watt incandescent lights on five-cluster ornamental standards was abandoned in favour of the high intensity arc lights along 7th and 8th avenues from 4th Street W. to 4th Street E. along with the adjoining streets between 6th and 9th avenues. However 9th Avenue retained incandescent lighting between 1st Street W. and 1st Street E. fronting the CPR properties using five-cluster ornamental standards. The intense white light, shielded from human eye by opaque glass enclosures, flooded the surrounding areas without the benefit of optical control which would come in later years. The two major downtown avenues became Calgary's "Great White Way." In

The "Flaming Arc" lights which turned 7th and 8th Aves.
into Calgary's first "Great White Ways." c. 1912.
Source: Provincial Archives of Alberta

8th Ave. and 4th St. W. c. 1911.
A 1906 arc light is seen on the nearest pole. Along 8th Ave. the new
"Flaming Arc" lights have been installed.
Source: Electric System Archives

"Cluster-mounted" incandescent standards on 9th Ave., c. 1915.
Source: Electric System Archives

1927, after an extended trip into the United States, R.A. Brown, general superintendent of the city's Electric Light and Street Railway departments, noted the
following in his detailed report to council:

> Street lighting in Chicago, particularly on State Street was the best seen in all of the
> towns visited...the class of lights used on 8th Avenue in Calgary, compare very
> favourably with the white way lighting of the cities visited. The number of high
> class electric signs are not as plentiful in Calgary...and I believe that we should put
> forth an effort to encourage the installation of more signs in this City, for a well-
> designed and illuminated sign is not only a good advertisement; but it is a real asset
> from the point of view of street illumination.[33]

Anyone who can remember back to the 1930s will recall those luminous arc
light units and the unusual characteristic clattering noise they produced each
evening as the internal mechanism struggled to establish an electrical arc. Smoke,
reminiscent of old kerosene lamps when the wick was over-extended, poured out
of the chimney on each unit as the carbon rods were slowly consumed. Occasionally,
a unit would go into a frantic sputtering phase as it attempted to maintain or
re-establish its arc. The main problem was the need for constant maintenance.
The carbon electrodes lasted about 300 hours and "arc trimmers" made regular

daily rounds to replace carbons, clean the glass enclosures and ensure that the temperamental electro-mechanical devices used to establish the arc in each lamp were functioning properly. Yet despite these "drawbacks" they flooded downtown Calgary for nearly four decades with a quality of light still unequalled to the present day. Unfortunately, not a single unit escaped the junkyard and all that remains of their existence is a photographic record.

"Toronto type" lighting units, consisting of clusters of five incandescent lamps enclosed by separate white glass globes and mounted on top of an ornamental standard, were installed in March 1911 along 1st and 2nd streets east between 8th and 17th avenues. These units were largely missing by the end of the 1930s, their major problem being the high breakage rate of the low-mounted glass globe enclosures. By the end of World War II the only places where these lighting units were still in operation were along the approaches to the railway subways at 1st and 2nd streets east and 1st and 8th streets west. As with the old arc units none of these lighting units have survived. If they had they would have been wonderful additions to the streets of Calgary's Heritage Park.

After 1923 the older series-operated arc and incandescent lighting units gave way to lighting units which were operated in parallel (or multiple) from the ordinary secondary voltage source already in place to provide electrical service to residential homes or commercial buildings. These lamps were controlled in groups by streetlighting "relays" which in turn were operated from a low voltage "pilot" wire circuit carried on the secondary voltage crossarms of the overhead distribution system. The "pilot" wire usually had its origin in a local substation where it could be conveniently switched on or off. Switching the pilot "on" turned the lights off with the opposite operation having the reverse effect. The switch was replaced often with a photo-electric device which would perform the operation automatically — an action which in 1923 was often viewed as quite mysterious.

By 1922, 628 incandescent streetlights were in service in Calgary, increasing to 1,824 by 1946. That year marked the beginning of a renewal of the streetlighting system although another seven years would elapse before any dramatic effects became obvious. Up to 1929, Calgary's streetlighting system, with the exception of the downtown commercial core, was merely one of "corner or intersection" marking with one 200 or 250 watt incandescent lamp burning at each location. These lights, either series or multiple, were installed and operated as an expense to the city's general revenue accounts. The additional costs incurred by the "white way" lighting in the downtown core were covered by local improvement by-laws under which the adjoining property owners paid for the capital costs of the installation with the general city revenues covering the operating costs.

Concurrent with the city policy of lighting street intersections only, a few residential areas embarked on programs to upgrade their lighting. The earliest of these were the Rideau and Roxboro districts where spherical white globe fixtures

Ornamental lighting standard in Mount Royal, c. 1929.
Source: Electric System Archives

were mounted on the top of fluted pre-cast concrete pedestals spaced fairly regularly throughout the subdivisions. No record remains of how these installations were financed but they were probably part of the original development costs when both of these areas were privately developed shortly after the First World War. Petitions to the city were received in 1929 for the installation of "ornamental" streetlighting in south Mount Royal east of 14th Street W. between Prospect Avenue and Premier Way and along Crescent Boulevard, overlooking Sunnyside. These installations were completed in the same year, using Union Metal Lamp Standard No. 1523 topped with a "Novalux" Form 18 cast bronze lantern. Without question they were the most elegant streetlighting units ever installed in Calgary. In later years the same units were extended to cover all of south Mount Royal to 34th Avenue S. Because large parts of Mount Royal did not have curbs and gutters along the streets, the cast iron standards suffered a high degree of damage from the bumpers of parking automobiles. Fortunately, when Mount Royal was relighted with new streetlighting standards in the 1960s, enough of the old standards were reclaimable and were reinstalled in Memorial Park where they still operate as a reminder of earlier days.

Restored Mount Royal ornamental standards in Memorial Park.
The South African War Memorial was erected under the supervision of J.F. McCall,
chief engineer of the municipal power plant.
Source: Bilodeau/Preston Commercial Photographers

By 1933 the Great Depression had dipped to its lowest level and city council decided to curtail streetlighting by reducing the number of hours the lamps burned and by having the lamps turned off completely on clear moonlight nights. (This was reminiscent of the time when Peter Prince had his "moonlight" schedule as part of his contract with the city.) This action prompted the city electric light superintendent, Bob Mackay, to write into his annual report of 1933 the effect on department revenue:

> We are of the opinion that economy in street lighting also affected the income of the Department in other ways. The average person is more or less governed by procedure and fads, fancies and fashions usually have quite a following. Seeing the City economize on street lighting undoubtedly interested the average citizen along the same lines.[34]

Mackay went on to point out that the savings were negligible in relation to the fixed costs already incurred to install the lighting. He was as frugal a Scotsman as ever lived but when it came to his department's revenue accounts he never hesitated to turn into a fighting Scot. As early as 1935 Mackay was anticipating the replacement of the downtown luminous arc streetlights with newly-developed mercury vapour lighting, and an experimental installation of nine mercury vapour lights around the city hall was made in 1937. At the same time it was decided to experiment further by installing low pressure sodium vapour lights at all level railway crossings in the city, anticipating that the distinct yellow-orange light from the lamps would provide an additional warning factor to automobile drivers. Because of the novelty associated with these lamps, Calgarians made regular visits to these locations to experience their ghastly greenish appearance under the monochromatic light source. During the depression years anything new and free created a diversion akin to entertainment.

There is little doubt that the curtailment of streetlighting during the depression years served to raise public awareness of the value of such lighting. By the end of 1939 a group of aldermen, spearheaded by J.C. Mahaffy, began asking for cost estimates to improve streetlighting facilities in those areas where trees were interfering with the existing lights. Bob McKay prepared his estimates offering several alternate proposals for council's consideration but the report was premature and was filed. Then the war intervened and for the next five years all activity ceased except for some improvement of public lighting around new military establishments such as Currie Barracks in southwest Calgary. In 1941 the East Calgary Taxpayers' Association complained to the council of the difficulties people were having in locating residential addresses at night and advocated a plan whereby citizens would leave their porch lights burning during the night hours to alleviate the problem. In return, co-operating citizens would receive a compensating discount on their regular electricity account.[35] Although the request was filed the idea would resurface after the war ended.

Most streetlighting units up to 1940 were not optically designed to focus and direct the bulk of the light produced by the light source to the street surface where it was most needed. Most residential lighting units in use in Calgary consisted of a simple "goose neck" bracket supporting a rippled porcelain coated reflector and a 200 watt incandescent lamp with no enclosure. In fact, the lighting units were not very different from the original ten units installed for the town of Calgary in 1887 except for the increased wattage of the lamp. Later, as the light source was enclosed in a glass envelope for improvements in appearance and maintenance, some attempt was made to direct the light by the use of internal metal reflectors thus providing the first crude measure of light control. Taking advantage of this development after 1939, many of the old bare lamp installations, particularly those which were still operating in series circuits, were replaced by the newly available streetlighting luminaires incorporating some internal method of light control. Mackay, in his 1940 annual report, wrote that these new units had provided noticeable improvement in streetlighting. As mercury vapour and other gaseous discharge lamps of high light output began to supersede the incandescent lamp, the potential for introducing light control by means of optical glassware was greatly enhanced and by the early 1950s almost all lighting sources

First mercury-vapour lighting installation on 8th Ave., c. 1948.
Source: Provincial Archives of Alberta

were enclosed in optical glass which efficiently and effectively directed the light uniformly to the road surface.

From 1905 to 1945 Calgary accumulated just over 3,000 streetlights. Of this total, 159 luminous arc lamps and 1,080 series incandescent lamps of 1910 to 1920 vintage were still in operation. The remainder consisted of multiple incandescent units of various types and ratings, nine mercury vapour units around the city hall and fifteen sodium vapour lamps at level railway crossings.

The first visible evidence of Calgary's second streetlighting renewal came in 1947 with the relighting of 1st Street W. from 10th Avenue to 17th Avenue S. using mercury vapour lamps housed in vertical "tear-drop" style luminaires. Similar lighting was extended along 7th and 8th avenues during 1948, ending almost four decades of service by the old luminous arc lights which had been installed in 1910. Many of these original mercury vapour units are still in service. Interest in improved residential lighting was also evident when the Sunalta district was relighted with properly spaced incandescent lighting units on modern steel standards. Any comprehensive plan to relight the entire city was delayed, however, until late 1953 when Alderman P.R. Brecken requested "that the Light Superintendent submit a report on what he considers necessary in order to provide adequate street lighting, particularly with reference to lighting in the centre of long blocks."[36] For J. Harvey Wilson, who had followed Mackay in 1948 as superintendent of the Electric Light Department, Brecken's request was like waving a red flag in front of an angry bull. He made a preliminary report to the city commissioners in which he detailed the existing policies of the city regarding the installation of streetlights. Next he stressed the complete inadequacy of existing streetlighting for a city like Calgary which was now faced with increased volumes of vehicular traffic. He recommended that all of the major traffic thoroughfares be lighted to the "minimum standards approved by the Canadian Electrical Association which are practically identical with those of the American Standards Association and the Illumination Engineering Society."[37] A new city planner and a traffic engineer were now part of the civic bureaucracy and Wilson recommended their assistance in planning a new lighting program to accommodate traffic flow and city growth. He recommended a $750,000 program which would light all major traffic corridors. Without any further comment the city commissioners forwarded Wilson's report to council where the matter was tabled on 4 January 1954 pending the receipt of an additional "all embracing plan to cover the residential portion of the City and an alternative to the present expensive system of ornamental lighting." The seeds of what would develop into the most comprehensive streetlighting program undertaken in a North American city were sown.

Wilson's second report expanded substantially on the material he had previously submitted. It was prefaced with a particularly ingenious appeal so characteristic of his approach to matters politic:

It is assumed in presenting this report that members of Council are already convinced of the necessity for improved street lighting in the City. No attempt is made therefore, to present any selling arguments for street lighting, which might be summed up briefly as increased safety to vehicle traffic and pedestrians, a decrease of crime, particularly molestation of women and holdups, and the enhanced value of property.[38]

Wilson's "soft sell" approach to the alderman was a masterpiece of rhetoric. In fact, Wilson, accompanied by two aldermen, had already undertaken a streetlighting "fact-finding" tour around the Province of Alberta and we can be certain that he used the opportunity to convince the captive councillors of the advantages of the programs he would be recommending. Wilson's first recommendation was a restatement of his earlier report. Thirty miles of major thoroughfares required modern lighting using mercury vapour lamps spaced along the roadways to produce a minimum illumination of 1.2 foot candles. The estimated cost of the program was the same as in his first recommendation with the capital costs being shared between the city and the adjoining property owners. His second recommendation was for the use of incandescent lighting in all residential districts, using modern luminaires supported by thirty-five foot high shaved pine wood poles spaced to produce the minimum lighting levels recommended by the Illuminating Engineering Society. Since residential lighting benefited local residents only they would bear the brunt of the capital costs. A "free porch light" alternative, reflecting a recommendation from the depression years, was also offered, this having come from a practice which the city of Medicine Hat had used for many years. Wilson did not agree with such an alternative but included it in deference to the aldermen who had been with him on the provincial tour. The report envisioned 1,680 lights for the thoroughfares at an annual operating cost of $92,400 and 14,000 lights for the residential program with a corresponding annual cost of $560,000. The costs were based on the experience of the 4,000 lights already in operation in 1954 but Wilson was confident that these costs would be substantially lower.

Mayor Don Mackay (left) and J.H. Wilson inaugurate the comprehensive street lighting program on 4th Ave. and 3rd St. E., 1954.
Source: Electric System Archives

Council, however, vacillated when the report reached them. They were obviously stunned by the magnitude of the costs and referred the entire matter back to the city commissioners. This resulted in a third report from Wilson which focused entirely on the costs of the program and ways by which the costs could be recovered.[39] The ball was again in council's court and to help them make a decision Wilson persuaded the commissioners to allow him to erect a number of streetlighting units in a selected "test" area where the public could view the various combinations of available luminaires and standards and submit their comments.

The area selected was along 17th Avenue S. between 2nd and 4th Streets East. The public response indicated that the citizens were more than ready to accept a comprehensive streetlighting program. Interestingly, the citizen response to Wilson's least costly residential alternative, which would have utilized shaved wooden poles on which to mount the lights, was rejected in favour of steel standards, underground wiring and mercury vapour luminaires. As fortune would have it, Calgary's phenomenal post-war growth had begun and a new city policy was implemented which provided for prepayment of the cost of local improvements in the purchase price of residential building sites and this policy could easily accommodate the capital cost of streetlighting in newly developed districts. With this concern settled, the city commissioner recommended that $153,000 be included in the 1954 capital budget to initiate the relighting of selected arterial streets. It was accepted by council on 25 April.

The new program to renew the streetlighting system was inaugurated in a simple ceremony held in August. Mayor Don Mackay and Harvey Wilson were elevated to the top of a pole on 4th Avenue between 2nd and 3rd streets east by means of a new "giraffe" man-lift device. Both men assisted in placing a lamp into a previously installed luminaire and the resulting glow announced to those assembled that the program to relight all of Calgary's streets was off and running. The first major roadway to receive the new horizontal-burning mercury lights was 4th Avenue S. between 9th Street W. and 4th Street E. The lights were turned on for the first time in December 1954 by Mayor Mackay from a switch installed for the purpose at the corner of 4th Avenue and 4th Street W. This marked the first visible sign of a comprehensive program which, in the next ten years, would relight the entire city to standards which exceeded the minimum recommendations of the Illuminating Engineering Society.[40]

The first residential area to be serviced by the use of mercury vapour lighting was Lower Briar Hill followed quickly by Spruce Cliff, Glendale and Thorncliffe. By the end of 1957 the number of mercury vapour lights in service had increased to 2,238 from 696 at the end of 1954. It did not take long before the city administration was flooded with petitions for the extension of new lighting into the older residential areas. Rather than waiting for local improvement petitions to determine which areas would be serviced, the city took the initiative and began to publish the names of those areas proposed, in the current year, for relighting under local improvement by-laws. Opposition to the advertised by-laws was non-existent and the citizens of Calgary gave their aldermen a blank cheque to proceed with the lighting program as quickly as possible. Installing the lighting using underground wiring was much more difficult in well-established areas because of the existence of sidewalks, pavements, driveways and landscaping and so highly innovative construction practices were developed to keep damage to these amenities to a minimum.

Another part of the streetlighting story began in the summer of 1954, when a Calgary youth, a student engineer at the University of British Columbia, was hired for the summer. In an earlier interview with Mr. Albert Bishop, the electric light department engineer, the writer could not help but overhear the proceedings. This slim youth lacked nothing when it came to self-confidence and at the close of the interview another contemporary, who had also overheard the conversation, remarked dryly, "Some day that little 'so and so' will be running the entire city." He did not realize how prophetic his off-the-cuff assessment would prove to be. Twenty-five years later, George Cornish became the city's most powerful administrator when he was appointed Chief Commissioner. When Cornish finished his engineering degree in 1956, he came to work for the Electric Light Department. When the engineer who had been in charge of the new streetlighting program resigned to take a position in Seattle, Cornish was attracted to the vacant position like a honeybee to sweet clover. It was an instant love affair and in the atmosphere of the clamour between the council and the citizens as to who would get the new lights first, Cornish found himself in the centre of a tailor-made environment which assured his success. Cornish soon gained many admirers for his expertise and no nonsense coordination of a program which was now growing like a rolling snowball. In the years that followed, Cornish became an international authority on streetlighting and his advice was widely sought. In the mid 1970s he became the international president of the Illuminating Engineering Society with headquarters in New York City, the highest honour that the lighting industry of North America can bestow.

By mid 1960 the program to relight the older parts of the city under local improvement by-laws was completed. The prime complaint from both the public and their elected representatives was that the program had not proceeded quickly enough. An average of 2,500 new streetlights were added each year and this required a coordinated field effort that ran like clockwork. Field crews used the frost-free months to install underground wiring and the concrete lighting standard foundations. During the winter months the same crews erected the standards and luminaires and spliced all the previously installed wiring and circuits to operate the lights. Every possible field operation was mechanized. The workmen, caught up in the enthusiasm of this huge program, produced a flood of ideas to increase the efficiency and productivity of the operation.

For example, all underground wiring which crossed under street pavement was installed in a plastic raceway so that it could be easily withdrawn and replaced if it failed in future years. Often these enclosed electrical circuits could extend for long distances depending on the location of the nearest splicing point. One enterprising tradesman developed a simple method by which the wires could be blown through the conduit in a matter of seconds using the compressed air source which was always available on the work site. The time saved over the old method of "fishing" the wiring through the pipe was enormous. In residential areas, streetlight wiring was commonly installed directly behind the inside edge of the sidewalks. Worried home owners would call in the morning to express the fear that their beautifully landscaped lawns would be destroyed by crews moving in to install the underground wiring. They could hardly be blamed for their apprehension as backhoes, trenchers, compressors and vehicles descended on the district to perform various duties. By the end of the day everything was back in place and the sidewalks and roads had been swept clean. The same citizens often called back to express amazement at what had transpired. It was an exciting period and the dispatch with which the job was so carefully accomplished created an unsolicited favourable public relations image for the city's electrical department which has not diminished to this day. The Electric Light Department (City of Calgary Electric System) became synonymous with the streetlighting system even though the streetlighting assets were never part of the electric utility. The City of Calgary Electric System has always acted as a contractor, charging an annual rate to recover the costs of operation and maintenance including energy, relamping, pole painting and other repairs as needed.

In 1966 a radically new development in lighting sources appeared. It was the high pressure sodium (HPS) lamp which combined twice the efficiency of the mercury vapour light source with a light quality that was almost fully chromatic, i.e., it contained all of the colours of the visible light spectrum so that objects under the light looked much the same as they would in daylight. The low pressure sodium lamp is remembered for its high efficiency but the monochromatic quality of the light output left much to be desired. The first commercial North American application of the new HPS lamp was scheduled for the 1967 World's Fair in Montreal. Cornish, because of his reputation in the lighting industry, persuaded the manufacturer of the new lamps to release them one year earlier for an experimental installation in Calgary along Macleod Trail from 34th Avenue to 58th Avenue. To compensate for the additional light output the lights were mounted at twice the height of the standard mounting height used for the mercury vapour lamps. The early Calgary installation of 400 watt HPS lamps presented many problems which the manufacturer had not anticipated during the development stage. Engineers from eastern Canada and the U.S.A. spent a lot of time in Calgary during that first winter and the knowledge gained translated into manufacturing modifications resulting in HPS lamps that became as reliable as the mercury vapour lamps. Their use was standardized for all additional main thoroughfare and highway lighting applications in Calgary. In 1974 its use was extended to all new residential subdivisions when lower wattage HPS lamps were introduced. Residential streets were lighted to exactly the same level of illumination as before but with one-half of the energy input, resulting in substantial savings in annual operating costs — a very important feature as energy costs soared after 1974.

When mercury vapour streetlighting was introduced four decades ago, Calgary had about 3,000 streetlighting units in operation and almost all of them were incandescent lamps of low efficiency. By 1984 there were 48,000 streetlights burning in Calgary, of which a mere 107 were incandescent. High pressure sodium units counted for 15,000 of the total and are now standard for most streetlighting applications. The distinctive golden colour of the HPS lighting system has completely surrounded the core of bluish-white mercury light and the next decade will likely see the end of all mercury vapour lighting.

The annual cost of the lighting system has remained fairly constant at about one mil of the total property taxes collected. It is a small amount to pay for the security and safety of Calgary's citizens. The complaints which always follow when any light ceases to function are indicative of how much its presence as a nighttime sentinel is appreciated. From the initial ten dim lights installed in 1887 we might well wonder what Peter Prince would say today if he could see what his early contribution to the lighting of Calgary's streets has grown into. At the very least he would have a difficult time to find some hidden obstacle over which to trip!

References

1. Council Minutes, 17 December 1884, v.1, p.41.

2. Editorial, *Calgary Herald*, 23 August 1887.

3. "Report on Council," *Calgary Herald*, 9 September 1887.

4. "Of Local Interest," *Calgary Herald*, 7 October 1887.

5. "What Is Going To Make Calgary A Great City?" *Calgary Herald*, 18 April 1888.

6. Council Minutes, 20 January 1890, v.3, p.35.

7. "Light Contract Completed," *Calgary Herald*, 26 January 1890.

8. "Where the Lights Will Be," *Calgary Tribune*, 29 January 1890.

9. "The Town Council," *Calgary Herald*, 19 April 1893.

10. "The Town Council," *Calgary Herald*, 16 May 1893.

11. "Last Night's Council," *Calgary Tribune*, 15 November 1893.

12. Council Minutes, 7 November 1893, v.4, p.452.

13. "The Town Lighting," *Calgary Herald*, 14 November 1893.

14. Council Minutes, 1 May 1894, v.5, p.74.

15. "Electric Light," *Calgary Tribune*, 23 May 1894.

16. City Clerk's Records, By-law 235, 5 June 1894. "Prince Contract." Additional quote from same source.

17. City Clerk's Papers, b3.f15. Letter dated 5 November 1894, P.A. Prince to City Clerk.

18. City Clerk's Papers, b6.f50. Letter dated 17 October 1899, P.A. Prince to City Clerk.

19. "City Council Meets," *Calgary Herald*, 2 May 1903.

20. City Clerk's Papers. Letter dated 28 May 1903, Prince to City Council.

21. City Clerk's Records. By-law 519. Quote from handwritten note on original.

22. City Clerk's Papers, b12.f100. Letter dated 28 July 1904, F.W. Thorold, City Engineer to E.H. Harrison, Westinghouse Electric Co., Winnipeg, Manitoba.

23. Statute No.33 of 1893, "An Ordinance to Incorporate the City of Calgary." Under "Power of the Council to pass By-laws," Section 117, subsections 54 and 55 it reads, "The Council of the said City of Calgary may pass bylaws for: (54) Providing for lighting the municipality or any portion thereof in any way the Council may appoint and providing the necessary plant therefore, subject to ratification by electors," and (55) "authorizing the Mayor and Clerk to sign any contract with any person or corporation to supply light or water for the use of the Corporation for any period not exceeding five years." Sub-section (55) clearly limited the Council to a five-year contract. Prince's proposed five-year contract with options coming into effect at the end of five years was a condition covered by sub-section (54) requiring the approval of the electors.

24. "Street Lighting Franchise Practically Declared Off," *Calgary Herald*, 28 October 1904.

25. Council Minutes, 10 November 1904, v.9, p.136.

26. "Municipal Lighting Plant Substitutes Private Service," *Calgary Herald*, 25 November 1904.

27. "Mr. Prince Makes New Offer in Regard to Electric Light," *Calgary Herald*, 17 March 1905.

28. "Municipal Light Plant is Ready for Business," *Calgary Herald*, 11 November 1905.

29. City Clerk's Papers, b20.f159. Memo dated 23 April 1906, J.H. McCall to City Clerk.

30. "East Calgary Now Lighted with Gas," *Calgary Albertan*, 10 May 1911.

31. No photographic record of the gas light installations in East Calgary could be located either at the Glenbow Museum, the Provincial Archives, or the Archives of Canadian Western Natural Gas Company Limited. If any person reading this possesses such a record, it would be greatly appreciated if it could be forwarded to the author, c/o City of Calgary Electric System, Calgary, Alberta.

32. City Clerk's Papers, b39.f300. Letter 15 August 1910 Mayor Jamieson to City Council.

33. City Clerk's Papers, b245.f1376. Letter 17 November 1927, R.A. Brown to Mayor and Commissioners.

34. Electric Light Department. Annual Report 1933. B1240.f811.

35. Council Minutes, 15 September 1941, p.559.

36. Council Minutes, 7 December 1953, p.886.

37. Council Minutes, 4 January 1954, p.24.

38. Council Minutes, 1 February 1954, p.98. "J.H. Wilson - Report on Street Lighting."

39. Council Minutes, 15 March 1954, p.225. Wilson's third report is essentially similar to that of 1 February 1954.

40. The decision to exceed the recommended residential lighting levels seems, on the surface, one which ignored operating costs. After all, additional light equals additional cost. There were two main mercury vapour light sources available in 1954: 250 and 400 watt horizontal-burning lamps. The 250 watt lamp was widely in use for streetlighting purposes but the 400 watt lamp was generally restricted to main thoroughfare lighting where higher levels of illumination were required. A detailed analysis showed that the overall costs utilizing the 400 watt lamp for residential service were competitive because it allowed greater spacing of the lighting standards while retaining the correct ratio of maximum to minimum light level on the street surface. The only unknown was the future cost of the 400 watt lamp, which, at the time of the economic analysis, was about $40.00 per lamp. A gamble was made that the price of the lamp would come down drastically which it did, to about $8.00 per lamp, by the mid 1960s, making the 400 watt lamp actually cheaper than the 250 watt. The city designers also wanted a lighting system which was obsolescent-free for at least twenty-five years. Energy costs in 1954 were very cheap. No one could have forecast the energy crunch of the 1970s. The advent of the HPS lamp enabled all lighting after 1970 to cut energy consumption by one-half and, with minor modifications, the new lamp could be used as a replacement in the older mercury luminaries.

Chapter 2

EARLY PRIVATE ENTERPRISE
AND COMPETITION
FOR SUPREMACY

The entrepreneurs who introduced electricity to Calgary were equally interested in extending its benefits to the citizens for lighting the interiors of their homes and businesses. The broader use of electrical energy as a public utility soon gained a foothold. At this early stage, the use of electricity for means other than lighting had not been seriously considered. In a letter appearing in the *Calgary Herald* on 11 February 1887, a citizen argued that "Electric light is just as applicable as gas lighting and is less initial and permanent expense and (has) far more potential." Shortly thereafter, on 18 February, the following item appeared in the *Calgary Herald*:

> It is probable that before many weeks the electric light will be in operation in Calgary. Mr. McMullen, representing the Northwest Electric Company, arrived in town yesterday but was called away to Victoria by telegram and therefore was not able to lay his plan before the citizens. He will return here in a week or so when the scheme will be fully explained. This light is in use in Victoria, Vancouver, and Brandon and said to be well adapted for lighting buildings as well as streets.

Mr. F.P. McMullen returned to Calgary six weeks later for the purpose of floating a company to light the town by electricity. McMullen was cooperating as part of a syndicate to bring the benefits of electricity to Calgary together with financial benefits which were likely to accrue to those who initiated the project. The new enterprise was legally established under the name "The Calgary Electric Lighting Company, Limited," with Letters Patent issued under the seal of the North-West Territories on 2 September 1887. Incorporated into the Company were:

> John Stewart of the City of Ottawa, in the Province of Ontario, Gentleman, George Clift King, of the Town of Calgary, in the North-West Territories of Canada, Merchant, William Thomson Ramsey of the same place, Land Agent, and Donald

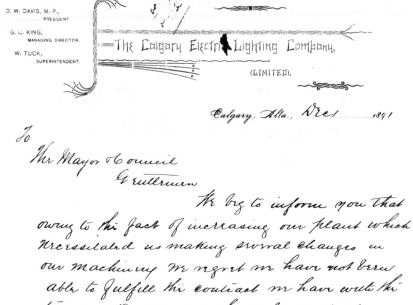

D. W. DAVIS, M. P.,
PRESIDENT.

G. C. KING,
MANAGING DIRECTOR.

W. TUCK,
SUPERINTENDENT.

The Calgary Electric Lighting Company,
(LIMITED).

Calgary, Alta., Dec 1 1891

To
The Mayor & Council
Gentlemen

We beg to inform you that owing to the fact of increasing our plant which necessitated us making several changes in our machinery we regret we have not been able to fulfill the contract we have with the town as strictly as it should be and also regret very much that on several occasions during the past month some of the lights were out. In a few days we shall have everything in good running order We will then have no reason for asking your indulgence.

We have the honor to be
Gentlemen
Your obedient Servant
The Calgary Electric Lighting Co
A. G. Van Wart
Secretary

**The only surviving evidence of the Calgary Electric Lighting Company.
Van Wart became one of Calgary's early aldermen in 1899.
Source: Glenbow Archives**

Watson Davis, of Fort Macleod, in the said Territories, Merchant, for the purpose of the lighting of the Town of Calgary.[1]

The company was capitalized at $25,000, divided into two hundred and fifty shares of $100.00 each. John Stewart is unknown but he was likely an Ottawa friend or associate of Donald W. Davis. Davis was a native New Englander who served in the American Army during the Civil War. After his discharge he moved to Montana where he became a representative for the I.G. Baker Company in Fort Benton. This association produced many trips into Canada until he became general manager of that company in Fort Macleod. He became a naturalized citizen in 1886 and was elected the first member of parliament for the Alberta District of the Territories in 1887. George C. King is considered Calgary's "first citizen," having arrived as part of the first contingent of the North-West Mounted Police. King was the local representative of the I.G. Baker Company in Calgary and there can be little doubt that this mutual association between King and Davis propelled him into the syndicate that proposed to establish Calgary's first electrical utility. No information exists about Ramsey.

If considered in its generic sense, Calgary's original "electrical" utility had been installed in 1885 when James Walker, of North-West Mounted Police fame, erected the first telephone line between his store at 8th Avenue and 4th Street E. and his lumber mill at 9th Avenue and 16th Street E., a distance of some two miles.[2] During the ensuing eighteen months, Walker installed telephone service to several other business firms with a switchboard which could accommodate twenty lines. Early in 1887 George Clift King, mayor of Calgary, had convinced the Bell Telephone Company of Montreal to extend telephone service to the city and, on 12 May 1887, Bell was granted permission to place telephone poles along Stephen Avenue on the express condition that the company "would not lease use of poles to Electric Light or other companies without the consent of Council."[3] It seems that Mayor King was already anticipating the needs of the infant electrical business of which he was a part.

The shares of the new electric company were offered to the citizens of Calgary. The *Herald*, in an editorial on 14 October 1887, commended the stock issue very highly as a good investment for the town citizens: "Users of the light would benefit themselves and share in the profits by taking stock in the Company." One leading citizen, Mr. A.W. Braithwaite, first manager of the Bank of Montreal from 1880 to 1892, must have thought the new company was a good investment because he became one of its principal associates and its spokesman. Other leading citizens associated themselves with the new company including Mr. Charles Watson and Dr. James D. Lafferty, a prominent early physician. On 1 June 1887, the Calgary Electric Lighting Company sought permission from the town council to erect poles for electric lighting. The Committee on Public Works and Property recommended:

That leave be granted to F.P. McMullen and Co. to erect poles for Electric Lighting of the Town on the various streets, but they must be placed upon the opposite side to that on which the telephone poles are placed, and the Council to reserve the right to have them or any of them removed at any time they consider it in the public interest to do so.[4]

The Calgary Electric Lighting Company never entered into a franchise agreement with the town as did its successor, The Calgary Water Power Company, a matter which would soon cause trouble for the first company. By late summer of 1887 work was underway: "A carload of material for electric lighting has arrived here. Among the rest is a large engine and several dynamos. The erection of the buildings and the stringing of wires, it is understood, will be begun at once and pushed forward rapidly to conclusion."[5]

The extent of the original area serviced by electricity is unknown but the earliest photographs of Stephen Avenue show pole lines on both sides of the street. Telephones were on the north side with electric service on the south. Joint use of poles was still in the future although an early report on the progress of the new company stated that, "The Electric Light Co. would be willing to use the telephone poles if an agreement could be come to, but it is not likely that the telephone company will agree to that."[6] The boiler and engine house were located, by present-day description, half-way between Centre Street and 1st Street W. on the south side of 7th Avenue, or just east of the present Central United Church. The company chose to utilize the direct current, low voltage Edison distribution system which was at this time in fairly wide use in North America. The Edison system had a inherent fatal disadvantage because of the limited distance over which the electricity produced by the generators could be utilized. A newer system of distribution using alternating current had already appeared in the early 1880s. Developed by Nikola Tesla, an electrical wizard with the Westinghouse Electric Company, it soon became the overwhelming choice of electricity producers. The failure of the Calgary Electric Lighting Company to select this more advanced system was one of the factors leading to its eventual demise.

The Town of Calgary was one of the company's first customers. The fact that George Clift King was a councillor on the first town council of 1884-85, and the mayor of the town during 1886-87 does not seem to have prevented him from actively negotiating contracts for the town with the Calgary Electric Lighting Company, of which he was the managing director. Later, when the company began to reel from the effects of competition, there were occasions during which the respected gentleman declined to vote on related matters while in council sessions. Public streetlighting by the Calgary Electric Lighting Company was overwhelmingly accepted by the town's citizens, as was its domestic use. Calgary's first fire chief, "Cappy" Smart, remembered when electricity was introduced into Calgary:

The most unusual and best attended social event of the month of February, 1889 (was) the 'Bachelor at Home' in the Royal Opera House and hailed as the most brilliant event ever held in the North West Territories at the time. The hall was beautifully decorated for the occasion. A short time before the first electric light plant had been launched successfully and in place of the coal oil lamps which were formerly used to illuminate the hall, strips of coloured electric lights were hung.[7]

The challenge to the Calgary Electric Lighting Company came from an unexpected source. Interest in timber stands west of Calgary had led an Ottawa lawyer, with the rather unique name of Kutusoff MacFee, to visit those areas in the early 1880s. Impressed by what he saw he consulted with lumbering interests in Eau Claire, Wisconsin, who in turn dispatched their experts to follow up the possibilities seen by MacFee. A favourable report resulted in the formation of the Eau Claire and Bow River Lumber Company. MacFee had, of course, secured the lumbering rights.

Peter Anthony Prince was born in Three Rivers, Quebec in 1836 and, following his father's trade, became a millwright and pursued his vocation in the lumber business in Ontario. Moving to Wisconsin, he joined the Northwestern Lumber Company where his career continued to be successful. He had visited western Canada in 1885 during a vacation and upon his return to Wisconsin was invited to become associated with a new business venture. This was the Eau Claire and Bow River Lumber Company in Calgary and Peter Prince became its manager in late December, 1885.

It was originally intended that the logs would be sawn into lumber near Kananaskis but a later decision moved the site of the sawmill to Calgary with the Bow River being used to transport the logs. The sawmill was located on what became known as the Eau Claire Flats, an area from 4th Avenue northward to the Bow River between the present Centre Street and Hillhurst bridges. The sawmill required power which came from steam boilers and steam engines. Steam boilers require fuel and Mr. Prince had plenty of that in the form of sawdust and log cuttings. It was an ideal plan which prospered from the very beginning. Theodore Strom arrived in Calgary early in the summer of 1886 to superintend the erection of the machinery for the sawmill. He remained with the company as lifelong superintendent of operations. Fortunately for us Mr. Strom took time in the late 1930s to record his memories of those early days and we shall rely on much of what he had to say as we proceed with our story.[8]

According to Strom, the original Calgary Electric Lighting Company started running into difficulties in the spring of 1889. It seems that its boilers had not received very good care and were leaking badly. The management of the Calgary Electric Lighting Company made overtures to the Eau Claire Company for steam power to drive the dynamos from the boilers that were being installed to operate the new planing mill. The new boilers and steam engine would be able to run the planing mill during daylight hours and at night could run the dynamos for lighting purposes. At this time electricity was utilized solely for lighting and, therefore, it was not important to have its supply available during the daylight hours. While there was some genuine agreement respecting this scheme, the Calgary Electric Lighting Company's representatives were somewhat surprised that the Eau Claire Company would not install its new machinery on the site of the Calgary Electric Lighting Company plant on McIntyre Avenue. Prince explained that it would be much easier to extend electrical lines to his location rather than hauling lumber into the centre of the town to be finished in a planing mill. The Calgary Electric Lighting Company protested and Prince quickly decided that, since they were in trouble anyway, he might as well get into the business of supplying electricity to the town and so the battle lines were drawn for what was to become a major political event in the town of Calgary.

To counter the new threat to its business enterprise, the Calgary Electric Lighting Company petitioned the town council for a ten-year franchise under which it would have the "exclusive right to place and use poles on the streets for Electric Lighting purposes."[9] As an inducement to the councillors to view its petition favourably, the company also proposed a 27 percent price reduction to private consumers of electricity and a 33 percent reduction in the cost of streetlighting. At the same meeting on 2 July 1889, Peter Prince also requested the privilege of placing poles on the streets of Calgary for electric lighting purposes and included a proposed schedule of rates for private consumers. The *Herald* reported the following discussions between the mayor and councillors and Prince:

Councillor: "Will your works be within the Town limits and subject to taxation?"

Prince: "Yes."

Councillor: "Do you want any monopoly?"

Prince: "No. I just want the privilege of putting up and using poles so long as I furnish light at the above rates or less. I expect to be able to furnish it much cheaper as soon as I get water power."

Councillor: "Would you make special contracts for churches and other places where the light is only used occasionally?"

Prince: "Yes, I will quote special rates before you grant my request, if you wish."[10]

Mr. Prince appeared to impress the council with his forthrightness because the Calgary Electric Lighting Company's request was deferred until the council's next regular meeting. However, before adjourning, the council asked their solicitor's opinion as to whether the "Council would be legally justified in entering into a ten year's contract as Company do (sic) not say whether they intend maintaining works and plant within the Municipality."[11]

Appearing before the council meeting on 9 July 1889, Mr. Braithwaite, managing director of the Calgary Electric Lighting Company, argued his case. Since

8th Ave. and 1st St. W., c. 1892 with Calgary Electric Lighting Company poles supporting electrical conductors for street lighting and distribution service.
Source: Provincial Archives of Alberta

Prince had made no reference to his special system of lighting at the last meeting, could it be that the alternating system that Prince was proposing might result in "igniting fires, and destroying the present works by electric contact?"[12] Braithwaite further challenged the prices quoted by Mr. Prince and, based on prices charged in other towns in Canada and the United States, thought that safe lighting "could not be given at Prince's schedule of Prices." Braithwaite also reminded council of the heavy taxes his company paid. In fact, "they were prepared at once to increase their plant" provided they were treated fairly. He also argued that the company "had been a great advertisement for the town." Council still could not agree on what should be done with these proposals and deferred the matter for another two weeks for further consideration. At the same time the council was advised by the town solicitor that it had no authority to grant an exclusive right for a term of ten years as had been the original request from the Calgary Electric Lighting Company.

When the council convened again on 20 August 1889, it approved two motions, first "that Mr. Prince be requested to put his proposition in the form of an Agreement," and second, "That the Solicitor be instructed to prepare for the next meeting of the Council a by-law and agreement authorizing Mr. Prince to erect poles and string wires within the Municipality on conditions agreed on between him and the Council."[13] The *Calgary Tribune* defended Prince's pro-posal by dismissing one councillor's argument "that the erection of poles on the street gives a very bad appearance" as rubbish. It proceeded to state, "If poles are good enough for Toronto and Chicago, then they must be good enough for Calgary.... By the way in which the people are taking the matter up, it seems that instead of Mr. Prince having to run after the Town for the privilege, they are determined that the Council should run after him now."[14] Prince clearly had a lot of public support for a proposal that would place him in direct competition with the Calgary Electric Lighting Company.

A meeting called on 23 August 1889 to deal with the proposed draft agree-ment between the town and Prince also ended in a stalemate. Mayor D.W. Marsh argued that any delay in approving the draft agreement would delay Mr. Prince in his efforts to "get the works in operation" before winter and Prince agreed with the mayor on that point. Councillor George Murdoch was opposed to approving the agreement until someone explained, "more definitely what system Mr. Prince would put in and what danger there might be from possible contact of wires."[15] Since the idea of danger from the wires of the Calgary Electric Lighting Com-pany did not attract much attention, it can be concluded that some of the council-lors were somewhat uneasy with Prince's proposed use of an alternating current system and bearing in mind that these deliberations took place during the earliest period of electrical distribution technology, one can readily understand such concern. Councillor James Bannerman was of the opinion that once Prince had his agreement with the town, he might "run the other company out (and) then we would be at his mercy as to prices and service." Then the question arose regarding Councillor King's right to vote because of his position as managing director for the Calgary Electric Lighting Company. The town solicitor was asked for an opinion but it was finally left to the discretion of King who decided to remain as a voting councillor. Mayor Marsh then left the chair, asked King to preside and moved that the by-law and agreement allowing Prince to operate in Calgary be introduced. It was seconded by Councillor W.F. Orr but the resolution was lost and the matter was referred to the next meeting. The *Calgary Tribune* recorded the reaction of Prince: "Mr. Prince who was present, thanked the Council and said he would not trouble them again, and the meeting adjourned,"[16] and the newspaper was quick to come to the defence of Prince:

> It should be the right of Mr. Prince to publicly demand of the people of Calgary the privilege he asks for, as the statutes expressly forbid a municipality to grant a monopoly of rights to any company or corporation for any purpose whatever, and for a municipal council to refuse an equal right to another company to put in and maintain another system of electric light certainly is fostering and maintain (sic) a monopoly, and can only be construed as a distinction without a difference.[17]

Prince had other powerful allies and they quickly rallied their forces to requisition a public meeting of the council. Prince had obviously been facetious when he had made his earlier comment to the council that he would not bother them again. He wasted no time in marshalling public opinion on his side to force the council to consider his request for a franchise to operate his electric company.

The special meeting convened on 3 September 1889, in the Fire Hall on McIntyre Avenue, between McTavish and Osler Streets. The Fire Hall was packed to capacity. The requisition called upon Councillors Murdoch, Bannerman and King to explain their previous opposition to Prince's new proposal. Mr. Murdoch was late arriving and both Bannerman and King declined to explain their positions until their "accusers" spoke first. Those who requisitioned the meeting included some of Calgary's most respected and notable citizens. Mr. J.R. Castigan wondered why the ratepayers should not be given reasons for the council's action in not allowing the introduction of a by-law to permit Prince to operate. Mr. James Reilly also posted the same argument when he said the council should be protecting the interest of the citizens who were consumers of light: "He thought it was too much for a little five-year-old town to be putting on more airs than great cities of the Continent in the matter of poles on the streets."[18] Mr. James Lougheed, later Senator Lougheed, argued that Prince was supported by very large capitalists: "Mr. Prince himself was a man of substance, and that it was not through any objection on the part of Mr. Prince's associates their names did not appear in the agreement, as he, Mr. Lougheed, had advised that it would be more convenient to have only the one name." When Lougheed went on to say that Prince was not asking for any monopoly he was supported by an unknown voice from the audience shouting, "You (the council) are supporting the old monopoly by not allowing competition."

Mayor Marsh, a Prince supporter, focused his remarks on two of the major objections voiced by Councilmen Murdoch, Bannerman and King. They objected to additional poles on the streets and queried the safety of alternating current systems. Mayor Marsh claimed that it was not practical to put all of Prince's poles in the lanes as had been suggested since "there were only three lanes north of the track (CPR) and two south if it." He then read extracts from papers purporting to report on investigations and experiments carried on in the state of New York to determine the power of electricity to destroy life, particularly the use of alternating current as a means of executing criminals. This had been abandoned because of its inefficiency and because "1,000 to 1,500 bolts (sic) had passed through a human body without producing death." When the time arrived for the three opposing councillors to speak, they had lost much of their thunder. Councillor Murdoch spoke at great length, quoting his references to the dangers of alternating current systems and "closed by saying he was not opposed to Mr. Prince's scheme, but wanted to have the interests of the town made as safe as possible." The *Tribune* smugly remarked, "he failed to convince a single ratepayer that he had acted in the interests of the town."[19] Both Councillors Bannerman and King expressed the view that their purpose was not to oppose Prince but to be certain that the interests of the town were being served first. They were loudly applauded for their stand even though Councillor King was still the managing director of the Calgary Electric Lighting Company.

Another curious twist which showed up at this meeting was the stand taken by Dr. James D. Lafferty who was an early supporter of the original Calgary Electric Lighting Company: "He said he did not and would not accuse the Councillors who voted against the introduction of the by-law of any improper motives, and conceded that they had acted in good conscience, but at the same time they had not acted in the interest of the ratepayers."[20] Dr. Lafferty moved that the meeting request the council to complete the agreement with Prince at the next regular meeting and to grant the privileges that Prince had requested. The motion was seconded by Mr. Reilly and the mayor asked in voting that those in favour of the resolution should take one side of the room. The *Tribune* reported: "On this the whole audience moved across, leaving empty benches on the one side, thus practically carrying the resolution unanimously." In his memoirs, Theodore Strom, who was present at the meeting, recorded: "The greater part of the audience crowded over to the east side, leaving about a dozen people, mostly shareholders in the first Company, on the west side. The Mayor declared that the Eau Claire Company should be allowed to start a light plant."

The Calgary Electric Lighting Company was doomed. One might ponder why the company could not have survived since, like Prince's enterprise, it was privately owned and was directed by Calgary businessmen of substance. Men like Braithwaite, who went on to an illustrious career with the Bank of Montreal, were surely the equal of Prince and his associates in business matters. Part of the answer must lie in Prince's image as a highly successful partner in the Eau

Claire and Bow River Lumber Company, a pioneer industry in Calgary, and one which must have had an exotic appeal to Calgary citizens because of lumbering operations on the eastern slope of the Rocky Mountains combined with exciting and sometimes dramatic log drives down the Bow River to the sawmill at Calgary. But more plausibly Prince brought with him expertise and his associates, like Theodore Strom, were men who intuitively knew how to make things work and keep them working. Prince also gambled and won by using the newer alternating current technology instead of the direct current system of the earlier company. The severe limitations of the direct current system were completely overcome by the newer alternating current technology and stacked the cards in Prince's favour from the beginning.

Finally on 9 September 1889, By-law 107 was approved and Prince had his franchise:

> ...to sink, erect place and maintain poles, to string wires, and to place lamps for electric light purposes; perpetually, upon, over and across any or all of the streets and lanes within the limits of the Municipality of the said Town of Calgary, provided he shall not place any poles upon Stephen Avenue save and except where he shall be requested to do so by the said Corporation.[21]

Part of the agreement which accompanied the by-law stipulated that Prince must provide electric service on or before the first day of January 1890. Also included in the agreement were the rates to be charged consumers for variously rated electric lamps ranging from 80 cents per month for a 4 candlepower lamp to $2.50 per month for a 32 candlepower lamp, with "all night" service. Lighting circuits were to be extended to any part of the limits of the municipality with an 8 percent per annum rate of return allowed on capital invested in extending the circuit. Both by-law and agreement were made exclusively with Peter A. Prince. At this time the enterprise was legally separate from the Eau Claire and Bow River Lumber Company although, according to Theodore Strom, it had financial backing from the North West Lumber Company of Eau Claire, Wisconsin, the parent company of the Calgary firm.

At the council meeting that granted Prince his franchise, Braithwaite sought clarification from the town solicitor as to why his company could not capture the right to a ten-year term to place their poles in town streets, whereas Prince was being granted the same right in perpetuity. The answer, of course, was that Braithwaite's Calgary Electric Lighting Company had asked for an exclusive right whereas Prince had only asked for the privilege. The perpetuity clause, however, would be challenged in future years. Questions arose as to whether Prince could meet his agreed deadline of 1 January 1890, to which Prince addressed a letter to the public in the *Calgary Tribune*:

> It appears that an idea prevails that I am not going to fulfill my contract with the city by putting in electric light by January 1, 1890. I wish to say that I will be ready

to furnish electric light to the consumer by December 1, 1889 and I would advise those who intend to use electric light not to contract for any length of time as very cheap light is what I am going to supply.[22]

Prince was not only determined to meet his deadline but his appeal to wait for his service was a further direct blow to the older company. Competition had begun in earnest. The *Calgary Tribune* hailed the anticipated battle between the two companies: "The prospect of the new company...has already had the effect of bringing down the prices of the Calgary Electric Light company to less than one half of their former prices.... There is no reason, as far as we can see, why both companies should not, to use a vulgarism, make a living out of the thing."[23]

Prince, not being one to shun publicity, quickly became the focus of public attention. He defended his choice of an alternating current system in a public letter appearing in the local press. Prince made a masterful presentation of the advantages of his chosen system in words that were easy for a layman to understand. From this letter we learn that the primary distribution voltage of his system was 1,000 volts, alternating current and that transformers reduced the voltage to 50 for utilization in residential and commercial premises. Prince concluded, "All the wires which I will use in installing my plant will be heavily insulated, both line and house wire. The poles will be the best I can buy and it will be my earnest endeavour to put up as good an electric light plant as can be found."[24]

Prince ordered the steam engines and dynamos for his power plant from the Royal Electric Company in Eau Claire, Wisconsin. He was up against a very critical deadline for getting his electric plant in operation before 1 January 1890 so as not to default on the conditions of his agreement with the town. Theodore Strom tells us that it was not possible for poles to be delivered to Calgary in time so an order was placed in Vancouver for three carloads of 6 x 12 inch rectangular cedar timbers. One week after the order was placed, the timbers arrived and were re-sawn to size in Prince's sawmill. According to Strom this was "how the first Eau Claire poles were square cedar ones." Mr. Walter K. Freeman, a contractor from Eau Claire, Wisconsin, came to Calgary to install the new system and Prince met the deadline with some days to spare.

It would be of great interest if we could determine exactly the extent of Prince's system and, for that matter, the limits of the system installed by the original company but unfortunately no records remain and we can only attempt a reconstruction by applying some reasonable assumptions. By 1890 most of the settled area in Calgary was bound by Angus Avenue (6th Avenue) on the north and Van Horne (12th Avenue) on the south. Drinkwater Street (2nd Street E.) and Ross Street (4th Street W.) formed the eastern and western limits respectively. We know that there were no joint-use agreements in existence which means that the telephone and electric light interests did not share common poles as they do today. Under these circumstances there was no place for Prince to go with his lines except into the three lanes north of the CPR tracks and the one south of the tracks, all in Section 15. Prince may have extended his lines along the avenues or streets where the old company had not bothered to extend their lines to connect new customers. Prince did, however, use the lanes to great advantage because he was able to capture customers of the old company since his lane construction allowed him easy access to the sides of two avenues. In fact, many customers on the old system moved over to Prince when they observed the benefits that his alternating current system had over the direct current Edison system. The battle for supremacy had begun in earnest.

The competition between the two companies was fierce from the start. Prince made an effort to influence his friend and legal counsel, James A. Lougheed, recently appointed to the Senate in Ottawa, to reverse the decision which gave the Calgary Electric Lighting Company the contract to supply electric service to the Mounted Police Barracks. Senator Lougheed replied to Prince on 27 January 1890 explaining that the contract arrangements had been completed by Sir Hector Langevin who was unaware of the existence of the new company.[25] All future contracts for supplying electricity to Calgary's public buildings, Lougheed assured Prince, would be opened to public bid, including the newly planned Court House. Strom records in his memoirs that the Eau Claire Company "had all the hotels" along Atlantic Avenue (9th Avenue) and that the initial load on their plant was two hundred, 16 candlepower lamps which burned brighter than those of the old company, resulting in all of the hotels "except the Alberta," transferring their business to Prince's company. He relates the antics of some of the older company's linemen in climbing their rival's poles and disconnecting the transformer fuses in order to disrupt the new services. Things were finally straightened out, however, and "as time went on we got more and more business." In desperation, the Calgary Electric Lighting Company finally decided to install an alternating current dynamo, ordering it from the same company from which Prince had purchased his machines. However after its new dynamo was in operation, Strom remarked that the only customers the old company attracted were those "bad customers that Eau Claire had cut off."

On 22 November 1889 the franchise held personally by Peter Prince under By-law 107 was translated by an Act of the Territorial Legislature into a joint stock company, with the first or provisional directors being Peter Prince, his son John Enoch, Frank H. Moon, all of Calgary, and Delos R. Moss and Isaac Kerr, both of Eau Claire, Wisconsin. The new company was called "The Calgary Water Power Company Limited." The powers granted to the company were extremely broad, enabling it to engage in almost any enterprise, including water works, electric light works, woolen mills, flour mills, shops and factories for working in all kinds of material, pulp mills, paper factories and smelting works of all descriptions. The company was capitalized at $100,000 divided into 1,000 shares of $100 each. The town council was not at all happy with this turn of events and attempted to oppose the bill creating the new company, believing that exclusive privileges and monopoly rights were being granted by the Territorial

MORTGAGE SALE

OF THE

Premises and Plant of the Calgary Electric Lighting Co., Ltd.

UNDER and by virtue of certain mort-gages, certified copies of which will be produced at the time of sale, and under the Territories Real Property Act, there will sold be at public auction at the office of Bourchier & Gouin, Stephen Avenue, Calgary, on

SATURDAY, NOVEMBER 26th, 1892,

Lot 10, in Block 50, Sec 15, Calgary, up-on which the said Company's Electric Lighting Station is erected, together with with 2 Steam Boilers. 2 Engines, 1 Steam Pump and Heater, one No 12 Dynamo, 1 No 10 Dynamo, two Spare Amateurs, all the furniture, fixtures, fittings tools, etc. upon said Lot. Also all poles main wires, interior wires and fixtures of every description used by the said Company in connection with their business in Cal-gary. whether on the streets or on any of the premises where they are furnish-ing light.

Intending purchasers may inspect the premises at any time. The property will be sold subject to a reserved bid. Terms 20 per cent cash, balance in one month with interest. Other conditions made known at time of sale. For further particulars apply to Bourchier & Gouin, Auctioneers, or to

LOUGHEED, McCARTHY & McCARTER, Vendors' Solicitors, Calgary, N W T. Calgary, Oct 26th, 1892.   oct26td

Sale notice of the Calgary Electric Lighting Company Ltd. assets.
Source: Glenbow Archives

Legislature. However, by the time they reacted to this concern at the council meeting of 29 October 1889, James Lougheed, Prince's attorney, had already returned from Regina with the news that, "The Calgary Water Power Co. has been incorporated, giving the company power to expropriate lands in the vicinity of their mill but granting them no monopoly of the river (Bow) or its tributaries."[26] It was the matter of a monopoly over the use of the Bow River and the originally proposed wide powers of land expropriation in the Territories which were of major concern to the town council and so upon Lougheed's announcement the matter was dropped. The two companies coexisted throughout 1890 and 1891 and competed for streetlighting service to the town of Calgary with the old company being successful in tendering on a contract for additional public street lighting on which it finally defaulted. The consumers were getting a break in the price of domestic lighting and although it appeared that the competitive market was working in fact the Calgary Water Power Company was becoming more successful while the older company was starting to suffer financially.

A letter from the Secretary of the Manitoba Board of Underwriters appeared before council at its 31 December 1890 meeting and drew attention to the use of uninsulated electric light wires. The letter concluded that, "It seems incredible that any company should use bare wire, but if such is really the case you should immediately serve a notarial protest on the civic authorities to have the practice put a stop to and those wires already placed taken down."[27] This letter provoked a heated editorial debate between Calgary's two newspapers, the *Herald* and the *Tribune*. The *Herald* argued that since there had been no unfavourable experience due to the use of bare wires replacing them with covered wires would simply be another financial burden on the users of electric lighting and that the *Tribune* was simply using the issue to promote a monopoly for the Eau Claire Company, a charge the *Tribune* vehemently rejected as "ineffable bosh." It was manifestly clear that the *Tribune* was a staunch Prince supporter, with the *Herald* tending to favour the older company. Both papers claimed to be defenders of an anti-monopoly position so why the issue of insulated versus non-insulated wires should have precipitated such a debate is puzzling. By 12 February 1890 the *Calgary Tribune* conceded that both Prince and the Calgary Electric Lighting Company were using uninsulated wires: "We very much regret to see that the Eau Claire company are following the example of the Calgary company in using bare wire also, but they say it is as fair for one as the other. We leave the matter in the hands of the council." Nothing further was ever done to resolve the matter and that was the end of it.

By the late fall of 1892, the Calgary Electric Lighting Company was in financial difficulty and appeared to be headed for bankruptcy. The Fire, Water and Light Committee reported to the town council "that they have not yet been able to get any definite information as to whether the old Electric light plant will be started again or not."[28] In fact it looked as if foreclosure on the company was already in progress since on 4 November 1892, notice of a mortgage sale of the company's assets to be held 26 November, appeared in the local newspapers.[29]

The town council, having a vested interest in the now bankrupt company because of the street lighting contract, decided on 16 January 1893 to approach the company (whose assets were still intact despite the public notice of auction) to see what could be done to keep it running. The best it could muster was a promise from Cave, King and Lafferty, agreeing to place a proposition before the council at an early date. Mr. Cave was a solicitor acting for unknown parties who were apparently interested in keeping the old company operational. He appeared before council on 24 January 1893, advising them that, subject to the completion of the foreclosure proceedings against the original owners, the parties he represented would accept the sum of $15,000 for the property. If the town was interested in buying the plant the vendors would accept payment by the issue of mortgage bonds at 5 percent interest spread over fifteen years with the additional option that the town could extend the purchase period to twenty years with interest charges at 5 percent, payable for three to five years on the extension.[30]

The town retained a consultant to evaluate the old power plant and the offer made by Cave and his associates. There are no existing records detailing what the council did with the proposal but later events would confirm that it wanted no part of the deal. There was a growing trend within that body favouring a municipally-owned plant. The town fathers had been initially motivated by citizen opinion in allowing Prince to compete with the original private company on the principle that competition would produce direct cost benefits to the users of the service. Now with the older company going into bankruptcy there was certainly some residual memory of that earlier decision since the principle of competition was now facing a major compromise. The *Calgary Tribune*, always a staunch supporter of Prince's Eau Claire Company, took a fairly moderate stand on the matter and conceded that, "If...the Council is assured that money will be saved by merely purchasing a plant for streetlighting, it should make the purchase," but cautioned against going into full competition with Prince for commercial business. It further argued that "The Calgary Electric Light Co. certainly did not find its business profitable, and the town with the same patronage could scarcely hope to do so."[31]

While these debates were going on the town streets had gone unlighted. This loss of public service, which by mid 1893 was attracting public criticism, was further complicated by the appearance of another privately organized group, calling itself the Calgary Electric Light, Power and Heating Company, whose legal representative, Mr. P. McCarthy Q.C., appeared before the council requesting that public streetlighting be submitted to public tender. This new company had originally planned to purchase the plant of the old, now bankrupt company but decided instead that a new plant was required. They tried to negotiate a site on CPR property for a plant location but were unsuccessful. The long delays finally convinced the council that the McCarthy company would not be successful and late in 1893 council terminated negotiations and gave the streetlighting contract to the Calgary Water Power Company.

On 15 May 1894, By-law 233 was passed to remove the poles and wires of the Calgary Electric Lighting Company from the streets of Calgary on the premise that it had "ceased to furnish electric light" and the "poles are an obstruction on said streets and avenues and a source of danger to the inhabitants of said City."[32] It is not known who undertook to remove the poles and pay the costs but two months were allowed for the work to be completed with the owners of the poles facing a penalty of $50.00 for each day beyond the end of the two month period of grace. The fortunes of The Calgary Electric Lighting Company, Limited had come to an end and for the next decade Peter Prince's Calgary Water Power Company would enjoy all the privileges of a monopoly.

References

1. *North West Territories Gazette*, 1885-87, v.2-4. (Glenbow)

2. Council Minutes, 12 May 1887, v.1, p.435.

3. Details of early telephone service in Calgary are found in *Singing Wires*, chap. 3, 4.

4. Council Minutes, 6 July 1887, v.1, p.478.

5. "Local Intelligence," *Calgary Tribune*, 8 July 1887.

6. "From Monday's Daily," *Calgary Herald*, 12 August 1887.

7. "I Remember Calgary When," *Calgary Albertan*, 14 April 1933.

8. T. Strom, "A Few Memories of When Calgary and I Were Young." *Relay* 1936. This article also appeared under the title, "With Eau Claire in Calgary," *Alberta Historical Review*, 12 (Summer 1964).

9. "Council Meeting," *Calgary Herald*, 3 July 1889.

10. Ibid.

11. Council Minutes, 27 June 1889, v.2, p.352.

12. "The City Fathers," *Calgary Herald*, 17 July 1889. Additional quotes from same source.

13. Council Minutes, 20 August 1889, v.2, p.378.

14. "Electric Light," *Calgary Tribune*, 28 August 1889.

15. "Council Meeting," *Calgary Herald*, 28 August 1889.

16. "Council Meeting," *Calgary Tribune*, 28 August 1889.

17. "The Council's Action," *Calgary Tribune*, 28 August 1889.

18. "Electric Light Meeting," *Calgary Herald*, 4 September 1889. Additional quotes from same source.

19. "Public Meeting," *Calgary Tribune*, 4 September 1889.

20. "Electric Light Meeting," *Calgary Herald*, 4 September 1889.

21. City Clerk, By-law 107, with attached agreement, 9 September 1889.

22. "Rival Electric Light Companies," *Calgary Tribune*, 25 September 1889.

23. Ibid.

24. "The Alternating Electric Light System," *Calgary Tribune*, 2 October 1889.

25. City Clerk's Papers. Letter dated 27 January 1889, Senator James A. Lougheed to Anthony Prince.

26. "The Calgary Water Power Company," *Calgary Tribune*, 13 November 1889.

27. "Town Council," *Calgary Tribune*, 8 January 1890.

28. Council Minutes, 15 November 1892, v.4, p.199.

29. "Public Notice of Mortgage Sale of Assets of the Calgary Electric Lighting Company, Limited," *Calgary Herald*, 4 November 1892.

30. "Council Meeting," *Calgary Herald*, 25 January 1893.

31. "Electric Lighting," *Calgary Tribune*, 15 March 1893.

32. City Clerk's Records, By-law 233, 15 May, 1894.

Chapter 3

PETER PRINCE
AND THE CITY OF CALGARY

With the demise of the Calgary Electric Lighting Company in 1893, the Calgary Water Power Company became the sole supplier of electricity for both public and private purposes. This monopoly survived until 1906 but it was under attack almost before it was established. The arguments about the benefits of competition, which had worked in Prince's favour when he sought his original franchise, were quickly turned against his company when it became a monopoly. The Calgary Water Power Company made a number of strategic errors over the next four decades which contributed to its eventual downfall. The first of those errors was a display of arrogance and disregard for the customer. In an astonishingly frank admission Theodore Strom described the reaction of his employer to the failure of the Calgary Electric Lighting Company:

> Both companies operated for some time and then finally the first company had to shut down. We had only the one machine and were carrying about the right load. When the old company went broke applications kept coming in to get on our system. We were already running to capacity, so, when the old company finally gave up, notices went out from the Eau Claire Company that the price of lights would be raised. There was a great kick about that from the people. Quite a number could not afford to pay the new rate and had the lights cut out. Those who had to have lights had to pay the price. While the people were complaining the company said, 'When we are able to make as much money carrying 500 lights as 1000, we would be very foolish (not) to take advantage of it.'

The sparkling style demonstrated by Prince when he went after the franchise for a new electric company in 1889 seems to have diminished with the attainment of a monopoly. The loss of personal control by the founder may have been a factor. Prince started the electrical business entirely out of his own initiative but when his idea showed signs of success control of the new enterprise was wrested from him, willing or otherwise, by the officers of the Eau Claire Company. After

51

the legal incorporation of the company in November 1889, Prince remained as a director with the titles of vice-president, treasurer and manager but the Calgary Water Power Company was now a subsidiary of the North Western Lumber Company of Eau Claire, Wisconsin.

A municipal takeover of the assets of the defunct Calgary Electric Lighting Company had been considered and rejected but the idea of a municipally-owned electric utility had taken root in Calgary. Council minutes contain no record of the public meeting called on 6 June 1893 at the request of a signed petition of Calgary citizens "for the purpose of getting an expression of opinion from the citizens on the project of the municipality purchasing and operating an electric lighting plant,"[1] but a newspaper account verifies that such a meeting was convened under the direction of Mayor Alexander Lucas. The mayor explained to those present that the town now had three options available for its consideration. First, the streetlighting proposals of Prince's company could be ratified. Second, there was a proposal by Councillor W.F. Orr to establish a municipal lighting plant, and last, the town could consider the proposal to supply electricity from a new group represented by a local lawyer, Peter McCarthy, which included a streetlighting option. Councillor Orr, who had been a staunch supporter of Prince when he had sought his 1889 franchise, was now of the opinion that a monopoly existed and said that his "position on the question was activated simply by his desire to do the best for the town." He had invited submissions from eastern electrical manufacturing firms, all of whom had confirmed that by owning the plant the town could save up to 20 percent on the prices being offered by Prince for streetlighting. A further argument for municipal ownership, Orr maintained, was that there were "over a hundred cities in Canada and the States with their own plant working most successfully." The issue soon became a choice between a municipally-owned plant or perhaps another private company operated in competition with the Calgary Water Power Company. Dr. James D. Lafferty put a motion to the floor that "this meeting is in favour of the council submitting a by-law to the ratepayers to enable them to purchase an electric light plant for lighting the streets and for domestic use, and that the municipality operate the same, and that said by-law contain the fullest information as to cost, etc." The motion was carried unanimously.

In just four years since the decisive public meeting in 1889, which had forced the town council to grant a franchise to Prince, public opinion was again divided with considerable support surfacing for a municipally-owned utility as an alternative to breaking the monopoly now perceived to be held by the Calgary Water Power Company. The polarization of opinion is illustrated by a letter to the editor of the *Calgary Tribune* on 7 June 1893 under the nom de plume of "Ratepayer" and a response on 14 June 1893 in the same newspaper under the nom de plume of "Another Ratepayer." "Ratepayer" staunchly defended Mr. Prince and his company and argued very rationally that "if the present company is making more than a fair profit, it is absolutely certain competition will arise independent of municipal intervention." The letter presented a classic case for the separation of government and the marketplace that could not have been stated more succinctly. In an equally lucid reply, "Another Ratepayer" took the opposite view and castigated Mr. Prince for enjoying his monopoly:

> The moment the old company died Mr. Prince raised his prices by 50 to 75%. ...the rapacious advances in prices on the death of the old company will be remembered and now, with his (Prince) deceptive offer exposed, under which so large an area of the town is to be shut out altogether, or only lighted at a great additional expense to the citizens, it will go hard with the few who support his pretensions to find an excuse for moving in the direction of giving him a monopoly of electric lighting in this town.

The problems which exist today with respect to the monopoly characteristic of a public utility in a competitive marketplace were understood nearly one hundred years ago by a small frontier community.

The scheme proposed by lawyer McCarthy under the name of the Calgary Electric Light, Power and Heating Company to relight the town streets and to supply electricity for domestic use failed, leaving the town with two options. By-law 230 was initiated by the town council to raise $35,000 "for the establishment of an Electric Light plant by the Corporation,"[2] but it was withdrawn after two readings when on 5 July 1894 the council decided to contract with the Calgary Water Power Company to supply the town's public streetlighting. For the next five years, which was the term of the new contract, very little transpired between the town, now incorporated as the City of Calgary, and the Calgary Water Power Company. A few complaints were addressed to the council from citizens about the charges of the company for service but the council seemed relieved to be free of the dispute that had occupied so much of its time in 1893 and 1894. However, when the contract approached the end of its life, the issues flared up again and on 2 November 1899, the city council renewed the contract on a month-to-month arrangement in order to keep the streetlights in operation until either a further contract was negotiated with Prince or an altogether different alternative took the place of a contract. Matters were finally resolved when the city built its own power plant in 1905.

The city, however, still had to live with the "perpetual" lease[3] which it had given to Peter Prince in 1889 and in the years up to 1926, the city and the Calgary Water Power Company coexisted in a relationship which, at times, appeared to be anything but friendly. Robert Mackay, who was employed by the City of Calgary Electric Light Department from 1908 until he retired as its superintendent in 1948, commented: "There is no doubt if the Calgary Water Power Company had given way on this contract (i.e., the streetlighting contract) that the installation of an electric light plant for the city would have at least been delayed for some time and perhaps, like the telephone business, the city would never have entered the field of distributing electrical energy."[4] Mackay's comment is valid for the evidence supports the conclusion that Prince, as negotiator for the Calgary Water Power Company, tended to be quite inflexible particularly in recognizing that the City of Calgary, under its existing charter, was limited in the manner of contractual agreements into which it could enter for the supply of long-term services. The evidence further supported Mackay's comment because it is clear that from the beginning the town citizens and their elected representatives were favourable to private enterprise. Prince and his associates bore the greater burden for the final separation because they failed to give sufficient weight to the local political climate during their negotiations with the city.

Although Prince and his colleagues chose the name Calgary Water Power Company when their utility was incorporated in 1889, the initial power generation was provided by steam produced by burning sawdust and scrap from the lumber mill. The choice of the name was, however, an early indication that the company planned to develop hydro power. The transportation of the Eau Claire Lumber Company logs which were harvested on the eastern Rocky Mountain slopes, upstream from Calgary, depended on the Bow River. The logs were driven down the river to a point just west of the present Hillhurst Bridge, creating huge log jams often extending westward to 14th Street. These log jams were a regular feature of the west Calgary landscape in spring when water flows in the river were at their highest.

The Eau Claire "Dam" immediately above the present Hillhurst Bridge.
Originally built in 1892, it diverted the water in the foreground
along a canal to the sawmill.
Source: Electric System Archives

In 1893 in order to move the logs from the river to the sawmill, a dam, or "weir" was built across the Bow River just upstream from the Hillhurst Bridge. The weir formed a pond and the water was directed into the intake of a canal which followed the south bank of the Bow River east for about one-half mile. At that point advantage was taken of several small islands or gravel bars at the entrance to the south channel around Prince's Island and with the aid of timber pile structures the logs were directed along the south channel to the sawmill located just west of the point where the south channel again joined the main one. The sawmill was located on the south bank of the southern channel where another timber dam formed a pond from which the logs were fished into the mill. The water license agreement between the Territorial Government in Regina and the Eau Claire Company gave the company the right to the total low flow of the river at the sawmill site which meant that during the summer months almost all of the flow of the river was diverted into the canal, leaving the north channel of the Bow around Prince's Island essentially dry. It was the twelve foot difference in elevation between the canal intake west of the Hillhurst Bridge and the point where water was returned to the main channel near Centre Street that gave rise to Prince's first hydro-electric power plant on the Bow River, thereby enabling the company to augment its initial steam power generation. Today the old canal, which operated into the mid 1930s, is no longer visible, having been filled in with south bank Bow River improvements. At the same time sawing operations ceased at the Eau Claire site and the old timber dams and structures gradually fell into disrepair until they were finally removed shortly after World War II.

The Eau Claire Lumber Company Plant c. 1892.
The sawmill is on the right and the planing mill, which housed
Prince's first electrical generators, is on the left.
Source: Provincial Archives of Alberta

Prince's hydro plant went into service in 1893. It could be described as radically unostentatious. It consisted of a two-storey wooden shed, spanning the weir between Prince's Island and the south bank of the river at the point where the water from the canal was returned to the main river channel. "Leffel wheels, set in an open timber wheel case, spanning the channel, are geared to two jack shafts, bolted to two generators," was the description of the plant contained in Hendry's *Water Resource Paper No.2*, published in 1914.[5] This description seems to contradict actual photographs of the interior of the plant which show belt-driven generators rather than "jack shafts bolted to two generators." Robert Mackay remembered the hydro plant and recorded: "The vibration and noise in the hydro plant would almost scare one to death and it seemed almost a death trap to the uninitiated with the whirring open gears and belting."

The hydro plant was never successful. The problem was that winter ice jams forming upstream from Calgary caused severe water shortages for the plant. Theodore Strom later remembered:

> The load kept increasing and more power was needed so more wheels were added until we had seven. The wheels and machinery worked fine, but the water proposition was a different thing. When the water came to Calgary we managed to help it along but when it jammed up west we couldn't do anything but wait till it came through, which sometimes took a week. We were then running with both steam and

The Calgary Water Power Company Hydro Plant c. 1900.
Source: Glenbow Archives

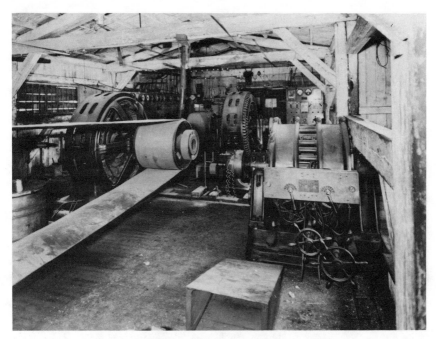

Interior view of Calgary Water Power Company Hydro Plant.
Source: Glenbow Archives

water. The steam plant always worked perfectly but when the river ran dry some of
the lights would go out as the steam plant could not carry them all.

Strom causes some difficulty with his reference to "seven" wheels. Hendry's
1914 report makes mention of only two water wheels and, unfortunately, no
living person remains who can help clarify the matter from firsthand knowledge.
According to Hendry's report, the hydro plant reached an ultimate capacity of
600 horsepower and while there were some preliminary plans in 1914 to add
another 400 horsepower, that expansion never materialized. The fortunes of the
Calgary Water Power Company continued with the expansion of its steam generation capability and by 1903 a new steam plant was taking shape on 1st Avenue
between 2nd and 3rd streets west. This steam plant grew to an ultimate capacity
of 4,000 horsepower and the hydro plant provided what assistance it could. The
name "Calgary Water Power Company" was a misnomer since most of the
electricity supplied by that company over its life came from a steam-powered
plant.

By the end of 1906 the Calgary Water Power Company and the city's utility
were in direct competition. The city, with its phenomenal population growth
between 1905 and the end of World War I, extended its borders so that by 1910
its limits were north to 40th Avenue, south to 50th Avenue, east to 26th Street
and west to 37th Street, an area comprising twenty-five square miles, compared

The Calgary Water Power Company steam plant,
located on 1st Ave. at 3rd St. W. on north side. The plant was scrapped in 1943.
Source: Glenbow Archives

to an area of less than two square miles at the time of incorporation as a city in 1894. From 1901 to 1906, the population of Calgary increased threefold from 4,000 to 12,000 and the additional electrical demands created were carried by the Calgary Water Power Company. From 1906 to 1911, a similar five-year period, the city's population increased fourfold to well over 40,000. The extra electrical load generated by this extraordinary growth was largely supplied from the city-owned power plant which, in turn, faced a continual struggle to keep pace. While this phenomenal growth was taking place the Calgary Water Power Company was confined to an area defined by the Bow River on the north, 17th Avenue on the south, 6th Street on the east and 4th Street on the west, although some minor extensions of the company did cross those boundaries on the south and east. Whether or not the growth of the company was restricted by direct political pressure from the city council or because the company could not compete with the city is not clear but it was probably a combination of both factors. The area which had been, up to the time the city entered the power business, the exclusive domain of the company was invaded by the city's electrical department and this engendered friction between the company and the city. Trying to find room on the streets for both distribution systems, however, resulted in joint-use agreements so that each utility distributed its electrical power from the same set of poles.

Joint-use power lines on 1st St. W. looking south to 17th Ave., c. 1912.
Calgary Water Power Company lines are located on the top
short cross arms with city lines on longer cross arms.
Source: Glenbow Archives

The first joint-use agreement came in 1909 "to prevent the duplication of poles on certain streets and avenues of the City,"[6] and provided for the future designation of joint-use poles as required. Photographs from 1912 clearly show joint-use poles with the Calgary Water Power Company's electric lines located in the topmost pole position on short cross-arms and the city's distribution lines attached at a lower level, using longer cross-arms to allow adequate clearance for linemen to reach the upper circuits. In 1914 the city issued a permit to the company to erect poles along 9th Avenue between 1st and 4th streets west but it was not without some concern that the wires should be buried since the poles were considered to be both unsightly and dangerous in that location. The city, however, found itself bound to the terms of the original 1889 franchise which permitted the company to use the streets for erecting their poles. In fact, up to the time it ceased to operate in 1938, the company had not buried any of its distribution system and as the city-owned electrical utility competed for new customers in those areas in which the company had traditionally operated, it became necessary for the city to place much of its facility underground, particularly in the developing central commercial core south to 17th Avenue.

Overhead power lines in downtown lanes c. 1912.
City-owned lines are on the right with Calgary Water Power Company
lines on the left.
Source: Electric System Archives

Just why the Calgary Water Power Company did not become a major provider of the electricity demands in the new areas of city remains a mystery. It is equally surprising that it did not become involved in larger hydro developments which, by 1909, were being developed or touted on the Bow and Elbow rivers. In each case the company was either out-maneuvered by other private developers or remained indifferent to the alternatives. Simply put, the Calgary Water Power Company allowed itself to become "boxed in" and made no serious attempt to provide for the future growth of Calgary's electrical needs. The total combined hydro and steam capacity reached about 4,000 horsepower with the steam plant consisting of two vertical cross-compounded Corliss steam engines, and a 1,875 kilowatt turbo-generator unit installed in 1926 as the last unit. The number of customers served by the Calgary Water Power Company at the time it ceased to operate in 1938 numbered about 2,000. Unfortunately all customer records have vanished and there is no way to reconstruct the final extent of the distribution system.

Peter Anthony Prince died at the age of eighty-nine on 12 January 1925. He was duly honoured by both the public and the press as one of Calgary's prominent citizens and rightly so. His personal vision and enterprise had introduced

Interior view of Calgary Water Power Company Steam Plant.
The machine shown was an 1800 kw turbo-alternator which was moved
to the Victoria Park Power Plant in 1944.
Source: Glenbow Archives

Calgary to the advantages of alternating current electricity, utilizing central plant generation. The *Calgary Herald* eulogized: "The passing of Peter Anthony Prince is regretted by a wide circle of friends and business associates, but who realize that he leaves behind a record of faithfulness to his trusts in life, and has contributed materially toward the upbuilding of his adopted country."[7]

Calgarians in particular can be justly proud that Peter Prince will be remembered in perpetuity by the "island" in the Bow River, west of Centre Street, which bears the name of Prince's Island Park. And to those interested parties who saw to it that the magnificent old Victorian-style Prince home, once the pride of 4th Avenue S.W., was saved from the bulldozer and beautifully restored in Heritage Park as another memorial to one of Calgary's most illustrious early citizens, we tender our sincere gratitude.

When the City of Calgary finally decided to break with Peter Prince and establish its own power plant, no one could have foreseen just how successful that new enterprise would become. Not only was the new municipal electricity service acceptable to the citizens but, of even greater importance, the enterprise became a moneymaker, and there never seems to be a time when local governments have an adequate supply of that commodity. In the years up to 1906,

Interior view of Calgary Water Power Company Steam Plant.
Source: Glenbow Archives

successive councils espoused their ideology of free enterprise and the evils of monopolies with great rhetoric. But ideology soon changes to pragmatism when money becomes a factor. To assume that this newfound source of needed revenue did not change the attitudes of the city council toward the Calgary Water Power Company would be less than honest and, as was suggested earlier, that change was also a likely factor in determining how the directors of that company viewed their opportunities for future expansions.

The wedge which various city councils used from 1906 onward to dislodge the company from its solidly entrenched position was to question the validity of the 1889 franchise agreement in two important areas. Questions were directed at the company's right to distribute electricity for ''power'' as distinct from ''electric light,'' which was the sole provision of the original franchise; and whether the town of 1889, prior to incorporation as a city, had the right to grant a ''perpetual'' franchise. Electricity had its first commercial application as a medium to provide a new, radical and convenient means of lighting and when the Calgary Electric Lighting Company started in 1887, it was solely for that purpose. The purpose was the same for Prince's company and that purpose was recited in the original franchise agreement. The developments in electrical technology following Edison's first practical application of electricity to lighting were quick in coming. It took only a short time before it was realized that the same primitive machines designed as electrical generators could also be utilized in reverse as highly efficient sources of power to operate machinery. Progress in the development of all types of rotating electrical machinery was simply staggering. The use of alternating current technology ensured the early development of electric motors which were simple, reliable and efficient and it did not take long before their application in manufacturing rendered the steam engine obsolete.

In a letter to the mayor and aldermen, dated 11 June 1906, the city solicitor, in response to an earlier enquiry, expressed doubts that the Calgary Water Power Company had the right to distribute electricity for power since the original 1889 franchise only gave the company "the right to erect poles and string wires for electric light purposes." He recited Section 15 of North-West Territories Ordinance No. 23 of 1889, later confirmed by the Dominion Government in 1891, which gave the company full power to operate works for the production, sale and distribution of electricity for purposes of light, heat, and power but "only upon and subject to such agreement in respect thereof as shall be made between the Company and the Municipal Corporation within whose jurisdiction the same are situate and under and subject to any By-law or By-laws of the Council of the Municipality passed in pursuance thereof."[8] The city solicitor's argument was that while the company may have the right under its charter to distribute power, that right could only be exercised in the municipality by virtue of a by-law and the right under the original By-law 107 did not extend to power distribution.

The matter surfaced again in 1909 when, on 22 November, Mayor R.R. Jamieson wrote to City Solicitor D.S. Moffat, asking for an opinion on the same question. Unfortunately the solicitor's reply cannot be located. Early in 1911, Mayor J.W. Mitchell made overtures to Peter Prince for the sale of the Calgary Water Power Company to the City of Calgary. In reply, Prince offered to sell "the Eau Claire Lumber Company and all its possessions"[9] including the power company for $1,500,000. The mayor only wanted the power company but Prince said, "all or nothing." The Calgary Albertan commented: "The city could really manage without the power plant as it is installing...new machinery at Victoria Park but the business of the Power company and the elimination of the possibly dangerous competition is a point that strikes the (city) commissioners forcibly."[10] The matter, however, was dropped and both city and company power plants continued to operate side by side for the next decade and a half without any further take-over incident.

The undercurrent of friction between the city and the Water Power Company publicly surfaced early in 1926 when the city commissioners, who were by this time elected rather than appointed administrators, announced that it was the intention of the city to cancel the franchise agreement by applying to the provincial government for amendments to the city charter thus permitting the city to expropriate the company after a ten-year period. "It is evidently the intention of the city to gain complete control of the distribution of power and electrical energy in the city," reported the *Herald*, "as the Commissioners have for some time...been carrying on negotiations with a view of acquiring the system of the Calgary (Water) Power Company."[11] Two days later Commissioner A.G. Graves augmented his earlier announcement with an offer to negotiate with the Calgary Water Power Company for the acquisition of its property but there is nothing to suggest that the company was prepared to negotiate with the city.

The existence of the smaller privately-owned Calgary Water Power Company had become somewhat of a nuisance to the City of Calgary with its own expanding electric utility. At a council meeting on 4 February 1926, called to discuss the commissioners' proposal to acquire the electrical plant of the Eau Claire Lumber Company, Robert Mackay, superintendent of the City Electric Light Department, reported that a "gentlemen's agreement" of long-standing between the company and the City of Calgary electrical department was more often than not ignored by the company. The understanding between the parties was that "when either the city or the company got a contract to supply energy the other was not to interfere to get the contract."[12] Two separate instances where the "agreement" had been violated were described by Mackay as the Universal Garage on 11th Avenue W. and the Traders Building on the corner of 12th Avenue and 1st Street W. In each instance Mackay held that the company had supplied electrical connections to both establishments despite prior commitments made to the city. One can be certain that this sort of gerrymandering was common to both parties.

Mr. Frank Kay was a young accountant with the Calgary Water Power Company at the time the company was finally taken over by the city and, at his retirement in 1981, was assistant treasurer of TransAlta Utilities Corporation. He recalled his early days with the Calgary Water Power Company when the city, and particularly its Electric Light Department, did its best to harass the company in its pursuit of business by the premature extension of city facilities into new areas thus preventing the company from any access to new customers beyond the traditional area it already served. The city, he claimed, would also use the provisions of the joint-use pole contract to replace poles earlier than the company felt was necessary and at costs which the company considered prohibitive but which they were forced to pay as a party to the agreement. It was not a happy coexistence and neither party appeared to be in the mood for conciliation.

By February of 1926, City Solicitor L.W. Brockington, who eventually left the city to become the first chairman of the Canadian Radio Corporation (later the Canadian Broadcasting Corporation), had brought down a report requested by the council's legislative committee giving his opinion of the legal status of the Calgary Water Power Company. In his report Brockington contended that in 1889 the Town of Calgary had no authority to grant a perpetual franchise and that the company's rights within the city amounted to no more than a revocable license.

However he conceded that if the original by-law was challenged in the courts, it would require "lengthy litigation for its adequate determination." Brockington further questioned whether the original franchise could be extended beyond defined limits, meaning those boundaries as defined by the town limits of 1889. Brockington concluded, "It is very doubtful indeed whether this Company has had at any time, any right to distribute power except by sufferance."[13]

There were other allied reasons which the mayor and commissioners advanced for the dissolution of the Calgary Water Power Company. One of these related to the desire of the city to have complete control of its streets but an even more compelling reason seems to have been the fear that the company might fall under the control of the same American interests who, in 1925, had acquired the local Canadian Western Natural Gas, Light, Heat and Power Company, Limited. Mayor G.H. Webster was convinced that this American utility-holding company, International Utilities Limited of Philadelphia, had also taken an option on the Calgary Water Power Company. An option to purchase the local company was also ascribed to the Calgary Power Company Limited but that rumour was denied by G.A. Gaherty, its managing director. "We do not sell power within the city," Mr. Gaherty said, "and therefore the city's action does not affect us."[14] Since the Calgary Water Power Company shares were largely held in the United States anyway, it seems strange that the council would be so concerned but it was a time when feelings of loyalty to the British Empire ran very high.

At the 15 February 1926 meeting the aldermen decided to proceed with an appeal to the provincial legislature to approve amendments to the city charter which would allow the city to gain control of the Calgary Water Power Company. The draft charter amendments they proposed would give the City of Calgary the right to purchase, without approval of the ratepayers, the distribution plant, machinery and equipment (exclusive of real estate and buildings) belonging to the Calgary Water Power Company, "used and useful in the distribution of electric energy whether for light or power purposes or both within the limits of the City of Calgary."[15] Provisions were also included for the use of evaluators. The existing franchise under By-law 107 would be extended to 1 June 1936, when all rights enjoyed by the company by virtue of the by-law "shall be forever terminated, extinguished, cancelled and annulled." The council, however, decided upon a two-pronged approach to the matter. Some of the aldermen reasoned that another approach should be made to the company to ascertain if the matter could be decided by direct negotiation for the sale of the assets to the city. Failing this, they decided on the arguments put forward by Alderman Andrew Davison, to proceed with their motion to request charter amendments from the Provincial Legislature, giving the city legal status to either buy or expropriate the company:

> As aldermen, we are elected to look after the interests of the city and the Calgary Water Power Co. is well able to look after its own interests.... It is necessary that the council take action tonight so that the bill can go before the legislature. The city

council has nothing to be ashamed of. If these people want to sell out they know where the city hall is situated.[16]

The decision to proceed with an application to the legislature brought a swift response from the Calgary Water Power Company. In a letter to the council, the company's lawyers, Lougheed, McLaws, Sinclair and Redman, outlined their intention "to oppose the application of the City to break the contract between the City and the Company and to terminate the Company's existence."[17] The letter outlined the exemplary behaviour of the company during its years of business within the city and its desire to cooperate to the fullest extent with the city during that period. It ended with a plea to the city to elucidate on "the particulars of the complaints against the Company, upon which you depend as grounds for asking the Legislature to put this Company out of business." The city council's response to the company's lawyers inferred that the company could hardly have been as surprised as it claimed since the city legislators had been making these overtures to purchase the company for "the past 18 months."[18] Needless to say these rumblings reached the ears of some shareholders, most of whom resided in the United States. They appeared to be ready to negotiate the sale of their shares to the city through an intermediary, a certain Mr. G.N. Black, of Winnipeg. In newspaper reports, Black was referred to as an "unknown gentleman" whom the mayor defended as a prominent citizen of Winnipeg who claimed to represent a number of shareholders in the United States and that the city was quite prepared to negotiate with him.[19] The "unknown person" was also identified as G.N. Black in a letter from the company solicitors to H.H. Irvine, Esq., of St. Paul, Minnesota, who was a shareholder and director of the Calgary Water Power Company. Mr. Irvine, who supported Black in his role as intermediary, was firmly chastised for engaging in such a clandestine matter:

> This has placed the officers of the Company in a very embarrassing position, as not knowing of the negotiations by Mr. Black, the President of the Company Mr. I.K. Kerr gave a statement to the press that there had been no negotiations with the City, and the General Manager of the Company. Mr. Carr in an interview we had with the Premier of the Province made the same statement. Mr. Black's negotiations without the knowledge of the officers of the Company has undoubtedly left the impression on the members of the Government and the public generally that the officers of the Company do not represent the majority of the shareholders and that the majority of the shareholders are willing to deal with the City over the heads of the officers of the Company.[20]

The city and the Calgary Water Power Company did not negotiate further with respect to the sale of company assets to the city. The resolution of the council to amend the city charter went before the Provincial Legislature and was given assent on 8 April 1926. Under its terms the City of Calgary was granted the right to purchase the assets of the company "without a vote of the ratepayers but with a vote of two-thirds of the Aldermen present and voting and subject to the approval of the Board of Public Utility Commissioners."[21] The city was not given the power to expropriate the company but upon negotiations for the purchase of the assets, the company was to be allowed a further ten-year extension of its franchise at the end of which "all licenses, rights privileges and franchises enjoyed by the Company under By-law No. 107 of the city of Calgary...shall be forever terminated, extinguished, cancelled and annulled."[22] The odd thing was that throughout the rest of 1926 and all of 1927, the council took no definitive action to finalize its newly acquired right to liquidate the Calgary Water Power Company.

Since 1910 the City of Calgary had entered into contracts with the Calgary Power Company for the supply of part of the wholesale electricity needs of the city. One of these contracts, signed in 1923 for a five-year term, provided that the company would supply 90 percent of the total electricity requirements of the city with the remainder to come from the city-owned Victoria Park power plant. This plant had not been expanded since 1916 and by 1918 it was only capable of providing about 18 percent of the city's total electrical load. The 1923 contract had a provision which required the city and the company to commence negotiations for a further contract not later than 1 August 1927 or one year before the contract expiry date. This contract requirement to commence negotiating with the Calgary Power Company coincided with the city's right to acquire the Calgary Water Power Company as a going concern which, if exercised, would have again placed the city in a strong position to generate more of its own electricity needs.

G.A. Gaherty, managing director of the Calgary Power Company, had denied any interest in the Calgary Water Power Company but on 14 April 1928 he and E.J. Chambers K.C., the solicitor who acted for that company had corralled almost 700 of the 1,000 outstanding shares of the Calgary Water Power Company. The share inventory of the Calgary Water Power Company showed that thirteen shareholders who held 406 shares had sold out to Gaherty while four shareholders holding 290 shares had sold out to Chambers. By 26 May 1928 both major shareholders were directors of the Calgary Water Power Company.[23] In the recently proclaimed amendments to the city charter, giving the city of Calgary the right to acquire the Calgary Water Power Company, there was a restrictive clause which prohibited the company from transferring or attempting "to transfer the control of its enterprise to any person other than the City of Calgary," except with the consent of the city. There is no record that Gaherty and Chambers ever approached the city for such consent. It was probably a moot point anyway if simply reshuffling the shareholders within the company constituted "transfer of control" to a different party. The move was never challenged by the City of Calgary, not even in 1928 when the city, during negotiations with Calgary Power Company for a new power contract, was formally requested by Mr. Gaherty to approve the transfer of the Calgary Water Power shares to the books of Calgary Power Company as part of the contract agreement. The Calgary Power Company also had a well-planned strategy in place. From the company's beginnings in 1909 there is no doubt that one of its main objectives was to secure the perpetual and exclusive right to supply electricity to the City of Calgary. With control of the Calgary Water Power Company Gaherty knew that it would never constitute any threat to the Calgary Power Company in achieving these objectives. The minutes of the board of directors' meeting of the Calgary Power Company, held in Montreal on 31 May 1928, dispel any doubts:

> The President reported that the Company had recently acquired the property of the Calgary Water Power Company, Limited through the purchase of its outstanding Capital Stock-consisting of 1,000 shares of the par value of $1000 each at the price of $600 per share, or a total of $600,000 for the property. He stated that the Calgary Water Power Company had been in successful operation in the City of Calgary for a number of years, supplying electricity retail in a substantial part of the city since 1888, and after careful investigation of the property by our engineers it was considered advisable and in the interests of this Company to acquire the property...which, *with our lease of the City of Calgary's steam plant and contract with the city for their power requirements, will result in our having full control of the power supply in the City of Calgary.*[24]

Apart from the primarily political reason for gaining control of the old Calgary Water Power Company, there may have been technical reasons as well. Mr. Ted Schulte, a senior hydraulic engineer with Calgary Power from the early years of its Bow River hydro developments, expressed the view that Gaherty saw the Eau Claire site in Calgary as an important adjunct to some future hydro development below Calgary. This was probably the Shepard site where water diverted from the Bow River at Calgary would plunge over a 300 foot drop south of Shepard, Alberta, developing hydro power as it returned to the main river channel. But Gaherty, being the brilliant and often enigmatic person that he was, never disclosed the reasons even to his closest associates.

On 17 May 1928 city council approved the transfer, to the books of the Calgary Power Company, of the shares of the Calgary Water Power Company. This constituted part of a new purchased power contract between the two parties. In a letter to council Gaherty agreed that upon such transfer of shares the Calgary Water Power Company would "continue to be bound by the statutory enactments of 1926, covering its operations in the City of Calgary."[25] Gaherty further guaranteed that the Calgary Water Power Company would not sell electric energy, whether for light or power purposes, at any rates less than those which might be fixed from time to time by the City of Calgary for its own consumers. And so it came to be that the Calgary Water Power Company, Limited became a wholly-owned subsidiary of the Calgary Power Company, Limited.

The steam plant of the Calgary Water Power Company was shut down immediately but it was not dismantled until 1944. The company continued to operate as a separate utility until 1 June 1938, the deadline set in the 8 April 1926 provincial legislation. The legislation also provided that the company could not make any new extensions to its distribution system and that its business must be confined to its existing pole lines but the company was permitted to make new connections from those lines. The Calgary Water Power Company, like the City of Calgary, now bought electricity wholesale from its parent, the Calgary Power Company and redistributed that electricity to its customers. This electricity was purchased in bulk from the 2300 volt bus bars at the city's Number 1 Substation at 9th Avenue and 7th Street W., where it was metered and deducted from the meters used for billing the City of Calgary. It was, at best, an odd arrangement since the Calgary Water Power Company's assets were to be purchased eventually by the city. One could well wonder why the arrangement was not terminated sooner. We can only conclude that neither party wished to disturb the amending legislation to the city charter and so it was tolerated. One very positive result accruing from the continued operation of two utilities in the downtown core was that the City of Calgary placed an increasing amount of its distribution facilities in underground ducts and manholes, and after 1938 these facilities evolved into the most modern and reliable of all electrical distribution systems.

In 1938, at the end of the period prescribed by the provincial legislation of 1926, the Calgary Water Power Company still had over 2,000 customers attached to its distribution lines. Most of these distribution lines were on overhead pole lines in the available downtown lanes. The transfer of the assets of the Calgary Water Power Company to the City of Calgary began in July, 1937 as part of the next purchased power agreement with the Calgary Power Company. At this time only the assets of the distribution system were transferred to the city for a negotiated sum of $325,000, secured by an initial cash payment by the city of $100,000 and monthly payments of $5,000. As time permitted and as former customers of the Calgary Water Power Company were transferred to the city's facilities, the overhead pole lines were dismantled until by the late 1940s little visible evidence remained of the old company. The employees of the Calgary Water Power Company were absorbed largely by the city with some tradesmen going over to the Calgary Power Company. The last manager of the company, Mr. W. Anderson, became the first industrial development officer of the city, a position he retained up to 1954 when he retired. A further agreement between the Calgary Power Company and the city in 1944 included the transfer of the remaining steam generating equipment in the old 1st Avenue W. steam plant to the city. An 1800 K.W. turbine, which was still in good running order, was installed at the Victoria Park Power Plant. The remaining machines were scrapped.

The vision of Peter Anthony Prince had came to an end. The company for which he was responsible still survives to the present day as a wholly-owned subsidiary of TransAlta Utilities Corporation. The Calgary Water Power Company is but a hollow shell but if the name serves, like Prince's Island and the Heritage Park house, to perpetuate the name of Peter Prince, let us hope that it will always so remain.

References

1. "The Public Meeting," *Calgary Tribune*, 7 June 1893. Additional quotes from same source.

2. Council Minutes, 1 May 1894, v.5, p.74.

3. A copy of this contract is available in the City Clerk's Record Division, Calgary. Prince's franchise of 1889 gave perpetual rights to his "heirs, executors, administrators and assigns." The contract between Prince and the Calgary Water Power Company assigned that right to the company exclusively, who in turn relieved Prince "forever harmless and indemnified from the performance and observance" of provisions and conditions contained in the original 1889 franchise agreement with the town of Calgary.

4. City Clerk's Papers, f.3565A. R. Mackay, "History of the City of Calgary Electric Light and Power Department," dated 1936, but obviously a document begun at an earlier date, say 1926, and updated periodically to 1938.

5. Murray C. Hendry, "Water Resources Paper No.2: Bow River Power and Storage Investigations," Ottawa: Dominion Water Power Branch, Department of Interior, 1914. [TransAlta Utilities Corporation Archives.]

6. Calgary Power Papers, b.2, file 80. In order to indicate the extent of the Calgary Water Power Company by 1909 the streets named in the joint-use agreement are recited as follows:

   17th Avenue from 1st Street E. to 7th Street W.
   12th Avenue from 6th Street E. to 7th Street W.
   4th Avenue from 4th Street E. to 10th Street W.
   1st Street E. from 9th Avenue to 17th Avenue
   4th Street E. from 4th Avenue to 8th Avenue
   Centre Street from 4th Avenue to 9th Avenue
   Lane No.1 from 1st Street E. to 4th Street W.

7. "P.A. Prince Old Timer in Calgary Passes Away," *Calgary Herald*, 13 January 1925.

8. Calgary Power Papers, b4.f8, No.23 of 1889. An ordinance to incorporate "The Calgary Water Power Company, Limited," assented to 22 November 1889, by N.W.T. Legislative Assembly.

9. "City Serious About Buying Out Eau Claire," *Calgary Albertan*, 3 March 1911.

10. Ibid.

11. "Aldermen to Deal with Power Topic," *Calgary Herald*, 2 February 1926.

12. "City Willing to Deal Fairly with Calgary Water Power Company," *Calgary Herald*, 5 February 1926.

13. Council Minutes, 15 February 1926, p.45-47.

14. "Calgary Power Company Not Interested in Local Power Sales," *Calgary Herald*, 5 February 1926.

15. Council Minutes, 15 February 1926, p.50.

16. "City Willing to Negotiate with Calgary Water Power Company," *Calgary Herald*, 16 February 1926.

17. City Clerk's Papers, b240. f1350. Letter dated 15 February 1926. Lougheed, McLaws, Sinclair and Redman, Solicitors, to mayor and city council.

18. *Calgary Herald*, 16 February 1926.

19. "Power Companies' Perpetual Right Open to Question," *Calgary Albertan*, 16 February 1926.

20. Letter, dated 9 February 1926, Lougheed, McLaws, Sinclair and Redman to H.H. Irvine, St. Paul, Minnesota. Copy in author's file, source unknown. This letter treats in great detail the reasons attributed to the city for wanting to terminate the company's franchise and the various options open to the shareholders.

21. Extracted from 1926 Chapter 75, Clause 13, An Act to Amend the Acts and Ordinances Constituting the Charter of the City of Calgary, assented to 8 April 1926.

22. Ibid.

23. Calgary Power Papers, b1. f1. Calgary Water Power share inventory.

24. Calgary Power Papers, b2.f4. Board of Directors' Minutes, 30 May 1928, p.19-20, (status:author).

25. Council Minutes, 17 May 1928, p.265. Letter dated 11 May 1928, G.A. Gaherty to mayor and city council.

Chapter 4

THE EARLY YEARS OF
THE MUNICIPALLY-OWNED
ELECTRIC UTILITY

In the first chapter we saw that the principal reason leading to the decision by the City of Calgary to become involved with a municipally-owned electricity generating plant was that no satisfactory agreement could be reached between the city council and Peter Prince for an expanded agreement to light the city streets. Consequently the city council authorized $60,000 to build an electric light plant and received the assent of the ratepayers on 20 December 1904. With public sentiment on its side, the council wasted no time. On 19 January 1905 the Fire, Water and Light Committee recommended that "the City Engineer be instructed to submit plans and specifications for an Electric plant capable of supplying 100 arc lights of 1200 candlepower and 2500 incandescent lamps of 16 candlepower."[1] The City of Calgary was intending not only to light its streets but to actively compete with Prince's Calgary Water Power Company for the supply of lighting for residents and commercial enterprises. The recommendations, according to the *Calgary Herald*, were "heartily endorsed," further predicting that "the Council is considering the advisability of ordering the Calgary Water Power Company to remove its poles and equipment from the city streets, in accord with the decision of the city solicitor (and) at the same time hastening the construction of a municipal lighting plant."[2]

During the first four months of 1905, while the city was progressing with the details of the specifications for its new steam power plant, residual sentiment in the city council remained for the renegotiation of a further contract with Prince for streetlighting. This was finally rejected on 27 March 1905 because Prince was offering a contract which, he insisted, must have the approval of the same ratepayers who had already cast their ballots in favour of a municipally-owned plant. The matter was closed.

Details of the specifications for the municipal power plant have long since

73

vanished and all that remains is the information in City Engineer F.W. Thorold's report to city council on 2 February 1905:

Contract "A"—One 225 kilowatt 2300 volts, 60 cycle, 2 phase, revolving field, generator, to be direct connected to a cross, compound, horizontal, corliss valve gear, engine running at 150 revolutions per minute, also 7 1/2 kilowatts exciter, belt connected with engine, suitable switchboards, arc regulators, 100 6.6 ampere series arc lamps with absolute cutouts and 60 two kilowatt transformers.

Contract "B"—Two 200 horsepower high pressure, water tube boilers, feed pump, connection, etc.

Contract "C"—Power house building and chimney.

Contract "D"—Supplying all necessary poles.

Contract "E"—Erecting all necessary poles, cross arms, etc. and stringing wire, hanging lamps, etc., also supplying all cross arms.

"It has been impossible," Thorold continued, "to have detail descriptive specifications of the apparatus prepared but I hope to be able to submit such specifications at the next regular meeting of your Council."[3] The size of this plant was comparable with the existing capacity of the Calgary Water Power Company. The area available for service by the municipal power plant was identical to that already being covered by the private company. By 1905 the limits of the municipality had not extended north beyond the south bank of the Bow River, or south beyond 17th Avenue, with eastern and western limits defined by 11th Street E. and 14th Street W. respectively. The next major expansions occurred in 1907, 1910 and 1911, with the 1911 surge remaining unchanged until 1951. This timing gave the city a tremendous opportunity to develop a market for electricity sales. Every effort appears to have been exerted by the city to inhibit the private company from expanding its facilities. In fact, the Calgary Water Power Company never enlarged its service area much beyond the limits established in 1894 when the town of Calgary was incorporated as a city.

When City Engineer Thorold completed the specifications for the municipal plant the *Calgary Herald*, on 17 February 1905, reported in some detail on the contents of his recommendation. Instead of a single 225 kilowatt generator, four generators and their boilers were said to be included, the additional ones being of 200 KW and 150 KW capacities. It is obvious that the city engineer had anticipated the early need for additional stages of capacity, notwithstanding that the plant started up with only one 225 KW machine; a rather risky venture since no allowance could be made for the machine being out of service. Continuity of service, however, was not too important at this time. Only as other uses of electricity developed did continuity of service became a major factor in user expectation. The same article went on to say:

The time limit for the completion of the entire plant is October 1st and a penalty is imposed for failure to comply with that particular part of the contract as it is the purpose of the council to be ready before next winter to light the streets as a metropolis of Calgary's pretensions should be lighted, and render an acceptable service to a large number of private buildings.

By the end of February 1905, public tenders had been called in newspapers in Montreal, Toronto, Calgary, Golden, B.C. and Cranbrook, B.C. The last two newspapers were probably chosen because of their proximity to centres of the production of wooden poles needed for the overhead power lines.

Thorold recommended to the council on 2 March 1905 that "all the tenders for Electric Light contracts "A", "B" and "C" (Generators, Engines and Boilers) be referred to an expert electrical engineer for his opinion on the best tenders to accept." The tenders were opened on Thursday, 16 March and reported to the council. The sum of all the contracts, excluding the powerhouse building, came to $45,423. When the estimated costs of the powerhouse, electricity meters, additional wiring for extra incandescent lamps, foundations for machines and inspection were added, the total came to $57,523, which was still short of the original debenture issue of $60,000 approved in December of 1904. A cost analysis by "two of the Electrical Engineers now in Calgary" estimated the cost of generating electricity at between 8 1/4 and 8 1/2 cents per kilowatt hour on "condition that the City takes 100 arc lights at $85.00 per year."[4] While the Fire, Water and Light Committee recommended the immediate awarding of the contracts, the city council tabled the matter pending the preparation of a city electricity rate schedule in order that comparisons could be made with those of the private company.

The aldermen were concerned that their municipally-owned utility should be fully competitive. The schedule of rates was produced at the 22 March 1905 meeting of the council and quoted the "house rate" at 14 cents per kilowatt hour, with commercial rates ranging from 12 cents to 16 cents per kilowatt hour, depending on the usage. Hotels, restaurants and churches fared a little better with rates varying from 11 cents to 13 cents. After much discussion, the council decided that the proposed rates were competitive. It was a difficult decision since most of the consumers on the private supply were charged on a flat rate governed by the number of lights being operated and their candlepower rating. The city rates, however, were proposed as metered rates where the number and rating of the lamps did not matter but only the actual metered energy consumed.

No further action was taken by the council until 27 March 1905, after the decision to break with the Calgary Water Power Company was finalized. After what the *Calgary Herald* described as an "acrimonious debate" during which charges and counter-charges were exchanged with Mr. Prince's supporters who wanted "to embarrass the city in this movement,"[5] it was agreed that the city would proceed with its plans to build its own power plant. On the advice of City Engineer Thorold, an electrical engineer, R.S. Kelsch of Montreal, was retained to recommend the awarding of tenders for contract. In addition, the council agreed to advertise for "an Electrician to supervise the whole building of the City Electric Light plant."[6]

It would be of great interest, at least to those whose minds have a technical bent, to learn where the city engineer, who almost certainly had a civil engineering background, obtained the information to prepare the power plant specifications as he did. Perhaps the two electrical engineers who had given advice on the costs of city-generated power had assisted Thorold in preparing his original specification. Thorold's own admission that the tender documents should be referred to a competent electrical engineer for assessment surely indicated his concern. R.S. Kelsch was very critical of the city's specifications and was not very helpful to the council in making its decision as to what equipment to buy for this new venture. Kelsch wrote: "Inasmuch as your tenders are drawn up so that there is no one contractor in Canada who makes a specialty of the work, the result is that all bidders have been placed at a disadvantage."[7] Kelsch wanted the council to prepare new specifications "in such a way that you can make comparison and select the best offer," but lacking the concurrence of the council finally made what he considered to be the best alternative decision under the circumstances. The council accepted his recommendations while at the same time giving strong support to the city engineer who had done, by all counts, a most admirable job for them.

The first engine and generator were ordered from the Allis-Chalmers Bullock Company "providing they satisfy this council that the portions of the plant referred to in Mr. Kelsch's report as being incomplete will be properly supplied and provided the city have the right to have an expert superintend the installation of the plant."[8] Some time later Kelsch wrote a letter to Alderman S.A. Ramsay, formerly Mayor Ramsay, who was chairman of the Fire, Water and Light Committee in 1905, and concluded with these rather caustic remarks,

> The Consulting Engineer's duty is to advise his clients in their best interests, regardless of the fact that it may not please everybody, and I hope you will consider it good advice and not unnecessary criticism, and hope that your plant, will not have to join the ranks of unsuccessful municipal plants, which are being published almost daily in the newspapers.[9]

Despite Kelsch's criticism which probably stemmed from the fact that he was not consulted from the beginning of the plant, the municipally-owned plant proved to be an instant success.

The location of the new coal-fired steam plant was fixed as Lots 31-38, Block 50, Plan A1 in Section 16, which gave it a municipal location on the northeast corner of 9th Avenue and 5th Street W. where it was known as the "Atlantic Avenue Plant." On 12 June 1905 the council awarded the contract for "a brick veneer power house" to a local contractor, E.A. Kettison, for the sum of $4,632 which was considerably less than the estimated $6,000. The building, with its subsequent extensions, served Calgary long after the power plant was relocated to Victoria Park, first as a municipal garage and later by some operating divisions of the municipal Electric Light, Heat and Power Department. In the early 1950s it was remodelled to house a retail outlet of the Alberta Liquor Control Board and it still serves this function. If a pun can be excused, the pioneering "spirit" has been symbolically replaced by the "spirit" of the Alberta Liquor Control Board.

The Fire, Water and Light Committee's report to.the council on 20 July recommended that E. Lionel White of Montreal be hired as the superintendent of the new plant at a salary of $100.00 monthly and that he assume his duties in August. Nothing is known of White's background but perhaps we can assume that the contact came about through one of the eastern Canadian contractors who worked on the new plant. Mr. White remained with the city until early in 1907 when he resigned for unknown reasons and left Calgary.

The supply of fuel chosen for the new power plant was "buck wheat size" coal from the Pacific Coal Company at Bankhead, Alberta, an early anthracite coal-producing town north of Banff. The decision to utilize anthracite coal required the addition of forced draft fans in the power house to ensure complete combustion. By mid July 1905, City Engineer Thorold reported that the contractors had arrived to start on the erection of the distribution system external to the power plant. Applications for service from the new system were to be accepted immediately "so that we may know where our current is to be used and where the transformers are to be placed."[10] The problem of where to place poles on the streets where those belonging to the Calgary Water Power Company already existed was solved by an agreement between the city and the company, and considering the hard feeling which existed between the parties, that was no small achievement. The city engineer reported that "wherever there is no lane...we (will) use longer cross arms so that our wires will be clear of theirs and I would ask your permission to order the longer cross arms." The city engineer confidently announced that the new streetlights would be turned on by the 15th of November.

In the middle of the frenzy to complete the new city plant and bring it "on line" before the end of 1905, another power offer was submitted to the city by Garnet P. Grant (of whom we know nothing) to supply 30,000 kilowatt hours of energy which would be available for "night loads." He demanded a ten-year contract from the city and this required the approval of the ratepayers. The Fire, Water and Light Committee gave grudging approval to Mr. Grant's scheme but when the offer reached the council on 3 July 1905, it balked. Council argued that it would be foolish to commit such a term to Mr. Grant when there was already the possibility of natural gas becoming available as a cheaper fuel for power generation and even the possible development of hydro power from the Kananaskis Falls on the upper reaches of the Bow River. Grant's offer was dismissed without further comment.

Meanwhile progress on the municipal plant continued. By 1 November 1905 it had reached a stage of development meriting glowing reports from the *Calgary Herald,* one of which carried the headline, "SOME INTERESTING DETAILS OF INDUSTRY WHICH BREAKS INTO AN ODIOUS MONOPOLY," referring obviously to the Calgary Water Power Company. The article reported gangs of men working day and night, boilers tested, engines in place and a smokestack five feet in diameter, rising to a height of ninety-five feet from the base. The second article was equally complimentary:

Calgary's civic electric light plant will soon be an active factor in solving the problem of street lighting as well as providing domestic services....When the plant is ready the citizens will have every reason to feel proud of their investment. Everything will be of the most up-to-date character, and arranged with an eye to efficiency and economy.[11]

The new plant went "on stream" for the first time on Saturday, 2 December 1905 when the new streetlights were tested. The first light switched on was on the corner of 8th Avenue and 4th Street W. and when it was found to be fully operative, the remainder of the lights were illuminated. The *Herald* recorded the event: "The many trials and vexatious delays which naturally attend the erection of an electric light plant came to an end Saturday evening...and about 80 arc lamps shone brightly in different parts of the city."[12] Formal dedication of the new plant took place on Wednesday, 6 December 1905 with Mayor John Emerson starting the generator and Alderman S.A. Ramsay, chairman of the Fire, Water and Light Committee, turning on the power to operate streetlighting circuits. The *Calgary Herald* reported that an "open house" followed for the citizens with "tempting refreshments...for all who attended the opening and were greatly enjoyed." The article continued:

There were a great many ladies and they appeared to take a very intelligent and lively interest in the workings of the plant. They were shown the workings of the different intricate pieces of machinery by the courteous staff of officials and if they understand all about generators, exciters, volts, condensers and vacuums, they are a whole lot wiser than the average male who visited the plant last night.[13]

Perhaps the reporter had enjoyed more than his fair share of the "tempting refreshments." The article concluded with an admonition to those not enjoying the benefits of the new electrical generating plant to make their requests soon since a single application requiring a long line extension could not expect service as quickly as those in a geographically concentrated group. An editorial also appeared in the *Calgary Herald*:

The formal opening of the municipal light plant last night marks an epoch of unusual importance in the progress of the municipality. The enterprise developed under rather unpromising conditions. The determination of the council to submit the proposition to a vote of the ratepayers followed lengthy negotiations with the private company for a street service. There were many level-headed citizens who disliked the suggestion that a second lighting plant be erected with civic funds. Others seriously questioned the ability of the city to compete with the private corporation as a business proposition. The appropriation of $60,000 was declared to be but a drop in the bucket. The adoption of the by-law by an overwhelming vote was the first evidence of the unanimous sentiment in favour of municipal ownership. Last night came the climax. The plant and the quality of the light supplied reflect credit upon every man connected with the project and every ratepayer who cast his vote for the by law which made the civic light possible. The city officials deserve the congratulations they are receiving.[14]

It was not long before a fundamental deficiency surfaced in the new plant. Many of the prospective users of power were concerned that the plant would not be operating on a firm twenty-four hour schedule. The use of electricity for supplying power as well as lighting was beginning to emerge and the matter needed urgent attention. The answer, which had been anticipated by City Engineer Thorold, was to have more than one machine in the powerhouse so that service could be maintained while a machine was shut down for maintenance. The Calgary Water Power Company was already providing continuous service to its customers and even though the rate was 20 percent higher than that proposed by the municipal plant customers of the older company were not likely to transfer their patronage to the newer one because of this advantage. While the municipal plant opened with a single machine, it would only be a short time before this deficiency was eliminated.

Lionel White of Montreal had been installed as the first city electrician with responsibility for overseeing the erection of the power plant. By the end of 1905 two other important names made their appearance. The first was James F. McCall who was retained prior to the official opening of the plant as chief engineer.[15] James McCall came to Calgary from Dumfries, Scotland, by way of Toronto and Vernon, B.C. where, as a competent machinist, he worked as engineer and mill superintendent for a flour milling company. He later installed the power plant at the International Coal Mine at Coleman, Alberta and from there he came to Calgary. He remained as chief engineer and superintendent of the municipal steam plants up to his death in 1952 although from 1928 onwards he was an employee of Calgary Power Company when it assumed the operation of the Victoria Park Power Plant under the contract agreement of 1928.

The second name is that of Charles A. O'Brien. Whether he was an employee of Calgary or of the contractor who was in charge of erecting the first city-owned outside electrical distribution system is not clear. Prior to 1905 Mr. O'Brien had been in charge of the Bell Telephone service in Calgary and in that capacity installed Calgary's first fire alarm system. Some time between 1905 and 1906 he joined the Calgary Fire Department as Calgary's first electrical inspector. In a letter authored by James McCall to the city commissioners, dated 24 May 1906, we learn of a confrontation between McCall and O'Brien. They did not seem to get along, perhaps because of their Scottish and Irish backgrounds. The problem arose when a fire alarm circuit broke and fell across the streetlighting arc circuit, rendering the fire alarm circuit inoperative until the break could be located and repaired. Fire Chief "Cappy" Smart and Charles O'Brien stormed into the powerhouse that night and demanded that the shift engineer on duty, a Mr. Watson, "pull one switch after another till they found out where their trouble was." Watson refused since such action countermanded his orders, insisting that it was not a "case of life or death or serious damage to property." However, the Fire Department officials prevailed after threatening to report Watson to the city council. Watson finally did as he was told but not before telephoning the morning papers to determine if the action being taken would "tie up the printing." The next day, McCall concluded his defence of Watson in the final fiery paragraph of his letter to the city commissioners:

> Engineer Watson has his orders from me not to cut lines in or out of circuit unless on orders from Mr. White or myself or in a case of life and death or serious damage to property, he told these gentlemen his orders and they wanted to know what in H__ I had to do with it. If they do not know they had better find out for they will not be allowed to put a hand on any apparatus here. When they want a line cut out we will always oblige them but we must protect ourselves. I gave Watson the orders and if there is any trouble go after me not him. Will you please give us written instructions governing our mixups in such cases. We do not want to throw the city in darkness because a fire alarm is grounded on our lines and it will save any further trouble between these *CITY OFFICIALS* and ourselves.[16]

The mere fact that McCall took the time to spell "city officials" in large capitals and underline them gives clear indication of how he viewed interfering outsiders. At the council meeting a few days later, a motion was carried "that the officer or officers in charge of the municipal electric Light Power house be notified to switch off power on any circuit at the request of the City Electrician in the case of trouble with alarm system."[17] McCall had made his point.

The municipal power system was an instant success. By May of 1906, City Electrician White was receiving requests for the extension of lines for industrial power loads, including motors. These extensions for power were designated by White as "three phase" and this confirms that a change was made to the original 1905 specification calling for a "two phase" power house generator. Either the original specifications were incorrectly recorded or a change was made after the machine was ordered, the latter being more likely. Many early alternating-current distribution systems on the Canadian Prairies were "two-phase" and some persisted well into the 1940s when they were changed to "three-phase" systems. The great advantage of a "three-phase" power system was the saving achieved in primary voltage conductors, one less being required for the "three-phase" choice. The addition of motor loads to the distribution system had a disadvantage because of excessive regulation. Simply stated, "regulation" means the voltage drop caused by starting electric motors resulting in "flickering" of incandescent lamps connected to the same system. City Electrician White sent a long handwritten treatise on this problem to the city clerk explaining the phenomenon of flickering lights and recommended the use of a "voltage regulator which can be bought and installed for about $550.00."[18] The city was learning that "quality" of service was just as important as the "availability" of service. Six months after the municipal plant opened, White reported on the extent of the system:

> At present the plant is carrying 310 places including motors and lighting. The lighting lines have been so extended that we can catch nearly any place from 4th St. W to 6th St. East from 5th Ave. to 15th Ave. We have also extended in all directions where the arc lamps are placed, so that while we cover the above mentioned part of the town we also cover a great deal of the town in the out-lying districts such as the West end and over the Elbow. We have up to date installed 240 new poles and 228 1/2 K.W. in transformers.[19]

The problem of maintaining continuous service to new customers was also being addressed. White was instructed to assume a shift in the power plant every day as an engineer, along with McCall and "the other engineer." The shifts were for five, nine, and ten hours respectively for a total of twenty-four, with White, we assume, taking the shortest period. Additions to the system to supply the demand for service were of some concern to the council throughout 1906 and well into 1907. The plant, in its infancy, could not generate enough revenue to cover all of its expenses, requiring frequent requests by the city electrician to city council for additional funding which had to be raised by money by-laws, the costs of which were charged directly to the power plant. In July 1906 the total revenue from electricity sales was just under $10,000. Expenses for the same period were $9,800, including coal costs, interest and sinking fund payments.

The city council was by no means unconcerned about the need for more revenue-producing customers and tried its hand at a bit of coercion. On 28 May 1906, the council instructed the city commissioners:

> ...to make representation to public institutions that are receiving grants of public monies or special favours from the City with a view of inducing them to install the City electric light and power. Further that in future no grants of public monies or special favours be granted to any institution, company, or persons establishing industries in the City unless they first agree to use the City electric light and power.[20]

When it suited their purposes some city councillors who had so zealously defended the principle of competition could turn a blind eye! By January 1907 the installation of the second steam engine and generator, a duplicate of the original machine, was complete and additional electrical load was being openly solicited on a voluntary basis. For example, a letter from the city clerk to J.J.

Young, managing director of the *Calgary Herald*, said in part: "As our City electric light plant is now running in first class order, we will be pleased to receive applications from all ratepayers to become patrons of this department."[21] It is ironic that the *Calgary Herald*, which so strongly supported a municipally-owned power plant, was still a customer of the Calgary Water Power Company.

Earlier we related the story of the interference by the fire chief and Charles O'Brien into the operational affairs of the power plant. The friction between O'Brien, the city electrical inspector, and White, the city electrician, was also considerable, as a series of letters between each official and the city commissioners illustrates. O'Brien reported a series of overhead line problems where he believed that insufficient clearances were being maintained. In what was the usual reporting procedure of the day, this report went directly to higher authorities instead of to the responsible official. The higher authority, in this case the commissioners, would direct the information back to the other subordinate authority, who would always take a defensive stand and accuse the originating authority, through the commissioners, of unfair practice. Lionel White reacted to O'Brien's report of unsafe overhead lines by countering that he should also inspect the lines of the Calgary Water Power Company for similar infractions. Further, Mr. White claimed that if the commissioners had approved his earlier request for enough money to do the extra "guying" required by Mr. O'Brien's report, the matter need never have surfaced in the first place.

Following the resignation of White, Charles O'Brien was separated from the Fire Department and appointed city electrician in February 1907, at a salary of $100.00 monthly. Later that year the council passed By-law 842 providing for the maintenance, management and regulation of the electric light plant and system of the City of Calgary by a "Light Committee or such other authority as may from time to time be designated by the Council."[22] The by-law also provided for the maintenance of the positions of city electrician and mechanical engineer, with the first having "superintendence of all the electrical works in connection with the plant and system" and the second having "supervision and control over the power house and the mechanical part of the system and property connected therewith." Whether the city electrician was superior to the mechanical engineer in the administrative structure is not clear but the evidence indicates that each official acted as if they were equal and separate entities. Each party reported directly to the commissioners and the council and each was paid the same.

On Sunday morning, 7 October 1906, there was a major accident in the new power plant. Engineer McCall reported in his usual forthright manner: "Owing to the wreck of the L.P. (low pressure) side of the engine at Power House...I beg to report the shaft and frame are in a much worse condition than after the first break, the shaft being more bent and the repairing that was done after the first break is badly shattered."[23] Evidently some repairs had been done but they were not successful and now one of the steam engines was in need of major repair.

Fortunately the second machine was now operating but McCall expressed concern over the ability of the remaining machine to carry the extra loading required of it. In the same letter, he also reported the following incident: ''I regret to have (to) report that Robert Rice lost the thumb of his right hand on Sunday night while assisting in cooling a hot bearing on the broken engine.'' Reporting a fairly severe occupational accident was only incidental to the main problem.

At the end of the first year of operation by the municipal power plant, Mayor John Emerson extolled the virtues of the municipal ownership of public utilities to a certain Joshua Dyke of Manitoba. ''The City of Calgary,'' Emerson wrote, ''established a municipal electric light and power plant one year ago, cut the price twenty per cent below that charged by private company, who have operated plant and had monopoly for fifteen years. Our municipal plant is today a paying concern.''[24] Indeed it was but on the other side of the coin were the financial problems besetting the small booming city because of the demand for extension of all manner of municipal facilities, including the power plant, which by early 1907 was carrying electrical demands almost equal to its capacity.

Help was sought in November 1907 by contracting with a newly formed private power enterprise, the Calgary Power and Transmission Company, for the provision of an augmenting wholesale electricity supply to the city as soon as the company's proposed hydro-power development was completed at Horseshoe Falls on the Bow River at Seebee, Alberta. This matter will be addressed in the next chapter but it is mentioned here because the contract between the company and the city marked the beginning of an arrangement which has survived to the present day. By the end of 1907 the city power plant was faced with the addition of a 175 horsepower pump for the city water department and it prompted the chairman of the Fire, Water and Light Committee to appeal to E.H. Crandell, secretary of the Calgary Power and Transmission Company, for the early supply of 1,000 horsepower under the terms of the contract: ''we find it necessary to refuse any further business that would tend to overload the plant; notwithstanding the demand for additional street and private lighting is still very great.''[25] Whether or not all of this panic was justified, it did not seem to have any effect on the undaunted Scottish spirit of James McCall, chief engineer of the power plant, who reported confidently, ''that (the) Power House is now in (a) position to guarantee an unbroken service.''[26] Since no contracted hydro power was available to the city until 1911 and since the Atlantic Avenue Power Plant was not significantly expanded until 1909, we can only conclude that much of the electrical load growth was picked up by the Calgary Water Power Company. Both James McCall and his counterpart, Theodore Strom of the Calgary Water Power Company, had reputations for being extremely knowledgeable and resourceful and it is reasonable to assume that they cooperated in operating their respective plants to the overall benefit of Calgary citizens despite the bad feeling which existed between company and city officials.

Calgary's population during its first major boom cycle increased four-fold from 12,000 in 1906 to 44,000 in 1911. It required another two decades before the population doubled again. In the spring of 1907 recommendations to increase the capacity of the power plant were made by R.R. Jamieson,the chairman of the Fire, Water and Light Committee. As a result, the powerhouse building was extended with the addition of two 250 horsepower boilers but this did not include new engines. By late summer Jamieson reported satisfactory revenues from the power plant even though prices for electricity had been reduced. Construction of new power lines into southwest Calgary had reached several miles and a start had been made on extending similar lines to the eastern limits of the city. This prompted a letter on 23 August 1907 to the city clerk from William Pearce, the pioneer land surveyor and outstanding administrator of the western affairs of the Federal Department of the Interior:

> Is the City prepared to furnish me electric light? If so I would desire to obtain same. The large plant now being erected by Cushing Bros. Co. will, I understand, likely require electric light to be supplied it by the City. To do so the poling will come within about an eighth of a mile of my place.
>
> Further, there are a number of houses erected or in course of erection on property sold by me, some of which are not more than a quarter of a mile from my house and probably some of those would desire to obtain light also.
>
> Kindly advise me as early as possible as to the probabilities of obtaining light.[27]

City Clerk Gillis replied that "should the firm of Cushing Bros. and others in the near future require light, it is more than likely that the same can be extended to your place."[28]

The following excerpt from a letter written by Ronald Fraser, an office employee in the Electric Light Department, gives us a post-Victorian insight into a grievance. Mr. Fraser addressed his letter of complaint to the mayor and aldermen:

> I regret having to inform you that on Saturday last the 3rd inst. your City Treasurer, Mr. T.S. Burns arrived at this office and after a bit of preliminary swearing, let the bolt of his wrath fall on my head in a torrent of abuse and black guardianism. I did not return it with interest but rather offered the other side to be smitten however I made up my mind that if such disgraceful affairs are to be tolerated in a public office and in presence of women, I would not be a party to it.[29]

Despite these minor irritations the enthusiasm of city officials was evidenced by the city clerk's letter to Mr. H.V. Jamieson, Barrister, of New Glasgow, Nova Scotia, who had written to Calgary for information about the electrical plant: "I have enclosed you a copy of the yearly report of the Electric Light Committee of the City of Calgary, which I trust you will find satisfactory. All I can say is that it is all true."[30] One could hardly fault these officials for their smug optimism.

By the end of 1907, nearly two years after the municipal plant had opened, the peak electrical loading on the two 225 KW generators was 527 KW. The plant and its line extensions were valued at $165,000 and the metered electricity customers totaled 1,480. Despite the contract held with the Calgary Power and Transmission Company for the supply of additional hydro-electric power, expansion of the municipal plant was a high priority item. The decision came in June when the Fire, Water and Light Committee recommended the purchase of a 1,000 horsepower, vertical cross-compound condensing engine, coupled to a 750 kilowatt generator for the combined cost of $36,126, which in 1908, was an enormous amount of money to spend on a single item. By contrast, the same meeting of the council produced the recommendation that, ''the Light Com.(mittee)

Erecting the stack and forced draft fans at the Atlantic Ave. plant for the 1000 kw
"A.L. Cameron" steam engine and generator 1908.
Source: Glenbow Archives

be authorized to sell the pony now used by the Arc Light Trimmers and purchase one that may be used for any work that the Department may require."[31]

The largest and last steam engine and generator to be installed at the Atlantic Avenue (9th Ave.) Power Plant was officially commissioned on Monday, 18 January 1909. It was christened the "A.L. Cameron" in honour of Calgary's mayor during 1907 and 1908. The opening was reported in the *Calgary Herald*:

> At one o'clock yesterday afternoon, the 'A.L. Cameron' started and made her first revolution of wheels, and at 3 o'clock she was carrying the entire load of the City Lighting Plant and doing it easily.... The engine is an enormous and marvelous bit of gigantic mechanism standing 20 feet high, with two decks and a ground floor.... The 'A.L. Cameron' is a vertical engine, working straight up, instead of along the level, like the other two horizontal engines in the power house. She weighs roughly speaking about 253,000 pounds, or over 120 tons...one thing is assured now. There is a sufficiency of engines at the city power plant to supply all the light necessary for the city, even though there is not as yet enough boiler power to run the three engines.[32]

A new and substantial electrical load for the municipal plant made its appearance early in 1909. It was the driving force required for the new municipal street railway which was planned to be operational by mid year. By the beginning of 1909 the highest load carried on the municipal plant was approximately 1,000

Interior view of Atlantic Ave. Power Plant c. 1908.
Source: Glenbow Archives

horsepower or 746 kilowatts. The initial street railway electrical load was esti-mated to require some 500 kilowatts of direct current capacity which would mean a major addition in generating capacity. The electric light department estimates for 1909 included 1,000 horsepower of additional boiler capacity at an estimated cost of $26,000 and an engine and generator set for operating the new street railway at an estimated cost of $22,000. The lack of any specifics in regard to the engine and generator indicates that initially no one was quite certain how this increased capacity would be provided. However by March the decision on the plant extension had been made and it was a most surprising and satisfactory one.

The street railway required direct current for its operation but the generators at the powerhouse supplied alternating current only for distribution to its users. One alternative was to install a steam engine driving a direct current generator of the required capacity but unless two such machines were available, the street railway would face unscheduled shutdowns. There was also the double cost for standby service. The alternating current generators, however, had additional capacity available during daylight hours and it was decided to use this capacity as the alternate electrical supply for the street railway. A motor-generator set, which could run on the alternating current supply and produce direct current for the railway, solved the problem quite handily. A 750 horsepower vertical steam engine, directly coupled to a 500 kilowatt direct current generator, was pur-chased from the Robb Engineering Company for $14,300 together with a motor-generator set of 300 KW direct current capacity, coupled to a 500 horsepower alternating current motor from the Allis-Chalmers Bullock Company at a cost of $15,950. The total cost was $30,250, some $8,000 more than the original vague estimate but this extra amount guaranteed an uninterrupted electrical supply for the new street cars, and their operation needed reliability if they were to gain widespread public acceptance.

In July 1909 James McCall was asked by city council to calculate the selling price of energy to the street railway. McCall submitted a rate of 3.5 cents per kilowatt hour based on a fairly elaborate cost analysis which recognized the various cost components that go into rate design. The rate provided for normal operating costs, including coal at $5.65 per ton, interest at 4 1/2 percent on the assets of the powerhouse used exclusively for street railway power, plant depreciation, and the efficiency of the new 300 KW motor-generator at various electrical loadings. McCall concluded, "I would recommend that a rate of 3.5 cents (per kilowatt hour) be charged the street railway for current supplied from motor generator; a much lower rate can be given as soon as steam set is in operation; this rate will allow the Power House a fair margin of profit as soon as we get back on Bankhead coal, and we will also profit from higher efficiency from motor generator as its load increases."[33] The rate advertised in 1909 for energy use of 5,000 kilowatt hours or over from the city system was a flat 6 cents per kilowatt hour. Clearly, the rate offered to the street railway was a preferential one because of the high energy usage which amounted to one-third of the total output of the plant.

The street cars which were to become the pride of all Calgarians went into service on Monday, 5 July 1909 and with that event the future of the municipal power plant was further assured. The wise choice of machines to supply the street railway system was demonstrated when the steam engine coupled to the direct current generator developed serious trouble with its valve gear in December. Electrical supply to the railway was unbroken while the necessary repairs were completed. In his annual report for 1909, McCall made the following recommendation to city council:

> I beg to call the attention of your Honourable Body to the fact that 2000 h.p. additional should be provided before the Fall of 1910, owing to extensions to street railway and lighting system, as we were just able to pull through the past winter's peak load with nothing to spare. I would not recommend adding to present plant as in my opinion it would be a menace to the water and sewage system of the city; furthermore there is no storage for coal should the plant be extended on present site. I would, therefore, recommend that if an additional steam power is to be installed, another power house site be looked for.[34]

The highest electrical load in 1909 was 1,600 kilowatts while the lowest was 165 kilowatts. The highest load included the street railway while the smallest load was largely that of the streetlighting system during the nighttime hours. The pole line extensions had increased to a total of twenty-seven miles using 1,100 poles and the total number of power and light services reached 2,971. The city electrician remarked that, "The work in connection with this department has over doubled itself over that of any previous year."[35]

The search for additional cheap power became a matter which occupied a great deal of the deliberations of the city council throughout the second half of 1909 and all of 1910. That body had to consider many genuine and fanciful proposals submitted by private contractors. The various committees of council established to examine these proposals were, without exception, very cautious due, no doubt, to the memory of the long and unsatisfactory negotiations between the city and the Calgary Water Power Company five years earlier but also because of the operating and financial successes of the municipal plant. In the end, however, one of the proposals from the Calgary Power Company was to win with a contract for the supply of hydro-power generated on the Bow River for 1911 delivery. (These matters will be dealt with at greater length in the next two chapters but the reader should be aware that these new outside pressures were beginning to impinge on plans for any expansion of the municipal power plant.) The city administration was on the horns of a dilemma. Calgary needed industrial expansion as well as population growth and the availability of a reliable and inexpensive power supply was a key to the development of the city. So while the city entertained and courted alternative power supply proposals, it continued to "cover its bets" by expanding its own plant until it could be assured that the hydro developments proposed along the Bow and Elbow rivers were indeed all that they were touted to be by their promoters.

While the power plant received most of council's attention up to the end of 1909, a new development started in the spring of 1910 with a recommendation that the city "construct a partial conduit system in the congested part of the City before any more permanent pavement is laid."[36] The recommendation was for $30,000 to install underground conduits on 9th Avenue between 4th Street W. and 6th Street E. and on 4th Street W. from 8th Avenue to 17th Avenue, as well as minor extensions into Lane 2, which was between 7th Avenue and 8th Avenue. The four lanes which were surveyed into Section 15 traversed the area with most of Calgary's commercial development and the lanes and streets were already host to overhead power and telephone lines. The conduits were added each year until, by 1915, there were over twenty miles of conduits interconnected by some 400 manholes along most of the lanes, streets and avenues of Section 15, between 17th Avenue and 4th Avenue. Major extensions into adjacent Section 16, as far as 8th Street W. were also completed. It was, by any standard, a major project for any city in western Canada. The conduit system quickly absorbed the overhead lines north of the CPR tracks so that by the mid 1920s most of the city's distribution system within the commercial areas of Sections 15 and 16 had been placed underground. The area south of the

From 1910 to 1914 Calgary's central core was underlaid with conduits for electric cables. View shows tile ducts being installed on Centre St. between 6th and 8th Aves., c. 1910.
Source: Electric System Archives

CPR tracks remained residential and did not fare as well. The conduits along 5th Street E. from the Victoria Park Power Plant into downtown Calgary served a particularly useful purpose in carrying high voltage feeders, using paper-insulated lead covered power cables. Up to the end of 1912, $170,000 had been raised in by-law debentures specifically for conduit extensions but after 1912, when the borrowing by-laws tended to be more general in nature, it becomes difficult to earmark the specific amounts spent in each successive year for the purpose of conduit extensions. It was a bold and imaginative venture for these early decision-makers and it made Calgary a pioneer in the application of underground electrical distribution systems.

By the end of 1909, the city electrical utility showed a substantial surplus on its balance sheet and it was not long before the civic administration made its recommendation to the city council regarding the distribution of this windfall:

...the earning capacity of the City electric light and power plant is such that a surplus revenue of $49,000 was on hand at the end of last year. After providing back sinking fund from the starting of the plant, which fund was formerly provided from the general rate, we have been able to take $25,000 from that revenue and apply to current revenue, thus reducing our taxation. After thus taking this amount of $25,000 there is still in this revenue or contingent fund a margin left over of some $24,000.[37]

This was the first occasion on which surplus funds were used to offset property taxes and it was to become formal practice in later years. By October of 1910, another idea had emerged, sponsored by Mayor Jamieson as chairman of the board of commissioners. In his letter to the city solicitor, the mayor addressed the matter of the distribution of surplus revenue from city utility operations. "Would it not be well," he wrote, "to incorporate a provision in the new charter authorizing surplus revenue from these utilities to be used in extending the systems and thus relieve, to some extent, cost against the City through having money by-laws voted and issuing bonds."[38] He argued that if some of the revenues of the utility enterprise were used for relief of taxation then there was a case for those receiving such relief to be expected to contribute something in the form of equity capital. It was another idea which was to gain favourable acceptance in later years.

Quite unexpectedly the electrical load on the city plant increased again at a faster pace than anticipated. To cover this contingency the city had the 1907 contract in hand with the Calgary Power and Transmission Company for delivery of 2500 horsepower of hydro power from their anticipated development at Horseshoe Falls on the Bow River. This company was unsuccessful, however, in financing the project and was the target of a takeover that included the contract with the city, by a new Montreal company, the Calgary Power Company Limited. City council was not about to acquiesce to the conditions of the contract without some further negotiations with the new company and much valuable time was lost before a replacement contract was signed in September 1910, advancing the delivery of the much needed power to April 1911. To further aggravate the problem the new company had construction problems at Horseshoe Falls in the form of a washout, prompting Chief Engineer McCall to write to the mayor informing him that the unfortunate event "is going to place the City plant in a very serious position this fall unless you have some absolutely sure source from which to secure power by October 1st."[39] McCall also recommended that the city stop soliciting new business for the power plant until the crisis was over. In the middle of these events, City Electrician O'Brien, seemingly unaware of what was going on, recommended to the commissioners that the city should promote the use of newly-available electric water heaters. Needless to say the commissioners did not take very kindly to the suggestion. It was one of several such events which eventually resulted in O'Brien's replacement as city electrician.

The beginnings of the Victoria Park Power Plant came in mid 1910 when a new 750 horsepower steam engine was ordered so that a further 600 kilowatts of direct current power would be provided for the municipal railway. Following the 1909 recommendation of Chief Engineer McCall, this machine was located in

Crews building brick superstructure for Victoria Park Steam Power Plant.
Scotsman Hill in background.
Source: Electric System Archives

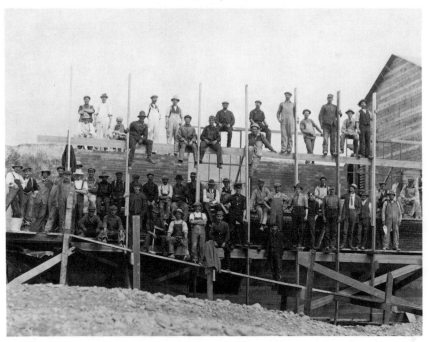

Victoria Park, a piece of land deeded to the city by the Crown for agricultural purposes. It was already the site of the Dominion Agricultural Exhibition. The power plant was located at the eastern extremity of the area adjacent to the Elbow River. Water for cooling would come from the Elbow River and a railway spur from the main CPR line would provide coal delivery. With adequate storage facilities and water available on the site, the disadvantages of the 9th Avenue site were overcome. By-law 1061 was passed to raise $125,000 for the new engine, auxiliaries, boilers, and a temporary building located on a permanent foundation. The chairman of the Power Development Committee, Mayor R.R. Jamieson, reported on 22 October 1910 that:

> Work on the new power station is progressing satisfactorily. Boilers are now being installed and the engine and generator foundations are now completed. The contract calls for the erection of the plant and to have the same in operation on the 15th day of December. At the present time we are consuming up to the limit of our output of electrical energy at our present power station. We are still taking on all private business and intend to do so, but it is not unlikely that the street lights will have to

Main switchboard of Victoria Park Power Plant c. 1912. Left hand panels controlled direct current supply to street railway while the right hand panels controlled the alternating current generators.
Source: Electric System Archives

be cut off during temporary heavy loads before we can use our new installation to relieve the situation.[40]

Despite Engineer McCall's earlier concern, the connection of new consumers to the municipal system continued throughout 1910 at the average rate of one hundred each month. Calgary was not only continuing to grow at an unusual rate but the municipal electric service was received enthusiastically by its citizens. On 4 November 1910, the *Calgary Herald* published a detailed account of the progress being made in Victoria Park:

> The new $100,000 home of the giant engines, boilers, generators, transformers and other machines through which the subtle and powerful electric fluid passes before lending its giant strength to the moving of hundreds of wheels of industry and traffic in the city and the illuminating of the streets and many homes, will be completed by Dec. 15, and is now standing with massive walls almost finished, awaiting the roof and other finishing touches of expert workmen.

The article then explained at some length the necessity of the new power plant as an auxiliary source of electrical power for Calgary if the anticipated hydro power from Horseshoe Falls was interrupted for any reason:

> Then as an auxiliary, 6000 h.p. will be ready in an adjacent room, stored in boilers under which banked fires lie, to come to the assistance of the power sent down from the Bow river when the peak load (or the time when the demand for electricity is greatest) is in progress, or when a breakdown occurs. There will not be another power-house in the west more modern.... Experts state that every detail is planned correctly, and the principle of automatum is carried out to as great an extent as possible.... Just west of the boiler room is the room where the switchboard, generator and other machines will be placed, with coils of snaky black wires, great whirring wheels, little black dials with white faces and restless hands, and complicated devices for various electrical purposes.... The building is built fireproof in every detail. It is one well-fitted to house thousands of horse-power of electricity, and worthy of such a progressive city as Calgary.

City Electrician O'Brien's regime was now winding down and on 16 October 1911 the commissioners reported to council:

> During the last two years the growth and development of the City has increased the work of the Electric Light department to such an extent that it is necessary an electrical engineer should be appointed to supervise the department. We are very much behind in this year's work owing largely to changing over our installment (sic) from steam to hydro-electric power which is increasing our scale in the power end of the business, and this necessitates a large number of heavy copper feeders being erected, and there are prospects for large developments during the year 1912, therefore, your Commissioners would recommend that Mr. H.E. Kensit, M.I.E.E., now with firm of Messrs. Smith, Curry and Chace of this city, be appointed as Supervising Engineer at a salary of $225.00 per month.[41]

Boilers and coal stokers in Victoria Park Power Plant c. 1912.
Source: Glenbow Archives

Kensit, however, refused the position informing the commissioners that he could not accept the terms and conditions of the offer. The commissioners then decided to advertise for a suitable candidate and on 13 November 1911, recommended the appointment of Mr. R.A. Brown from the city of Nelson, B.C., as the new superintendent. "We believe," they reported, "that he will be of good service to the City of Calgary."[42] No one could possibly have imagined the scope of the contribution which R.A. Brown would make to the city of Calgary and to the pioneer development of the crude oil industry in Alberta. Charles O'Brien moved back into quiet obscurity in the fire department and remained there as fire alarm superintendent until his retirement in 1934.

Early in 1911, By-Law 1170 was enacted disbanding the Light Committee which had its origin in the Fire, Water and Light Committee of 1884. Under the new by-law, the administration of the electric light plant and system became the responsibility of the city commissioners chaired by the mayor. The commissioners assumed full responsibility "excepting the financial part" which remained with the city council. The officers who could be appointed were the city electrician and the mechanical engineer. In actual practice the titles electrician, superintendent and electrical engineer continued to be used interchangeably as were the titles chief engineer and mechanical engineer. Both city electrician and mechanical engineer reported directly to the commissioners and there was no further attempt to combine the administration of the electrical and mechanical power departments until 1923 when consolidation occurred under R.A. Brown.

The new power plant site at Victoria Park determined where the augmenting hydro-electric power supply would be received in order to meet the anticipated 1911 winter peak load of something in excess of 6,000 horsepower. But to ensure that the anticipated electrical load could be serviced, an order to purchase the first 2,000 horsepower turbo-generator set from the Allis-Chalmers, Bullock Company at a total price of $41,965 was approved on 1 April 1911, with a guarantee that the unit would be operational by 22 August. The recommendation for purchase was accompanied with the comment that, "While this price is considerably higher than other tenders, we do not feel that we should take any chances in case the hydro-electric should fail during the fall of this year." The continued expansion of the city power plant was undertaken as insurance against the unknown problems associated with a new hydro plant and a single fifty-mile long transmission line to Calgary. In his 1911 annual report to the city council, Commissioner Graves concluded, "With the completion of the Victoria Park Station, we will have one of the most modernly equipped and up-to-date buildings in Canada."[43]

The hydro-electric power contracted from the Calgary Power Company arrived in Calgary at 8:30 a.m., Sunday 21 May 1911, one month behind schedule. The *Calgary Albertan* reported that:

Mayor Mitchell was awakened from a Sunday morning nap at 8 o'clock and found an automobile ready to convey him to the power station where by the insertion of a little plug he turned the power on the bus bars at the switchboard and harnessed up the power generated by the water at Horseshoe Falls for the use of the City of Calgary. There was no demonstration of any kind, no cheering crowd to witness the interesting event. Only Superintendent McCall and the power house staff witnessed the ceremony but everything passed off without a hitch, and exactly as was intended.[44]

No sooner was the new hydro-electric power supply available to the city than work commenced on dismantling the (Atlantic) 9th Avenue Power Plant and relocating the boilers and two of the engines to Victoria Park. The two original 250 horsepower horizontal reciprocating steam engines and their generators were sold with one of them ending its days providing electricity to the coal mines at Canmore, Alberta. R.E.(Roy) Malcolm, who joined the city power plant in 1908 as a "coal trimmer," maintained that it had been a mistake to move the larger 750 KW machine (the "A.L. Cameron") to Victoria Park, but gave no particular reason. By 1912 the machine was gone from its Victoria Park location. An old-time operator, Walter Gillingham, who joined the power department in 1918, remembers that the "A.L. Cameron" was missing from the power plant when he started but that the memory of the machine was still very much alive with his older contemporaries. In view of these recollections and in the absence of any record of the sale of the machine, we conclude that it was scrapped, possibly because of an unsatisfactory service record or to make room for additional turbo-alternator sets.

The arrival of hydro-electric power did little to alleviate the concern over its reliability and the city continued enlarging the Victoria Park site. City Commissioner A. Graves focused the concern of the city, anticipating a second turbo-alternator in the near future. It was actually installed in 1913:

> With the installation of another Steam Turbine of 2,500 K.W. capacity, the City will then have a 'Stand By' Plant of over 6,000 H.P. Alternating Current, which although adding very materially to the overhead charges and consequently to the cost of power, puts the City in a most favourable position should any serious interruptions occur to the Water Power Plant. With the rapid development of this City I estimate

Interior view of Victoria Park Power Plant c. 1912. Machine in foreground is the first 2000 kw turbo-alternator set installed in 1911. The next machine is the "A.L. Cameron". The smaller machines at the back are direct current sets for street railway service.
Note: Gas lighting fixtures.
Source: Electric System Archives

that 6,000 to 7,000 H.P. will be required by next November to meet the demands. As there is a limited amount of power available at the present site (Horseshoe Falls) on the Bow River, it is necessary that the City should investigate other sources of power.[45]

Until the end of 1913 hydro power had been delivered to Calgary over a single 60,000 volt transmission line and the city power plant was a necessary adjunct to cover line outages. Another problem encountered by the city plant was the management of the annual load factor to produce minimum power costs when two totally different power sources, each having unique cost factors, were involved.

The "load factor" is a simple ratio of actual energy delivered over a defined period of time, usually annually, to the maximum amount of energy which could have been delivered if the plant or machine had been fully loaded over the same time period. A one kilowatt generator, for example, operating for one year at full load would be capable of delivering 8,760 kilowatt hours of energy, simply the product of its capacity and the number of hours. However if the actual demand for energy from the generator occurred for only one half of the total time available, the energy delivered would be only 4,380 kilowatt hours and the annual load factor would be 50 percent. This, incidentally, approximates the annual load factor under which most modern electrical utilities operate. Obviously both city and company wanted the highest possible load factors at each of their plants. Malcolm recalled that the problem resulted in a continuous squabble between the city and the Calgary Power Company as to how the load would be shared. The first contracts between the city and Calgary Power were simple "Horsepower per annum" agreements for which the city paid $30.00 for each horsepower delivered. This was a much better price than the power generated from its steam plant where the figure was closer to $60.00 per horsepower. The incentive was there for the city to purchase as much power as possible from the company because of the price advantage. However, because of the reliability required for the service, the power plant had to be kept available constantly which meant that steam pressure had to be maintained with associated fuel costs. One year after the delivery of the first hydro-power, the hydro source was supplying 70 percent of the total electrical requirements of the city with the remainder coming from the steam plant at Victoria Park at an annual load factor of just less than 20 percent. Chief Engineer McCall knew what was happening and in his 1912 annual report he included the following:

I beg to suggest to you, that as you are about to make arrangements for an increased supply of current, and as it has been demonstrated beyond doubt, that an auxiliary to the present source has to be maintained, and that the cost of operating this auxiliary plant would be very little more if it were run for the full twenty-four hours, the only increase in operating costs of any importance would be the extra fuel,...in this way you can get a fair efficiency from the steam plant, which has not been the case...as during the summer months the steam plant was only used

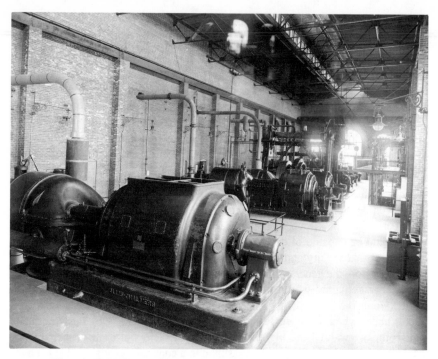

Victoria Park Power Plant at the height of its development c. 1914.
Source: Electric System Archives

for...cutting off peaks, and to keep the voltage of the Power Company's supply somewhere normal.[46]

It was also of major concern to city officials that the hydro development at Horseshoe Falls was at the mercy of low water conditions during the winter months when electrical demands were at their highest. R.A. Brown, who had acquired considerable experience with hydro power sites while superintending the hydro power installation at Bonnington Falls, B.C., recognized this pressing problem and informed the council in late 1912: "For the additional power we shall need over and above that which the Calgary Power Company can be relied on to continuously supply, we have the following means from which it can be generated."[47] Brown outlined his alternatives in some detail, expanding on the use of coal versus natural gas for fuel and the economic alternatives between moving fuel to the plant versus transmission of electricity. He recommended securing the services of an "eminent electrical expert" to advise the city further. The expert appointed was R.A. Ross and Company, consulting and supervising engineers of Montreal. Ross submitted his report prior to April 1913 but, unfortunately, it has been lost. However, City Commissioner A.G. Graves produced a summary of the Ross recommendations for the city council and this was published in the *Calgary News Telegram* of 21 April 1913. The cost comparisons showed that for a 50 percent annual load factor the most economical power cost could be obtained by a combined hydro power contract at $26.00 per annum per horsepower and a coal or gas fired power plant each sharing an equal portion of the combined energy requirement of the city. The Ross report recommended a municipal power plant expanded to an ultimate capacity of 45,000 KW in increments of 5,000 KW each year or year-and-a-half, to accommodate the electricity needs of a population of 200,000 by 1923. In retrospect this was rather optimistic since Calgary's population did not reach that figure until 1958. As a result of this strong report a further 5,000 KW turbo-generator set was added to the plant in 1914. Steam was supplied to the new machine from gas-fired boilers and a substantial addition to the north end of the building was required to accommodate them. While the extension was large enough to accommodate three 5,000 KW machines, only one machine was installed.

By 1913 the Calgary Power Company had completed its second hydro plant installation at the Kananaskis Falls site upstream from the first site at Horseshoe Falls. With this larger up-stream water storage capacity coupled with a second 60,000 volt transmission line to Calgary much of the concern of the city regarding the reliability of the hydro service was temporarily alleviated. At the end of 1914, Chief Engineer McCall, with a certain sense of finality regarding the future of the Victoria Park Power Plant, published an inventory that included the value of his engines and generators:

1-1,100 HP Cross Compound Engine and 1-750 KW Generator-	$36,126.
1-900 HP 3-cylinder Vertical Engine and 1-600 KW Generator-	$18,900.
1-750 HP 3-cylinder Vertical Engine and 1-500 KW Generator-	$19,300.
1-1,600 KW Turbo-generator set, installed 1911-	$44,000.
1-2,500 KW Turbo-generator set, installed 1913-	$42,750.
1-5,000 KW Turbo-generator set, installed 1914-	$75,000.[48]

The Victoria Park Power Plant had reached its ultimate electrical capacity except for a small 1,800 KW turbo-generator set relocated there in 1944 when the remaining assets of the Calgary Water Power Company were taken over by the city. In 1928 the plant was leased to the Calgary Power Company after which it ran spasmodically until the Second World War. In the immediate post-war years the plant, in one last heroic effort, was called upon to augment a critical electrical energy shortage in the province. The obsolete machines were unceremoniously scrapped in 1953 with the building serving out its days as a horse barn for the Calgary Exhibition and Stampede until 1972 when it was demolished.

By 1911 the city limits were 48th Avenue N., 50th Avenue S., 24th Street E. and 37th Street W., comprising one township or an area of thirty-six square miles. A small four mile square addition existed on the southeast corner of the city, encompassing Ogden and the CPR Ogden Shops, while another small one-half square mile extension south of 50th Avenue included Manchester. By a

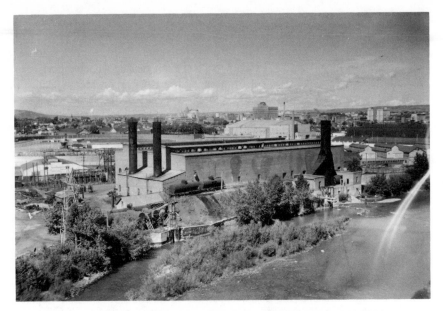

View of Victoria Park Power Plant before it was scrapped in 1954.
Source: Electric System Archives

stroke of genius either Charles O'Brien or R.A. Brown decided, in 1911, to erect a 12,000 volt power line around the perimeter of the city, one mile inside the limits, except on the north where it was two miles. It became known as the "ring main" and it was fed in two directions out of the Victoria Park Power Plant. It was so well located that, up to the mid 1950s, it serviced the entire electrical requirements, other than those of the downtown core, of Calgary. It had the inherent advantage that any substation cut into the line was supplied with a dual infeed thereby greatly increasing the reliability of service to electricity users. Many portions of the old "ring main" still exist, most notably along the lane immediately north of 16th Avenue N. between 6th Street E. and 14th Street W. and along 34th Avenue S.W.

Two major substations were built in 1912. Number 1 Substation at the corner of 9th Avenue and 7th Street W. was connected to the Victoria Park Power Plant by two parallel 12,000 volt underground cables. A transformer with 3,000 KW capacity was installed and thus transformed the voltage down to 2,200 volts for local distribution of electricity into the downtown core, south into the "Belt Line" area and north to the Bow River as far west as 14th Street. The newly-installed high intensity arc streetlights on downtown streets were also serviced from this location. The street railway needed more traction power and this was provided by two 1,000 KW motor-generator sets, installed in the substation in 1918. This building, now vacant, still stands albeit with a new facelift. (As a boy,

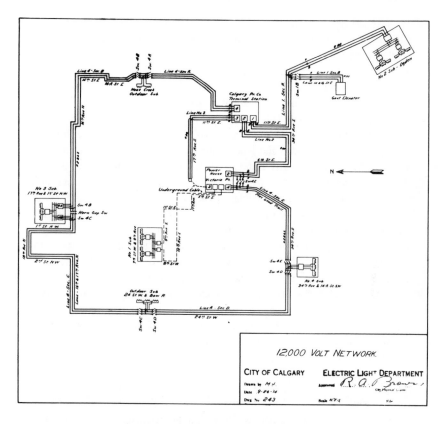

Schematic diagram of the city 12,000 volt network c. 1914.
The "Ring Main" is readily identified.
Source: Electric System Archives

I remember watching those large machines, through an open door resplendent with a polished brass "No Admittance" plate, as they went about their work of aggressively producing power to run the street cars. Years later I would have the job of supervising their removal and sale to a Vancouver junk dealer.) Across the city, in the extreme southeast, No.2 Substation was built opposite the new CPR Ogden Shops. One of the main reasons for the shops locating in Calgary was the city guarantee of street railway service for the workers. Between the Ogden Shops and the municipal railway, 3,000 KW of capacity was required and it was delivered to No.2 Substation over 12,000 volt overhead power lines from the central power station.

It would be difficult to close this chapter without recalling one of the more bizarre requests for electric power proposed in Calgary. In a 1911 letter addressed to the mayor and aldermen of the city, a Mr. Charles McAlpine, representing Dr. W. O. Farquharson of Edmonton, requested assistance:

We have just received our charter for a Company called the Magnetic Wheat-Food Co. Ltd. We have been manufacturing, in a small way, in Halifax, N.S., under another name and all those who have used our Wheat-Food have called for it again. The wheat we are using is grown in Ontario, but we want to get near the product. This wheat can be grown in Alberta Province. The process of manufacturing this wheat,—and only one kind of wheat will answer the purpose,—is done by our own mills that are magnetized. This food will never go sour, the magnetism keeps it continually fresh. This wheat is the most economical food in existence. It makes the most delicious porridge and gruel in the world. Food dishes can be made in great variety and the bread is unsurpassed. We will want a building and elevator that will cost from $12,000 to $15,000. The first year we will employ about twenty people and that number will be doubled up each year, as we increase in size...What can your City do for us, and can you raise from the City or Business Men, say, $50,000 in cash to buy that much worth of stock? There will be a dividend of at least 20% with 10% rest fund, and the Company is capitalized at $150,000. Also take into consideration the fact that every package that goes out advertises your City, and there will be millions of packages,—all over the world. We will use up from $15,000 to $20,000 in cash in advertising purposes throughout Canada, Great Britain, United States, etc., and every year the amount will be increased, in fact this advertising will be one of the largest items outside of the cost of manufacturing the Wheat-Food. Also, what can you do about power, heat, light and taxes, and how near the railway for shipping purposes?[49]

Was it a genuine promotion or just a scam? Whatever happened "magnetized wheat" does not appear to have reached the market unless by some other name.

In its first decade of existence, the municipally-owned electric utility had developed from a simple 250 horsepower generating plant, feeding into a primitive distribution system, into the beginning of a highly sophisticated and reliable electrical distribution network with a capacity in excess of 12,000 horsepower. It was an heroic effort on the part of all those who were involved and reflected a period of growth in Calgary's history which has never quite been duplicated. In fact it was this extraordinary growth that was responsible for attracting the attention of eastern Canadian financial barons and convincing them that they too should make every effort to get into the act.

References

1. Council Minutes, 19 January 1905, v.9, p.203.

2. "Tenders for Light Plant Will Be Asked By City," *Calgary Herald*, 20 January 1905.

3. Council Minutes, 2 February 1905, v.9, p.231.

4. Council Minutes, 20 March 1905, v.9, p.271. Names are unknown.

5. "Municipal Lighting Plant Will Be Erected At Once," *Calgary Herald*, 28 March 1905.

6. Council Minutes, 27 March 1905, v.9, p.281-82.

7. "Light Plant Plans Will Be Rushed," *Calgary Herald*, 22 April 1905. Additional quotes from same source.

8. Ibid.

9. City Clerk's Papers, b.15. f.22. Letter dated 27 April 1905, R.S. Kelsch to S.A. Ramsay.

10. Council Minutes, 13 July 1905.

11. "Municipal Light Plant is Ready for Business," *Calgary Herald*, 11 November 1905.

12. "Civic Light Now Shines in Calgary," *Calgary Herald*, 4 December 1905.

13. "The City Lighting Plant is Formally Dedicated," *Calgary Herald*, 6 December 1905.

14. "Dedication of the Municipal Light Plant," *Calgary Herald*, 6 December 1905.

15. J. McCall is probably best remembered as the father of Capt. F. McCall, D.S.O., M.C., D.F.C., of the Royal Flying Corps. McCall was one of Canada's illustrious World War I heroes. The name was given to Calgary's international airport.

16. City Clerk's Papers, b.19. f.139, 24 May 1906. McCall to city commissioners. Previous quotes from same source.

17. Council Minutes, 28 May 1906.

18. City Clerk's Papers, b.17. f.140, 29 May 1906. G.L. White to Gillis.

19. City Clerk's Papers, b.19. f.152. Letter dated 25 June 1906. White to mayor and council.

20. Council Minutes, 28 May 1906, p.352,353.

21. City Clerk's Papers, b.19. f.152. Letter dated 15 September 1906. City Clerk to F.J. Young.

22. City Clerk's Records, Calgary By-law 842, 30 December 1907. Additional quotes from same source.

23. City Clerk's Papers, b.18. f.147. letter dated 9 October 1906. McCall to commissioners. Additional quotes from same source.

24. City Clerk's Papers, b.18. f.147. Letter dated 29 October 1906. Mayor Emerson to Joshua Dyke.

25. City Clerk's Papers, b.28. f.207. Letter dated 3 January 1908. Chairman of Electric Light and Power to E.J. Crandell, Secretary, Calgary Power and Transmission Company. The copy is unsigned so the actual author is unknown.

26. City Clerk's Papers, b.22. f.172. Letter dated 20 January 1907. McCall to R.E. Speakman.

27. City Clerk's Papers, b.22. f.173. Letter dated 27 August 1907. William Pearce to E. Gillis.

28. City Clerk's Papers, b.22. f.173. Letter dated 27 August 1907. City Clerk to Pearce.

29. City Clerk's Papers, b.21. f.167. Letter dated 5 August 1907. R. Fraser to Mayor.

30. City Clerk's Papers, b.28. f.211. Letter dated 13 February 1908. City Clerk to Jamieson.

31. Council Minutes, 1 June 1908, pp.31-2.

32. "New 1,500 Horsepower Engine Takes Up Load," *Calgary Herald*, 19 January 1909. Additional quotes from same source. The Herald reported the capacity of the engine incorrectly. The engine was only 1,000 horsepower but perhaps the reporter confused the capacity of the "A.L. Cameron" with that of the entire plant which was, with the addition of the new engine, 1,500 horsepower nominal. Mayor Cameron was the only citizen to hold the mayoralty on two widely separated occasions: 1898 & 1907.

33. Commissioners Papers, Box 1, file 2. Letter dated 2 August 1909. J. McCall to Mayor.

34. City of Calgary. *Annual Report* 1909.

35. Ibid.

36. Council Minutes, 29 March 1910, p.32, Commissioners' supplementary report.

37. Council Minutes, 25 April 1910, p.74A.

38. City Commissioners Collection, b5. f:26. Letter 6 October 1910, Jamieson to Moffat, City Solicitor.

39. Ibid. b.43. f:331. Letter 19 May 1910, McCall to Mayor.

40. Council Minutes, 22 October 1910, p.241.

41. Council Minutes, 16 October 1911, p.259.

42. Council Minutes, 13 November 1911, p.280.

43. City of Calgary. *Annual Report* 1911.

44. "Calgary Now Supplied With Hydro-Electric Power," *Calgary Albertan*, 22 May 1911.

45. City of Calgary. *Annual Report* 1911.

46. City of Calgary. *Annual Report* 1912.

47. Ibid.

48. City of Calgary. *Annual Report* 1914. Smith, Curry and Chace was the consulting engineering firm acting on behalf of the Calgary Power and Transmission Company in its Bow River hydro development at Seebee.

49. City Clerk's Papers, b.47. f.365. Letter dated 24 November 1911. Charles McAlpine to mayor and aldermen.

Chapter 5

THOSE IRRESISTIBLE RIVERS

Constable George Clift King was part of "F" Troop, North-West Mounted Police and the first man in the troop to set foot on the southern flats at the spot where the Bow and Elbow rivers join to form a single stream. Later he described his first impressions: "Never will I forget the sight that met our eyes; the confluence of the two winding rivers with their wooded banks, the verdant valley and beyond, the wide expanse of green plain that stretched itself in homage to the distant blue mountains. A Garden of Eden! A place to live forever!"[1]

And so, with the beginnings of a Mounted Police outpost in the western extremity of the Canadian prairies, Calgary was established. King's glorious, idyllic vision included two rivers which were destined to play an important role in the development of the small tent community surrounding Fort Calgary into a prominent Canadian metropolis. Like most rivers around which communities of men have gathered throughout history, the Bow and Elbow rivers proved to be both blessing and bane. Being of glacial origin, both rivers could be raging torrents in the late spring and mere trickles for the remainder of the year. If Calgary was not to be continually at the mercy of the arbitrary nature of these rivers some upstream developments to even out the flow would soon have to be considered. Well into the 1930s, flooding on both rivers was an annual, sometimes catastrophic event that had to be reckoned with by Calgary.

The earliest commercial use of the Bow River was by the Eau Claire and Bow River Lumber Company. The original plan of the Eau Claire Company was to establish its sawmill at Kananaskis, near the lumbering operation, but Prince later decided upon Calgary for the location of the sawmill with the Bow River becoming the means of transporting the logs. "The Company's booms and arrangements for utilizing the Bow are on a large and most complete scale and it is more than likely that they will utilize the fine water power at no distant day," wrote a commentator in the *Calgary Herald*. "The establishing of this enterprise in Calgary is one of the greatest advantages which any town could desire and no doubt it will be duly appreciated.''[2] Prince and his associates did establish the original hydro power plant on the Bow River in 1893 but the plant was never reliable, particularly during the winter months when water was in short supply, or when excessive ice build-up rendered the plant useless.

As early as 1903 the city's Board of Trade was collecting information on the possible development of hydro power at Kananaskis Falls, about fifty-five miles upstream on the Bow River. The Board of Trade had asked Rodney J. Parke to speak to them on the subject of hydro power. Parke outlined his qualifications as a consulting engineer who had been retained by the City of Toronto in its scheme to transmit hydro power from Niagara Falls.[3] He was enthusiastically received by both the Board of Trade and Mayor Thomas Underwood who in turn instructed the city clerk to advise him whether the city had the right to develop hydro power from the Bow River. The clerk advised that under the Act of the Northwest Legislature the city could not only apply for that right but could also make arrangements with the Canadian Pacific Railway to utilize its right-of-way as a route for the transmission of the hydro-generated power to Calgary. Mr. Parke offered to make a preliminary ten-day survey of the scheme at a cost of $25.00 per day, with the city providing a man to assist him. The council proceeded to vote the sum of $300.00 for the survey and Mr. Parke promised a report which would be forwarded from Toronto as soon as possible. Unfortunately, the Parke report has not survived but the action of the city council must surely have served to focus the attention of others on the hydro power possibilities of the Bow River.

On 21 March 1905, the matter of water power came up briefly before the city council when the city was close to terminating its streetlighting contract with the Calgary Water Power Company and just prior to its decision to build a municipally-owned steam power plant. Alderman C.A. Stuart raised the question with the Fire, Water and Light Committee when he asked if it had any further information but the reply was simply that "the water power question was too far off and was unpracticable."[4] Mr. Prince was quoted by his supporter Alderman R.C. Thomas as saying that the Kananaskis site did not suffer from the formation of slush ice which was the greatest problem with Prince's small hydro plant in Calgary. Furthermore Alderman Thomas reported that, "The formation of a company to run a plant at the falls (Kananaskis) was considered by Mr. Prince as a much more dangerous competition than a civic plant." Obviously Prince had some knowledge of plans underway to develop the Bow River further upstream for hydro power and hoped that this advance information might discourage the council from proceeding with its plan for a municipally-owned power plant. Mayor John Emerson concluded the discussion, commenting, "there was plenty of (hydro) power on the Elbow but no money to develop it." This was most probably the reason why the city did not progress any further at this time in its investigation of the hydro potential of either the Bow or Elbow rivers.

The first hints of a proposal to develop hydro-electric power on the Bow River upstream from Calgary surfaced on 30 November 1906 with news items in the local newspapers. Two Calgary business and financial entrepreneurs, W.M. Alexander and W.J. Budd, had joined forces to propose a hydro-electric development about thirty miles west of Calgary, two miles below the CPR station at Radnor. They had retained the services of an expert hydro-electric engineer, C.H. Mitchell, C.E., of Niagara Falls, Ontario, to report on the details and feasibility of the plan. Mr. Budd was a prominent Calgary entrepreneur between the period 1883 and 1914, and had played a major role in the financing and development of cement plants in Alberta. These undoubtedly included the Alberta Portland Cement Company plant in east Calgary and a more obscure plant, Western Canada Cement and Coal Company at Exshaw, Alberta. Of W.M. Alexander little is known except that he seems to have been a local contractor for a short period concurrent with W.J. Budd's activities. He may have been involved in the construction of Budd's cement plants but this is pure conjecture. Despite the dearth of information surrounding the activities of these two men, their influence had a profound and lasting effect on Calgary. The *Calgary Herald* reported in detail on the proposed scheme at Radnor which was to have a capacity of 4,000 horsepower with the market for this output being the industrial development foreseen in Calgary: "The city of Calgary, with its large population, is now at that stage when its manufacturing interests are being quickly advanced, and presents with its increasing demand for power a most favourable point for the initiation of such a scheme for bringing in power, as these gentlemen propose."[5]

The proposal envisioned two power-receiving terminals in Calgary, one at the municipal power plant, where the city would buy power for redistribution for lighting purposes and the other in east Calgary from which the Alexander and Budd Company would sell power to the surrounding area resulting, they hoped, in the concentration of industrial development in the east side of the city. The proposal was essentially one in which Alexander and Budd would sell power to all of the new industrial potential of Calgary, leaving the city to supply the less advantageous lighting load from its municipally-owned plant, supplemented as required by additional power from the hydro scheme. The cost of the development was estimated at $396,000 and in deference to the fact that "the aldermen are now busy over the municipal elections, etc., and that changes are liable in the composition of the present Council," the proposal was delayed until a new council was installed.

The development attracted instant attention from the citizens of Calgary, some strongly in favour and some strongly negative. The *Herald* editorialized:

> ...that the principle of the civic ownership of public utilities has been laid down very emphatically of late years and, generally speaking this principle is the safest one from the point of view of safeguarding the ratepayers against monopolies, which too frequently, with full powers and a period of years in their favour, abuse their privileges.[6]

The editor, however, quickly capitulated in his support of the principle of municipal ownership, reasoning that the municipal development of a much-needed
power scheme coupled with a growing demand for a street railway system was
simply beyond the financial capabilities of the existing property assessment
which allowed borrowing power up to 15 percent of the current assessment.
Calgary also needed new water and sewer services, sidewalks and roads and "the
whole amount could easily be expended in these quarters before *THINKING* of
such an extensive proposition." Alexander and Budd, with their proposal for a
combined power development and street railway system, were viewed as the
financial saviours of a city which was in a boom cycle that was out of all
proportion to its ability to pay for expensive services solely out of municipal
financing capability.

A special meeting of the city council was held on 17 January 1907 to consider
the Alexander and Budd proposal at which "Lawyers, manufacturers, civil engineers,
doctors, labor and aldermen and the mayor all voiced their views and there were
a lot of them."[7] Alexander and Budd, through their solicitor, Clifford T. Jones,
wanted a thirty-five year franchise from the city for both the power and street
railway proposal with an option to sell the railway to the city at the end of ten
years at cost less depreciation plus 10 percent but this option was not extended to
the power proposal. The cost of power to the city was to be set at one-half the
cost of the power produced by the municipally-owned plant. The actual power
cost from both the city power plant and the proposed scheme became the subject
of much debate and was not agreed upon at the meeting. The problem, of course,
was that everyone was comparing apples with oranges. The labour representatives
were solidly opposed to the privately-sponsored proposal, especially regarding
the street railway.

Calgary Solicitor R.B. Bennett appeared at this meeting to defend his eastern
Canadian client, the Calgary Street Railway Company, who also had a proposal
before the council for the operation of a privately-owned railway for Calgary. He
maintained that Alexander and Budd had not demonstrated that they could fulfill
any contract and, in fact, were not incorporated. Under these circumstances, it
would be risky to grant them franchises. He referred to them as "a couple of
gentlemen, one of whom had only been here a few months, and the other less."[8]
Bennett, who also acted as solicitor for the Calgary Water Power Company, then
drew the council's attention to the fact that the experience of his client with the
water flow in the Bow River had forced him (Prince) into the use of auxiliary
steam power "to fall back upon in case the water gave out."

Bennett's intervention at this meeting is of interest because the principal
financial backer of his eastern Canadian client's street railway proposal was Max
Aitken (later Lord Beaverbrook), a longtime personal friend of Bennett, and one
who would shortly play a major role in the survival of the Alexander and Budd
scheme. Bennett suggested that implicit in the proposal of Alexander and Budd

was the abandonment of the municipal electric light plant which had cost the city $110,000, whereas his client's street railway proposal would happily utilize power produced by the municipal plant. Alexander and Budd countered by stating that they also would be willing to negotiate for the takeover of the city plant.

Dr. James D. Lafferty, who had been a strong supporter of the original Calgary Electric Lighting Company, and of the entry of the Calgary Water Power Company as a competitor, represented the Board of Trade and supported the continued municipal ownership of its power plant. He argued that, "The aldermen might be giving away innocently something which was worth untold wealth." Whatever the aldermen decided to do, Lafferty continued, must be for the benefit of the city but he stood opposed to the granting of any further franchises for electric power. Another early Calgary pioneer, A.E. Cross, founder of the Calgary Brewery and a local rancher, took a surprising stance on the issue by approving of a city-owned hydro power plant if the city felt it could do it. Ex-City Engineer Thorold, who had been responsible for setting up the municipal power plant the previous year, was obviously still piqued by the events surrounding his resignation. He took a solid stand in favour of the Alexander and Budd proposal, arguing that he had never heard of a city running any enterprise as well as a company could. "As soon as the City realized this fact the better," was his comment, and he favoured a good agreement being drawn up and the municipal power plant being sold to the Alexander and Budd Company. Dr. Lafferty took it upon himself to cross-examine Thorold, who admitted that the city-owned power plant was indeed a success despite his new bias toward private ownership. The debate continued until a motion by Alderman A. Moodie, referring the question to a committee composed of the mayor, the city engineer and various aldermen, was accepted. The committee was to meet with the promoters and if some agreement could be reached the matter would be submitted to a further meeting of the ratepayers. The mayor appointed Aldermen C. McMillan, J.W. Mitchell, W.H. Manarey and J.G.(Gravity) Watson, to the ad hoc committee and the long public forum ended.

The committee immediately commenced its discussions with the Alexander and Budd Syndicate and presented its report to council on 28 January 1907 at a meeting convened in a cold council chamber, prompting the *Calgary Herald* to remark that, "the usual flights of oratory which have been indulged in at previous meetings appeared to have suffered from the drop in the thermometer."[9] The report of the committee was read but all discussion was deferred until 4 February because of the absence of Alderman S.J. Clarke, who was considered to have a vital interest in the question. The most significant change by the promoters was their decision to drop the street railway part of their proposal. As it happened, the proposals for an electric street railway by Bennett and Aitken were also rejected by the council and the city went on to develop its own railway without the help of any outside developer, with initial service inaugurated on 5 July 1909.

The council reconvened on 4 February 1907 to consider the report of the ad hoc committee. The committee, in its meeting with the syndicate, could not reach a consensus regarding the cost of power but some measure of agreement was reached on the arrangements by which the private syndicate could market its hydro power in Calgary. It was proposed that the company supply only large industrial users with power. The city would continue to supply all lighting loads from its municipal plant and, when needed, purchase power from the company for redistribution to its own consumers. The council went into a Committee of the Whole to discuss the question and the participation of those present to view the proceedings was solicited. The *Herald* reported that, ''There were more different views on the cost of power than there were spectators at the meeting, and it was a full house.''[10] The confusion that prevailed among both council members and the public was overwhelming and centred largely on the costs the syndicate was proposing for its power as compared to the cost of power from the municipal plant. The syndicate was offering costs which on the surface seemed to be less than one-half of that produced by the municipal plant. Chief Engineer McCall, knowing exactly what the underlying cause of the problem was, advised those present that the $77.00 per horsepower year being used to calculate the cost of municipal power ''did not actually represent the cost of power. The plant ran without any load at first and now (power) was being manufactured at half that amount.'' In other words, the municipal plant was operating with a higher load factor them the one on which the $77.00 figure was based. It was not surprising that the council and many of those purporting to have knowledge of the matter were confused. Some eighty years later the issue still evokes misunderstanding. It all relates to the difference between electrical energy (work) and electrical power (the capacity for work) and the proper allocating of costs between these two components.

Many aldermen were opposed to the thought of having additional poles on city streets but despite this objection they were generally favourable to the proposal provided that it did indeed bring cheaper power into the city for industrial use. Engineer F.W. Thorold, representing the syndicate, was asked by Alderman Mitchell how much the rate of 5 cents per kilowatt proposed as a selling price would be if expressed in horsepower; presumably a horsepower year. Thorold was very cautious on this point and would not commit himself since, by his own admission, it was not an easy question to answer. Mr. Jones, the syndicate's solicitor, was much bolder and volunteered that the 5 cent rate would ''mean $24.00 per horsepower per year.'' How he arrived at that figure is unknown since a horsepower converted to kilowatts with a maximum energy output based on 8760 hours per year at 5 cents, would result in a figure of $326.00 per horse-power year. However, despite all the contradictions, the Committee of the Whole agreed to a recommendation which would allow the Alexander and Budd Syndicate to enter the city and supply power to the corporation at a maximum rate of $24.00 per horsepower per year, and to private citizens at a maximum rate of

$30.00 per horsepower per year.[11] It was a most generous concession on the part of the council considering the degree of confusion and uncertainty still surrounding the Alexander and Budd proposal. The matter was turned over to the Light Committee to resolve the final disposition in the form of a draft agreement. The following day the *Herald* made this editorial comment:

> The most noticeable feature in connection with the meeting was the utter incapacity of the council to discuss the technical details of power and light propositions, owing to the fact that only one or two knew anything about it and the information of those few was of a very conflictory nature. A commission of experts in these various lines would be in a position to straighten the awful bewilderment of certain stages of last night's meeting in a very few minutes.

To which the author, some eighty years later, would add, "I doubt it."

While the Alexander and Budd proposal had implied that the hydro power they hoped to develop would come from the Radnor site, an announcement in the local press on 7 March 1907 made it clear that during the first part of year, while negotiations were being carried on with the city, the syndicate was actually bidding for water rights at the Horseshoe Falls site, about eighteen miles west of

View of Horseshoe Falls before development c. 1907.
Source: Glenbow Archives

the Radnor site. Along with the water rights the site included 1,000 acres of adjoining land purchased from the Stoney Indians. The water rights were granted for a period of two years and provided that if 3,000 horsepower was in actual process of development by the end of that period a permanent lease would be granted by the federal Department of the Interior. The original application for the water rights at Horseshoe Falls was filed with the Minister of the Interior in Ottawa on 21 December 1906 on the letterhead of "The Builder's Supply and Construction Company Limited," which showed W.J. Budd as President, with offices in the Burns Block in Calgary.[12] The application involved both the federal departments of the Interior and Indian Affairs, precipitating no small degree of confusion between these departments and the applicant as to which department was ultimately responsible for granting the water rights on a site situated on Indian reservation lands.

C.H. Mitchell, C.E., the Toronto engineer acting on behalf of the Alexander and Budd Syndicate, submitted his comments to the Department of the Interior on 26 February 1907, accompanied by a short description of the proposed hydro development and a freehand sketch plan of the Horseshoe Falls site.[13] "The Department of Indian Affairs has now proceeded with this matter so that the negotiations are nearly to completion," he wrote, concluding that the Department of Indian Affairs "cannot grant land under water at Horseshoe Falls or give authority for diversion of water itself. From my interview with Mr. Young, I understand that the Department of the Interior is the proper authority to grant these privileges." Eventually the confusion was sorted out. The Stoney Indians agreed to sell one thousand acres of land for $10.00 an acre in a 2 March 1907 agreement, witnessed by Chiefs Moses Bearspaw, Peter Wesley and Jonas Two Youngman, and five Councillors, James Swampy, Amos Big Stony, John Mark, Hector Crawler and George McLean.[14] The water rights were granted to the syndicate in May in the name of the Crown, represented by the Governor General of Canada, Earl Grey. Since there is no evidence to show that the water rights to the Radnor site were ever applied for by Alexander and Budd, we conclude that they simply "borrowed" the Radnor site for publicity in order to achieve an early start in the 1907 proceedings with the City of Calgary.

The decision taken on 9 February by the city to entertain a contract with the Alexander and Budd Syndicate was barely news before another proposal came before council from the Alberta Portland Cement Company, "we contemplate development of water power on the Bow River at a point west of Calgary (Radnor), and electrically transmit some 3,500 to 4,000 Horse Power to your city. We will require to use about 2,000 H.P. of this at our cement works, the balance, 1,500 H.P. to 2,000 H.P. will be for sale."[15] To facilitate the sale of this excess power, the cement company requested a franchise similar to that being considered for the Alexander and Budd Syndicate, which included the use of city streets for the transmission and distribution of electrical power. If the city had concerns over the additional poles on its streets which the earlier request for a franchise involved, one can easily imagine the reaction to further proliferation. A curt reply to the cement company's proposal was forwarded by the city clerk on 22 February: "Yours of the 9th Inst was duly considered by the Council at a

Civil Engineer Mitchell's 1907 sketch of Horseshoe Falls Hydro Power Site included with his report to the Alexander and Budd Syndicate. Compare with Photograph 5.3. Source: Public Archives of Canada

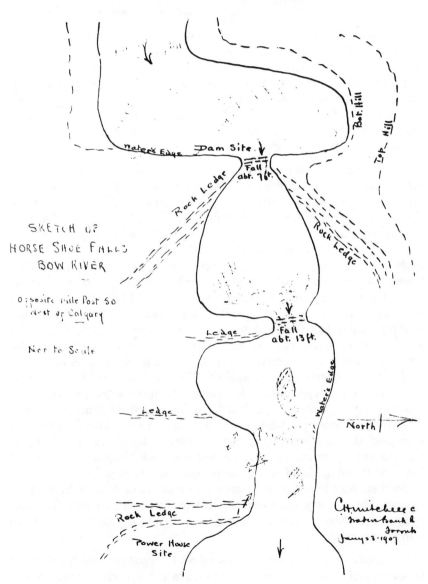

recent meeting and on motion it was resolved that the same cannot be entertained.'' However, the council changed its mind and agreed to at least reconsider the proposal of the Alberta Portland Cement Company. The company's lawyer, R.B. Bennett, appeared at the council meeting on 25 February 1907. The aldermen were given a long description of the company's proposal for generating hydro power for its own requirements with the surplus being available for other consumers in Calgary: "Mr. Bennett assured the Council that he was acting only as a citizen of Calgary, and his remarks were treated quite seriously."[16]

Meanwhile, the council continued its efforts to reach an agreement with the Alexander and Budd Syndicate. Alderman A.G. Graves submitted a draft contract between "The Calgary Power and Transmission Company Limited" (the name of the newly incorporated Alexander and Budd Syndicate) and the city of Calgary. The draft agreement, with few amendments, was ratified on 12 April 1907 and adopted by the directors of the company on the same day. This pioneer agreement was the prototype which ultimately determined the manner in which Calgary would obtain part or all of its future electrical power needs.

The contract obligated the company to start construction of the Horseshoe Falls project within six months of 12 April 1907 with 2,500 horsepower to be delivered to Calgary by 1 March 1909 and additional quantities provided on demand "as fast as the same may be applied for from time to time."[17] Failure to meet these conditions would be sufficient grounds for the city to annul the contract. While the company was enfranchised to provide electrical energy directly to the consumers that it expected to recruit, the energy so supplied was for "motive or power purposes" only and not for lighting purposes because the city retained this for its own municipal power plant. Had the arrangement been sustained, a great many electrical consumers would have ended up receiving their electrical service from both the new private company and the city, a most awkward arrangement. The city reserved the right, upon giving six months' notice, to "take over and purchase from the Company all the power required or used or to be required and used within the City...and deliver that power to the consumers...for such price as the city may see fit." It was an escape clause under which the city could consolidate all of the electrical service within the city limits under its sponsorship provided that the company's assets within the city limits were purchased at a mutually agreed or arbitrated figure. The company was regulated entirely by the city as to where it could place its poles on streets and lanes and in the matter of shared-use of poles already in place. The city also reserved the right to require the company to place its facilities underground in conduits. The company, under pain of forfeiture of all rights, contracted to supply power "continuously day and night" at a "cost per horsepower per ten hour day per annum."

The contract carried two prices: $24.00 per horsepower to the city should it decide to purchase power from the company, and $30.00 per horsepower to other consumers, "and no discrimination is to be made to other users or consumers within the City in the price, all are to be charged alike." It was also a condition of the agreement that the city would always receive power at the lowest rate and in the proportion that $24.00 bore to $30.00. Moreover, the city did not obligate itself to purchase power from the company but could do so by giving thirty days written notice for blocks of power not exceeding 500 horsepower. However, the city would be bound to a "take or pay" clause for such power contracted for a period of at least one year. Finally, the company would be required, upon the day of the contract approval, to deposit $10,000 with the city "as a guarantee towards the fulfillment of the construction and readiness of its plant for operation within the delays mentioned." On 17 May the contract was further modified to give the company the right to arbitrate the amount the city would charge for use of its poles or underground conduits and to include a "tariff of discounts" which would result in differing charges between small and large power users provided that the $30.00 maximum in the original contract was not exceeded.

Calgary had put absolutely nothing at risk in the contract with the Calgary Power and Transmission Company except perhaps the financing involved if the city exercised its option to buy out the company's facilities within the city limits. The contract carried no minimum term which is rather surprising since it is usual to negotiate a time period which would guarantee the recovery of the company's investment. This omission may have been compensated for by a contract the company also held with the cement plant at Exshaw for the supply of wholesale power. We can only admire the gambling spirit of the Alexander and Budd Syndicate. The company retained the services of Smith, Kerry and Chace, Consulting Engineers, out of Toronto, who enjoyed no small reputation for the hydro works they had designed and constructed in eastern Canada. The Horseshoe Falls project at Seebe appeared to have all the prerequisites necessary to commence construction.

In September of 1907, what the *Calgary Herald* described as a "lively war" erupted between the Calgary Power and Transmission Company and the Alberta Portland Cement Company. The *Herald* went so far as to predict a "price war" between the companies but at this stage of the rivalry the first company held all the cards with its possession of a signed franchise agreement and the preliminary work in progress on the Horseshoe Falls site. Throughout the ensuing debate it is significant that the cement company never once publicly disclosed the location of its proposed hydro development.

Earlier we suggested that the site was at Radnor, Alberta. This is deduced from the fact that only three suitable hydro sites had been proposed for development by Engineer C.H. Mitchell. These were the Radnor, Horseshoe Falls and Kananaskis Falls sites. The rights to the Kananaskis site were not granted by the Department of the Interior until 1912 so that rules it out. Since the Calgary Power and Transmission Company had already acquired the water rights at Horseshoe

Falls after initially announcing its planned development for Radnor, we can reasonably assume that the water rights at Radnor were under at least preliminary control of the Alberta Portland Cement Company, who had only announced that its development was geographically west of Calgary. Furthermore, while the cement company implied in one of its press interviews that it had retained the services of consulting engineers for the hydro project, there is no evidence to either confirm or deny that claim. For any hope of success, it was obvious that the proposals of both companies depended upon the Calgary market for their power, whether by way of a franchise to operate within the city or by selling excess power directly to the city for retail to its electricity consumers.

There was no unanimity between the mayor and the council on the matter of competing private enterprises. Some, including the mayor, felt that competition was paramount if the consumer was to benefit but the prospect of the proliferation of poles and other electrical distribution apparatus on city streets, and the deleterious effects likely to accrue to their own, now profitable, power plant made other councillors at least ambivalent to outside competition. The Calgary Power and Transmission Company, through its spokesman W.J. Budd, viewed the cement company's proposal as frivolous. "The city must take their power from us under the agreement, and I cannot see what advantage there would be to let a rival company in. There are sufficient poles in the city, and it would be utterly impossible to string their wires without their getting crossed somewhere," he argued.[18] The cement company countered, "All we want is a franchise similar to that given to the Calgary Power and Transmission company. The consumer would then have the advantages of competition."[19] On the pole question, Mr. J.W. Campbell, managing director of the cement company, pointed to the city of Portland, Oregon, as an example of how competing electrical utility companies handled the problem.[20]

The matter came to a stormy climax at the 23 September 1907 council meeting. R.B. Bennett, representing the cement company, raised a few hackles when he insinuated to the council that underhanded dealings had taken place between the directors of the Calgary Power and Transmission Company and some members of council in a conspiracy designed to defeat the franchise bid of the cement company. Mr. Bennett remarked that, "There is something beneath the surface of this affair and I am going to make it my business to find out what it is."[21] This provoked Alderman Graves into reminding Mr. Bennett that, as the chairman of the Light and Power Committee, he was not about to accept insinuations of covert behaviour. Mr. J.W. Campbell said that he and the president, Mr. A.P. Butchard, had discussed their proposal with the Light and Power Committee but had been advised to wait in order not to prejudice the Calgary Power and Transmission proposal. Campbell maintained that, unlike the Calgary Power and Transmission Company, the cement company had not watered down its stock issue by giving its directors large blocks of stock at reduced prices for their services and, in fact, were prevented from doing so by their incorporation under the English Companies Act, passed by the British Parliament. He concluded his remarks by insisting that the council had no right to grant a monopoly to the Calgary Power and Transmission Company and "if you think this is not so you do not represent the citizens of Calgary."

When all the rhetoric finally dissipated, both Mayor Cameron and Alderman Graves deferred to the arguments of the cement company, and this resulted in a motion giving consent "to erect poles and wires along certain streets for the conveyance of electrical power to their Works...and that the Alberta Portland Cement Co. be granted (the) same powers as the other competitors."[22] The same meeting also forced by a recommendation from the Light and Power Committee that, because of the inability of the municipal plant to keep pace with the larger than expected electrical demands, they "be authorized to negotiate with the Alberta Portland Cement Co. and the Calgary Power Transmission Co. for a supply of power for Civic purposes, the contract to be for a period not exceeding five years." The recommendation was approved and the remainder of council's deliberations during 1907 with respect to the "power question" was to determine which of the two competing companies would be chosen to provide what would become the first "purchased power" contract between the city of Calgary and a private company.

From the start of this new phase of negotiations the city clearly favoured the proposal of the Calgary Power and Transmission Company, because it appeared to have a better chance of success. The directors included several of the more prestigious names associated with Calgary's earlier development including Thomas Underwood, J.S.G. VanWart, E.H. Crandell and Dr. G. Ings, a prominent Calgary physician. Any suggestion that Calgary was not serious about its decision to entertain competing private electrical utilities is dispelled by the council's action in approving a recommendation from the New Industries Committee to provide city light, water and power at cost to S.E. Landry, Esq., providing that his enterprise would "continuously employ twenty-five hands or more a year." The letter from the city clerk advising Mr. Landry of the council's action concluded, "As to power, we beg to say that there are two power companies now having in contemplation the erection of works in the neighborhood of this city with a view of supplying power to manufacturers, and when their business is settled you will be able to make arrangements with them. The City at present is not in a position to sell power."[23]

The cement company immediately stalled on its offer to sign a contract with the city for a wholesale power supply. On 9 November 1907, Commissioner Graves informed council with regret "that we have not been able to arrange a meeting with the representatives of the Alberta Portland Cement Company, (and) we would therefore ask for an extension of time to prepare our report." By 18 November 1907 the Light and Power Committee was still reporting on delays by the cement company on the "power question." Whether or not it was a premeditated plan to·call the bluff of the cement company, the matter came to a head when the city council, on 25 November 1907, awarded the contract to the Calgary Power and Transmission Company for the supply of wholesale electric power to the city over a five-year period at $30.00 per horsepower for a 24 hour day.[24] One stipulation in the contract was that the company "agree to meet any competition in prices from any other company having the same agreement with the city during the period of the contract."[25] While no representatives of the cement company were present at the meeting, Thomas Underwood, president of the Calgary Power and Transmission Company was there and explained to council that his company was now committed to a half million dollar investment and "if they had a contract to furnish power to the City they could more easily dispose of their bonds."[26] It was an argument that the city would hear many times in the future.

The *Herald* found the action by the council in approving the contract most distasteful since the special meeting had been called to consider the "hospital question" only: "It arose like a breeze and was hustled through like a cyclone." The response came the following day in the *Herald* where J.W. Campbell, managing director of Alberta Portland Cement, replied in an open letter, "If the city will give our company a contract exactly on the terms of the resolution passed last night in favor of the Calgary Power and Transmission company, we will accept it and will substitute $25 per horse power for a 24 hour day instead of $30 as contained in that resolution."[27]

The *Calgary Herald* also took the stand that the council should call for tenders for the supply of power in the same manner as it did for other supplies. This view was supported by eleven major manufacturers in Calgary who submitted a petition to council maintaining that "the only manner by which this result (lowest cost power) can be obtained is by the calling of tenders before entering into any contract."[28] The response of the press and the petition from the local manufacturers combined to delay, temporarily at least, the final execution of the contract. The cement company finally submitted a formal proposal to the council on 2 December regarding its power development and the conditions under which electrical power would be supplied to the city. Alderman A.G. Graves complained that, "The Portland Cement Company, although requested to do so, had never made any proposition to the Light and Power Committee, except through the press."[29]

On 11 December the city council met again to discuss the cement company's proposal. After meeting as a Committee of the Whole, it passed a resolution requiring the cement company to agree, within ten days, to a contract similar to the one decided upon between the Calgary Power and Transmission Company and the city, and to deposit the sum of $10,000 within the same time limit. On the failure of the cement company to meet these demands, a contract with the Calgary Power and Transmission Company would be finalized at once. The cement company raised objections to many of the clauses contained in the draft contract arguing that the clauses were quite different from those of its competitor and that the $10,000 deposit carried a sixty-day limit that was not extended to the cement company. But by this time the city council was not in any mood to negotiate further with the Alberta Portland Cement Company and on 23 December they resolved:

> That owing to the fact that the Alberta Portland Cement Co. have not seen fit to accept the Agreement placed in their hands re furnishing this City with electrical energy, nor have they put up the necessary deposit of $10,000.00 and further, as the time for so doing has expired, this Council do now proceed to discuss a final Agreement with the Calgary Power & Transmission Company. [30]

A contract to supply wholesale power to the city was finally approved by the council. There was no representation from the cement company present not even their solicitor, R.B. Bennett. The *Calgary Herald*, which had been mildly supportive of the cement company's offer, reported sardonically: "The City Council has been jilted...just as it looked as though there was going to be something definite arrived at, the representatives of the company failed to attend the Council meeting."[31]

By-law 800 was introduced authorizing the agreement, given three readings and received a unanimous vote, and the "power question" was settled. At least that was what the council thought.

The Alberta Portland Cement Company came to the city council again on 3 September 1908 with another offer to supply power to the city. The company claimed that its plans to develop the Radnor site were complete and so it wanted another hearing "before any arrangement is concluded with the present applicants for rights to distribute power."[32] Unfortunately for the cement company those "arrangements" were concluded and while the council appeared to have given at least a cursory examination of the cement company's new proposal, there is no record of how it was finally resolved. We can conclude that after all the events of 1907 the council was content to leave the matter as decided on 23 December 1907.

A short summary of the events of 1907 is, perhaps, in order. At the end of 1907 the Calgary Power and Transmission Company (the Alexander and Budd Syndicate) held two contracts with Calgary. The contract of 12 April 1907 was a franchise agreement granting the company the right to operate an electrical utility in Calgary but supplying only industrial power. Lighting loads remained exclusively with the city power plant. The second contract of 23 December allowed Calgary to purchase power from the company in order to augment the electrical demand on the municipal plant. The Alberta Portland Cement Company wanted similar contracts but was unsuccessful in its bid to the city council. However, the

Calgary Power and Transmission Company had second thoughts about its contracts and returned to the council on 21 September 1908, expressing concern over
some "unworkable" clauses. By now the city council was quite receptive to the
company and on 28 December, the modifications deemed necessary to the contracts were agreed upon.

The most significant change was the extension of the time limit for delivery of
wholesale power to the city by one full year to 1 March 1910, while holding the
company to the 1 March 1909 delivery date applicable to its franchise agreement.
Other important changes gave the company a minimum five-year term on routes
of the pole lines before the city could demand either removal or re-routing, the
use of voltages up to 60,000 for the conveyance of electric current within the
limits of the city and a limitation clause whereby the company could not sell
power to any consumer, using less than 30 horsepower, other than the City of
Calgary. The "under 30 horsepower" clause was a concession won by the city
and assured a market of small power consumers for the city municipal plant, the
inclusion of which would have the effect of improving the load factor and thus
reducing the cost of power from the municipal plant.

Early in 1909 the aldermen suddenly revived their interest in the power
development on the Bow River and instructed their board of commissioners to
ascertain from the Canadian Pacific Railway whether that company had any
experience and views "as to the possibility of damming the Bow River for the
purpose of a water (power) supply."[33] The railway company in turn referred the
inquiry to William Pearce, who was a leading pioneer authority on hydraulic
matters, particularly irrigation in southern Alberta. To investigate the matter
further, the council appointed an ad hoc committee, which was known throughout 1909 as the Joint Power Commission, composed of aldermen and other
interested citizens, one of whom was William Pearce. What inspired the council
to take another look at the prospect of generating hydro power, utilizing a
city-owned facility, is unclear. However it may have stemmed from the apparent
slowness of the Alberta Portland Cement Company in concluding its application
to the Department of the Interior for water rights at Radnor, coupled with some
rising doubt about the ability of the Calgary Power and Transmission Company to
get its project beyond the initial development stage. By the end of February there
was no longer any doubt about the fears the city council may have harboured
regarding the Horseshoe Falls project. A letter addressed to Mayor Jamieson
from the consulting engineers, Smith, Kerry and Chace, confirmed that the
Calgary Power and Transmission Company was in financial trouble and that the
engineering firm was prepared to acquire a controlling interest in the company,
provide the funds necessary for construction to proceed, and complete that construction by 1 March 1910, provided that the council would enter into a new
"five-year contract for power on workable terms."[34] The letter was given to the
Joint Power Commission who met that same evening with representatives of the
Calgary Power and Transmission Company and the Board of Trade.

Minutes of that meeting were kept by the city engineer. Mr. Underwood, president of the power company, disclosed that they could not market their bond issues "owing to the stringency of the contract."[35] He estimated that the cost of completing the Horseshoe Falls project would be between $500,000 and $600,000 and that their consulting engineers, Smith, Kerry and Chace were "willing to finance the proposition if (the) contract was modified." The Joint Power Commission reported to the council on 8 March and recommended "that a workable franchise of which expediency shall be a main essential be granted to the Company, whom it is understood is to meet all competition in power."[36] The commissioner's recommendation also provided for reserving an option to the city for the purchase of 4,000 horsepower starting initially with a firm commitment for 1,000 horsepower. A sliding rate schedule was also included, starting at $30.00 per horsepower year for 1,000 horsepower and declining to $24.00 when 4,000 horsepower was reached. The Commission also recommended the appointment of an expert to assist in "Drafting and executing" a new agreement between the new principals of the company and the city.

On 6 April the Joint Power Commission, assisted by the expert, J.W. Campbell, submitted its report to council. Campbell had been, ironically, the manager of the Alberta Portland Cement Company during the time that company was attempting to extract a power franchise from the city. Mr. Cecil B. Smith, the negotiator and one of the principals of Smith, Kerry and Chace, demanded the use of city streets and lanes for an indefinite period as a condition for a franchise, and a contract to supply the City of Calgary with 1,500 horsepower at $30.00 per horsepower year. Smith also required that in the event that the city exercised its right to take over the company's distribution system, it must obligate itself to a perpetual contract to purchase all the power the company could supply.

The city negotiators countered with a proposal which would give the company a minimum six-year period before exercising the city's option to purchase the distribution system and to further contract for not less than 4,000 horsepower at $24.00 per horsepower year for a further period of ten years from the date of the takeover of the distribution system. Failing to exercise its option to purchase, the city would grant the company the right to "sell power throughout the City to consumers for a total period of 25 years."[37] Smith countered this offer with one for an eleven-year period for the city to exercise the option and a further fifteen-year contract for 4,000 horsepower at $24.00. The Commission however, could not close a deal with Smith, and the city commissioners concluded "that in view of the rapid growth of the City, it would be unwise to commit the City to any longer terms in an agreement with Mr. Smith than those suggested by the Joint Power Committee." If the offer of Smith, Kerry and Chace to obtain the controlling interest of the Calgary Power and Transmission Company from the original owners was conditional upon a new contract arrangement being concluded between the company and the city, it was not a major issue. By the end of May, C.B. Smith had acquired that interest in his own name through the transfer to him of 3,572 fully paid-up shares of the Calgary Power and Transmission Company and current liabilities in the amount of $8,569, all in promissory notes to bank creditors. The original directors of the company received nothing for their services and were not heard from again except for Dr. G.A. Ings who transferred his interests to another syndicate proposal to develop power on the Elbow River.

Smith, Kerry and Chace, despite their inability to successfully close with the city on the terms of a contract, did finally agree to a contract of sorts for the sale of power. While the details are sketchy, they seem to have accepted without alteration the modified 17 May franchise agreement between the city and the Calgary Power and Transmission Company. The purchase power agreement with the city covered the supply of power commencing with 1,000 horsepower on 1 August 1910 at a price of $28.00 per horsepower year for a five-year term, but when the agreement came before the council again in late 1909, it was declined "and the question was laid on the table to be considered at some future meeting."[38] The meeting with the new owners of the Calgary Power and Transmission Company never took place. In fact, the new owners were no more successful in completing the Horseshoe Falls project than were their predecessors. It appeared as if the Calgary Power and Transmission Company was doomed but in the next chapter we shall see that this was not the case.

The 1909 annual report of the city electric light and power plant ended with the following paragraph: "It will be absolutely necessary to have 1,000 more H.P. available early next fall in order to meet the demands upon the City's plant, and we cannot urge too strongly upon the attention of the Council the urgent need of promptly making some arrangement for this additional as well as cheaper power." The urgent need for additional electric power to meet the unusual city growth was settled by the expansion of the city's own power plant. The "cheap power" expectation from hydro development on the Bow River was still unfulfilled and early in 1910 the city council suddenly started to take a renewed interest in the development of both the Bow and the Elbow rivers for hydro power.

Looking back over seventy years it seems incredible that the Elbow River would have been considered as a possible source of hydro development. While the Elbow is the main tributary of the Bow River it has an annual water discharge of something in the order of 10 percent of the Bow, making any possible development for hydro power dependent upon a water storage basin. There was one site which lent itself to a power development scheme and it was described in some detail in Hendry's *Water Resources Paper No. 2*.[39] The location was given as "between the 20 foot falls in section 17, township 22, range 6, west 5th and the east boundary of section 14, township 22, range 6, west 5th." A gravity dam with a crest approximately 100 feet above the river bed would be needed a few hundred yards above the point at which Canyon Creek joins the Elbow. The powerhouse would be located from one and a quarter to two miles below the dam with a flume and penstock delivering the water from the dam to the powerhouse, resulting in an approximate 215 foot hydraulic head for power production. For those not familiar with the site by its survey description, it was the Elbow Falls site, about eight miles west of Bragg Creek.

Interest in the Elbow River as a possible source of hydro-electric power was evident in October of 1903, when the secretary of the Calgary Board of Trade wrote to the Department of the Interior in Ottawa, asking whether the city of Calgary held any franchises for water rights at both the Elbow River Falls and Kananaskis Falls on the Bow River. The inquiry probably originated out of the discussions held between the city's Board of Trade and Roderick J. Parke. The reply was that the municipality had made no such application for the water rights.[40] Nothing more occurred probably because of the priorities of the city in getting its power plant and distribution system into operation during 1905 and 1906. But in 1910, both the city and a newly organized private syndicate calling itself the Western Canada Power and Development Company became serious competing parties for the water rights on the Elbow River at the Elbow Falls site.

The Western Canada Power and Development Company was spearheaded by Dr. G.A. Ings. Calgary solicitors, Jones and Pescod, wrote a letter on 1 September 1910 to Frank Oliver, federal Minister of the Interior, in which the objectives of the Western Canada Power and Development Company were outlined. Beside Dr.Ings, additional directors were listed as Messrs. J.I. McLeod, William Astley, Frank Shackle and Jerome L. Drumheller (after whom the city of Drumheller, Alberta was named). The letter outlined the plans of the Western Canada Power and Development Company:

> The objects for which the Company wish to utilize the power from the site are the development of the valuable coal and iron deposits, which are under the control of the Company in the vicinity of Calgary. ...(to be) in a position to supply material close at hand such as rails, iron and steel for building purposes and other commodities, which at present has to be brought from long distances...(and) it is the intention of the Company to sell coal in the City at such a price that it will be within the means of the poorest residents.[41]

These were ambitious plans reflecting the optimism of the times. The widespread use of domestic coal in Calgary never reached great proportions because natural gas arrived in the city in abundant quantities shortly after 1910. As was common to hydro-power developments proposed on the Bow River, the surplus power would be available for sale to Calgary.

The Ings proposal gained the attention of city council on 21 June and was referred to the Joint Power Commission for consideration. The *Calgary Herald* reported that the submission was a proposal to supply the city with 4,000 horsepower at $25.00 per horsepower by 31 December 1911. The preliminary feasibility studies had been carried out by Mr. M.S. Parker, a member of the American

Society of Civil Engineers, described as an eminent hydraulic expert. Dr. Ings explained to the Joint Power Commission that the proposal would make available "at least 6,000 H.P. in low water and as high as 17,000 in high water."[42] Immediately a dispute arose between the Ings Syndicate, the Calgary Water Power Company and city officials as to whether this amount of power could be absorbed. While some said that the city's growth would be able to accommodate the amount in one year more conservative voices, including those from the city's own power plant, felt that five years was the more appropriate period. Concurrent with this proposal the city was also negotiating a contract for the purchase of power from the Calgary Power Company which had taken over the interests of the earlier Calgary Power and Transmission Company. Since that development was already a "bird in the hand" with tangible assets in place at Horseshoe Falls, the city showed greater partiality to the Bow River site. The *Calgary Herald*, however, was not so inclined, as its editorial of 23 July indicated:

> The sympathy of Calgary's citizens has been directed toward the Calgary Power Company, which has shown great enterprise in construction work up to date and its representatives do not appear to be prepared even to compromise. They have assumed an attitude which to the ordinary businessman looks pretty much like good hard bluff, with the result that not a few who were favourable to them a little while ago are losing sympathy with them, and rather hope that some other means of obtaining power may be found. The Western Canada Power company proposal, while cheaper than the other, is none too reasonable. It is, however, the best the City has yet had. The doubt that arises in many minds is whether the Elbow River can be depended on to produce a minimum of 5,000 horsepower the whole time. Old timers say that it cannot...Meanwhile the City is going ahead to put in an auxiliary power plant—a scheme in which the authorities will receive the endorsement of the people.

The "auxiliary power plant" was the new Victoria Park Power Plant. The Ings Syndicate, despite its offer to Calgary on 20 June 1910, still had not made a formal application to Ottawa for the required water rights although much discussion and correspondence had taken place between both parties. The city took advantage of this and on 25 July made its own formal application for the water rights at the Elbow Falls site. City Engineer Child had been a longtime admirer of the Elbow Falls hydro-power site and had persuaded Mayor R.R. Jamieson to proceed with the application. This was done without the prior knowledge of the city council. Engineer Child's proposal for the Elbow Falls site had some basic differences in layout from that of the Ings Syndicate. It claimed a minimum power output of 3,500 horsepower increasing to 25,000 when water flow was at its highest. The Western Canada Power and Development Company submitted its formal application to Ottawa for the same water rights two days later on 27 July.

For the remainder of 1910, a series of charges and countercharges ensued between the city and the Western Canada Power and Development Company, with both sides using all of the influence available to them to pressure Frank Oliver, Minister of the Interior, to accede to their particular application. James I. McLeod, one of the principals of the development company, attempted to discredit the city's application in a letter to the Minister of the Interior, dated 1 September, when he claimed that the municipal application was in reality only that of two private citizens who happened to be the mayor and the city engineer and did not carry the endorsement of the city council. "Application for a power site," wrote McLeod, "has never been brought before the Council of the City of Calgary at any of their meetings and there is no mention of such an application being made in the minutes of any Council Meeting."[43] Nevertheless, the matter came before the council on 11 September when a motion by Alderman C.B. Reilly, "that the City abandon its claim to the Power site on the Elbow River which the Western Canada Development Company desires to develop,"[44] was lost, indicating that the city's application to obtain the water rights did have the support of a majority of the council. A second motion, "That we await the decision of the Government re the granting of the Elbow River Power Site before we relinquish our claim on same," was carried. The development company wasted no time in sending a wire to the Minister of the Interior: "the City Council of Calgary at their meeting held last evening practically decided to withdraw their application,"[45] followed by a more detailed letter from their solicitor, J.I. McLeod, regarding the council proceedings.

What actually transpired at the 11 September meeting of council was that Alderman Dr. W.M. Egbert, who had seconded Alderman Reilley's motion, argued that in view of the city's need for money the power development would be better left to private enterprise.[46] City Engineer Child did not support this position, claiming that it would be entirely possible for the city to finance the project in the future. However, Mayor Jamieson seemed to have cooled in his earlier support of Engineer Child on the Elbow Falls water rights application, maintaining that the Bow River was a better power proposition. The city did, in fact, make a few brief excursions into the matter of Bow River water rights for hydro-power development but they were never pursued with any vigour. In any event, the acquisition of additional rights for power production on the Bow at other Bow River sites was beginning to weigh more and more favourably to the advantage of the Calgary Power Company.

A rift developed between Mayor Jamieson and City Engineer Child regarding the Elbow Falls power site on 24 October 1910. Before that evening's council meeting the mayor told the press that, "City Engineer Child has misled the city council in this matter," claiming that the engineer had prepared three different reports, none of which were in agreement.[47] Child, according to the mayor, was no longer looking after city interests. However, the mayor confirmed that he had wired the Minister of the Interior in Ottawa that same day, emphasizing "the fact that the city has not given up their claim on the Elbow River power site."[48] The mayor was protecting himself despite his disagreement with the city engineer.

The mayor further claimed that he had a chance street meeting with Dr. Ings earlier in the year and at that time they had casually discussed the power site on the Elbow River, after which he had mentioned the matter to Engineer Child. The mayor was of the opinion that Child never knew about the site before that time and consequently, in rushing to get an application to the Department of the Interior, the city had put the Ings Syndicate at an undeserved disadvantage. Mayor Jamieson also disclosed that he had subsequently talked to "old-time residents of the district, who had spent years of their lives to studying such matters," and in their opinion the proposal to develop water power at Elbow Falls was "preposterous."

So the battle lines were drawn for a heated debate at that evening's council meeting. Engineer Child fired the first volley calling Mayor Jamieson's earlier statements "uncalled for and most cowardly."[49] Mayor Jamieson and Engineer Child hurled unrestrained charges while the citizens who had crowded into the council chambers to hear the debate, "applauded the city engineer when he declared himself in favor of securing the Elbow River water power site for the city of Calgary at any cost." Mr. Child concluded that, "The poor engineers have usually to be the scapegoats and if I have to be the 'scapegoat' in this case I will glory in it because it will be in the interests of a municipal hydro-electric power plant for Calgary."[50] These were brave words but Engineer Child came perilously close to being dismissed. After all the bitterness had vented itself, a motion was introduced, "to appoint an electric-hydraulic expert to report on water sites on Elbow River,"[51] and the motion carried. Mr. William Kennedy, a hydraulic and mechanical engineer from Montreal, was retained to provide "expert opinion and advice" on hydro power sites in the vicinity of Calgary. His fee was $35.00 per day plus expenses while travelling between Montreal and Calgary, $50.00 per day plus expenses for the balance of the time and $200.00 for a written report.

On 1 December 1910, the city was granted the water rights, under the federal Water Power Regulations, to the Elbow River power site with stipulations that at least $150,000 be spent on power developments by the end of 1912, and 2,000 horsepower be available for use by 1 January 1914, with a maximum capacity of 5,000 horsepower developed after January 1914 if required for the public interest. The city was given thirty days from 1 December 1910 to accept the offer and close a contract with the Department of the Interior in Ottawa. But the city's expert, W. Kennedy, expressed doubts regarding the water flow at the Elbow Falls site and consequently the city requested an extension from the Minister of the Interior until water flows could be verified over the winter of 1910-11. The services of the local member of parliament, M.S. McCarthy, were solicited by the mayor to intervene on behalf of the city but to no avail. On 3 February 1911 the assistant secretary to the Department of the Interior wrote to the new mayor, J.W. Mitchell:

The City failed to accept the proposal within the time allowed and consequently now holds no priority over any other applicant....While the priority given the City...has lapsed, the Department is still prepared to accept applications for the development of Elbow River power...whether made by the City, the Western Canada Power and Development Company, or any other responsible person, corporation or municipality.[52]

The Department of the Interior left the door open but Calgary never again went after water rights for hydro-power production. Interestingly, the Ings Syndicate (Western Canada Power and Development Company), throughout their competition with the city had acted as if the rights were firmly under their control. They competed throughout 1910 with the Calgary Power Company for a contract to supply electrical power to Calgary although R.B. Bennett, counsel and president of Calgary Power, never took the Ings Syndicate seriously. Whether the Western Canada Power and Development Company survived as a corporate entity after Calgary Power Company succeeded with its first wholesale power supply contract to Calgary in 1910 is not known but it is known that Dr. Ings did not give up his plan to develop a hydro-power site at Elbow Falls.

After Calgary committed itself to hydro power from the Bow River the council redirected its attention to the use of the Elbow River as an enhanced source for municipal water supplies. A gravity feed, established in 1907, already existed on the Elbow River with its intake about ten miles west of the city limits. The city engineer had two schemes in mind. One was to augment the existing water supply intake with another source about two miles further upstream. He estimated that this would accommodate Calgary's population growth to about 100,000. However, the preferred scheme was the Elbow Falls site which, with the same type of dam as the one proposed earlier by the city for the power scheme, would provide the municipal water needs of a city population of 200,000. Calgary made new proposals to the Department of the Interior for the water rights at Elbow Falls for this purpose. F.H. Peters, commissioner of irrigation in the Calgary office of the Department of the Interior, wrote his superiors in Ottawa that he had advised the city to proceed with a new application and that "the question of priority will not enter into the matter."[53] He indicated that he considered that the matter of potable water for Calgary had priority over water use for power development. Dr. Ings, because of the failure of Calgary to proceed with the development of the Elbow Falls site in 1911, now held prior right to that same site for development of a hydro-power plant. This is certain because of a contract agreement drawn up in August 1914 by Mr. J.B. Challies, superintendent of the Water Power Branch of the Department of the Interior. Mr. Challies felt this was necessary to protect the Crown, Dr. Ings, and the City of Calgary because of the city's recent request to use the Elbow Falls site for a municipal water supply.

The preamble of the agreement confirmed that Dr. Ings had the right to develop the site for hydro-power but only if he made ample provision in his plans to accommodate the higher priority use of a municipal water supply and have 2,000 horsepower developed before 1 August, 1918. The agreement required that the contractor (Ings) come to an arrangement, satisfactory to the minister and the city, regarding the city's present and future municipal water supply works before a formal license to store and divert the waters of the Elbow River for power purposes would be granted. The agreement was signed by Dr. Ings but never executed by the Crown. Ings never reached an agreement with the city regarding the use of his proposed hydro-power development and, in particular, its related water storage. It would appear that in view of the hydro-power developments now on the Bow River at both Horseshoe and Kananaskis Falls, he simply withdrew from the field. Nothing further was heard from him. We might also suspect that the intervention of World War I dampened any further plans to develop the Elbow River for hydro-power purposes. The final blow came out of Hendry's *Water Resources Paper No.2*. It concluded that the "scheme of developing power on the Elbow is not an attractive one from an economic standpoint; there have been a number of applications filed respecting the development of power upon the river and in order that these might be dealt with the investigations were instituted with the above results."

For a brief period in 1923 Calgary again showed an interest in the Elbow Falls site. As a result of recent floods the city requested the Minister of the Interior to give priority permission to use the site for combined flood control, municipal water supply and hydro power development.[54] Fortunately the Elbow Falls site escaped development and to this day it has remained a spot of unequalled pristine beauty. Development in the early 1930s saw the dam proposed for Elbow Falls finally built on the southern extremity of Calgary. It was called Glenmore Dam and, with its modern treatment facilities, provided Calgary with a source of clear sparkling potable water, unsurpassed in quality. There was also the added benefit of permanent flood control on the Elbow as it snaked its way through the city to finally join the Bow River above St. George's Island.

Before concluding this chapter, we will consider one further development proposed for the Bow River downstream rather than upstream from Calgary. The development was offered on 13 November 1913 by a company incorporated as the Alberta Hydro Electric Company Limited. The scheme was the brainchild of Zephren (sometimes Zephir) Malhiot, described as a railway and hydraulic engineer during the early days of the construction of the Canadian Pacific Railway. He was a native of Quebec and after his service with the CPR was employed by the federal government as a hydraulic engineer in Saskatchewan and Alberta. Before coming to Western Canada he had been associated with engineering enterprises in Providence, Rhode Island and was an extremely colourful figure, as indicated by his memoirs.[55] He lived to the ripe age of ninety-six and was buried at St. Paul, Alberta in 1948.

Malhiot's plan was to dam the Bow River across its flood plain at four locations below Calgary, creating a continuous series of lakes from St. George's Island downstream to the location of the last damsite. The first dam would have spanned the eastern tip of St. George's Island and Malhiot, recognizing that this would flood the island, recommended a concrete "dyke" around the island to preserve it. The second dam was to be situated immediately north of the point where the present Bonnybrook Bridge crosses the Bow River, near 42nd Avenue S.E. The third dam was planned to span the river at the eastern projection of the present Heritage Drive with the last one located across the Bow River at the eastern projection of the present Anderson Road. As anyone who is familiar with the topography of the flood plain of the Bow River knows, these dams required fairly long adjacent earthworks to tie into the flood plain escarpments thus giving rise to a rather ambitious undertaking. Between the first dam at St. George's Island and the last one some ten miles downstream, a hydraulic head of about 100 feet would be created from which it was expected that nearly 12,000 aggregate horsepower could be developed from low-head power houses at each damsite. Malhiot later wrote in his memoirs about the advantages of his scheme:

a wonderful aid in the form of design or plan, adaptable to the City of Calgary's townsite, or city planning, which fortuitously.seriously agitated the public mind...(but) has not ceased to dominate the creative thinking inhabitants who have the welfare and advancement of the city in contemplation both as a foremost industrial center of trade and commerce and a residential city. If the A.P. & D. Co's plan had been carried out, a Dam below St. George's Island, called G. Dam, on plan, would have afforded power and raised the water about the island to such an elevation as to make it appear within a lake, and a proper and complete summer resort, having enough water for the navigation of small crafts. Also the building of another Dam, called E Dam on the same plan, and located above the Grand Trunk Ry. bridge, would have created another lake and constituted the islands and foreshores about Col. Jas. Walker's property ideal resorts, likewise navigable for small crafts. The construction of two more dams, one opposite Ogden Shops, and another below, would have produced two more identical lakes, with likewise adorable foreshores and islands that could have been reached by means of small craft, gasoline launches, etc. Within handsome clean tidy power houses, would produce noiseless, dustless, smokeless power, to generate the hydro-electric power much enjoyed by thriving industrialists, simultaneously reducing the cost of light and power, and it follows, the cost of living generally; and above all, of the greatest import to the tender, lovable, laborious house wife of fastidious taste and mind, would have thrown onto the market, thousands of acres, of most charming building sites, contiguous and overlooking the water of these lakes, from which the exhalation of pure fresh oxygen would flow, the health creating and restoring element; constantly renewed, by the permanent flow, fresh from the rocky mountains' melted snow and ice, supplemented by springs and virginal water sheds, through its natural discharge, the Bow and Elbow Rivers. This development would doubtless have accomplished a transformation of the site of the city of Calgary, instead of a turbulent, scowling dingy monstrosity of a stream, such as it appears today; calm almost still water would front and traverse the City, compatibly with popular appeal, and euphemistic intellectual power of enthralling pleasures, healthful and sanitary, fundamental of happiness.[56]

Surprising as it may seem, Malhiot's scheme had the enthusiastic support of many of Calgary's prominent citizens. The engineers of the Water Power Branch of the Department of the Interior in Ottawa examined the scheme very closely and conceded that it was possible. Hendry concluded his lengthy report to the superintendent of the Water Power Branch in Ottawa that "the scheme is one which does not offer any attractions from an economic standpoint," and estimated the power output at a reduced 6,000 horsepower.[57] Malhiot's company, however, had also retained prominent American engineering consultants from New York and Chicago who enthusiastically endorsed the plan. Unfortunately, the American consultants only knew the project from paper plans and never having visited the proposed hydro sites, their enthusiasm must be considered somewhat suspect. The Alberta Hydro Electric Company Limited was grudgingly granted a contract by Calgary for the delivery of electric energy with a minimum annual quantity of 5,000,000 kilowatt hours, commencing 1 December 1918. This was done despite the fact that the city commissioners and R.A. Brown, superintendent of the Electric Light Department, were extremely negative about the company and its prospect.

This turn of events was enough to give R.B. Bennett, now president of Calgary Power Company, some genuine distress. He wrote to Sir Max Aitken in London, England, about his concern since this downstream scheme could seriously prejudice his company's plan for a hydro plant at the Kananaskis Falls site. Unlike his contempt for Dr. Ings' scheme on the Elbow River, Bennett viewed the Malhiot plan with no small degree of apprehension: "If the four dams can be constructed for $1,500,000.00…it would certainly be a very wise thing for us to undertake the development instead of putting in the second dam at Kananaskis."[58] Bennett offered Malhiot $1,000 for an exclusive forty-day option on the downstream project: "The reason I paid him $1,000 was because he (Malhiot) was very hard up and I thought it better to get his good will at this time than to haggle about a few Dollars, and we are thus enabled to decide whether or not the enterprise is in any way worthy of our consideration."[59] Malhiot recorded the same event in his memoirs: "R.B. Bennett…agreed to pay me $1,000.00 for option in the ostentatious clarion like espotulation (sic) of the fact that I should firstly have transferred my water power designs to him." Bennett sent Malhiot's plans to his consultant for further evaluation. He was worried that the downstream scheme could seriously upset his plan for a new contract with the city. "If we dispose of that I propose to close a contract for fifteen years," confided Bennett to his Calgary Power superior, Max Aitken, on 16 October 1912.[60]

Malhiot combed eastern Canada and the United States searching for financing of his scheme but had no success. To make matters worse the directors of the Alberta Hydro Electric Company reneged on their agreement to pay Malhiot for his services. Malhiot was convinced that the city commissioners and City Electrician Brown, along with the Calgary Power Company, were, "a handful of converging conivers" in league to frustrate his project. Malhiot then tried to convince local citizens of substance to finance his plan and when that failed, he blamed the result on the "rivalry of the Calgary Power Company, espoused by the Member of Parliament, (R.B. Bennett) and followers, influences, subdued so many who would have desired to see my plans succeed."[61]

Malhiot was a romantic visionary and we must give him credit for a valiant effort. Despite his paranoia, the truth was that the upstream developments of Calgary Power Company had won the day. By the early 1920s, nothing more was heard from Malhiot and his Alberta Hydro Electric Company. The battle for the rivers was over.

References

1. Tom Ward, *Cowtown*. Toronto: McClelland & Stewart, 1975.

2. "The Eau Claire and Bow River Lumber Company," *Calgary Herald*, 29 April 1887.

3. "Expert to Report on Power Scheme," *Calgary Herald*, 21 October 1903.

4. "Council Still Nibbling at Mr. Prince's Offer," *Calgary Herald*, 21 March 1905. Additional quotes from same source.

5. "Cheaper Power Proposed for Calgary," *Calgary Herald*, 30 November 1906. This article outlines in detail the Alexander and Budd proposal which also included a street railway and an "up-to-date pleasure resort at some point along the river" complete with theatres, merry-go-rounds, lawns and flowers.

6. "The Proposed Power and Street Railway System," *Calgary Herald*, 8 December 1906. Additional quote from same source.

7. "Street Railway and Power," *Calgary Herald*, 18 January 1907.

8. Ibid. R.B. Bennett's comment lends credence to the possibility that both Alexander and Budd were but temporary residents of Calgary.

9. "Power Scheme Held Over," *Calgary Herald*, 29 January 1907.

10. "The Right to Sell Power," *Calgary Herald*, 5 February 1907. A degree of confusion has always persisted over the difference between power and energy (work). It has not been helped by the British and North American practice of retaining the archaic term of "horsepower." Early steam boilermakers in the eighteenth century England equated

the ability of their new engines to produce work to that with which they had previously been familiar, i.e., the horse. So a "horsepower" was assumed to be the
power of a horse and was later defined as 550 foot pounds of work per second. Power
is commonly defined as the ability or capacity to do work and always carries with it
the element of time. The faster that work is done, the greater the power required.
Work, or energy, on the other hand, has no time constraints. The same amount of
work is done by raising one kilogram weight through one meter irrespective of the
time taken but if the time to produce the work is critical, the power required will vary
accordingly. In electrical terms, a "watt" or "kilowatt" (1,000 watts) is a unit of
power. The work done by using that ability is expressed in "watt hours" or "kilowatt
hours." Since the ability to do work is related to the size or capacity of the machine,
it follows that the costs related to power or capacity are the capital costs associated
with owning the machine. Hence, in energy utilities, capital costs are "fixed" costs
because they continue whether the machine is used continuously or sits idle. The
costs related to operating the machine are "variable" and are therefore related to the
work or energy produced by the machine. In a hydro plant, the costs are mostly
"fixed" since no fueling costs (except for water rental) are involved. In a thermal
plant, "variable costs" are considerable because of the cost of fuel. But it does not
necessarily follow that the unit cost of energy is always higher from a thermal plant
which usually has a much lower "fixed cost" component than would a highly
capital-intensive hydro plant. So, without knowledge of all of the factors involved, it
becomes very easy to compare "apples and oranges" and that was the problem when
the city council tried to come to grips with power costs from two different sources.

11. Council Minutes, 4 February 1907, p.117.

12. Public Archives of Canada, RG85, v.737, file R1436-3-5. Letter dated 21 December
1906. W.M. Alexander and W.J. Budd to Minister of Interior.

13. Public Archives of Canada, RG85, v.737, file R1436-3-5. Letter dated 26 February
1907, with attachments, C.H. Mitchell, C.E. to Secretary, Department of Interior.
Additional quotes from same source.

14. Public Archives of Canada, RG85, v.737, file R1436-3-5. Agreement dated 12
March 1907 between the Stoney Band of Indians and the Crown for surrender of
reservation property.

15. City Clerk's Papers. Letter dated 9 February 1907. A.P. Butchart, Managing Director,
The Alberta Portland Cement Company to the Mayor and Aldermen of the City of
Calgary.

16. "Leave to Finance Committee," *Calgary Herald*, 26 February 1907.

17. City Clerk's Papers. Agreement between the City of Calgary and the Calgary Power
and Transmission Company, Limited, dated 12 April 1907. All quotes are directly
from the contract document. The rate based on cost "per horsepower per ten hour
day" did not mean that power was available for only ten hours every day since the

contract provided that the power supply was to be "continuous day and night." Therefore the "ten hour day" refers to an archaic way of expressing "load factor." The ratio presupposes that only 31 percent of the total available energy from the generating plant is actually delivered to the consumer annually.

18. "Power Question in City of Calgary," *Calgary Herald*, 23 September 1907.

19. Ibid.

20. In later years, Portland, Oregon still maintained two private competing electrical utilities: Pacific Gas and Electric, and the Portland General Electric Company. Joint use of poles by the competing companies was always practiced but in order to accommodate the lines required by both utilities the poles reached inordinate lengths, often over 70 feet. The poles had high visibility but not as bad as it would have been in Calgary where trees and other flora were the exception rather than the rule.

21. "More Power is Coming," *Calgary Herald*, 24 September 1907.

22. Council Minutes, 23 September 1907, p.20.

23. City Clerk's Papers. Letter dated 24 October 1907. City Clerk to S.E. Landry.

24. The award on a "horsepower per 24 hour day" rather than the "10 hour day" specified in the original franchise agreement with the Calgary Power and Transmission Company Limited simply had the effect of eliminating a specified annual load factor as a criterion for the unit cost of energy.

25. Council Minutes, 25 November 1907, p.94.

26. "Alderman Watson Has Resigned," *Calgary Herald*, 26 November 1907.

27. "Would Furnish Cheaper Electricity," *Calgary Herald*, 26 November 1907.

28. City Clerk's Papers, b.23.f179. Petition dated 28 November 1907, addressed to city council and signed by eleven major local manufacturers.

29. "Extended Water Mains," *Calgary Herald*, 3 December 1907. As was often the case in the early years, newspaper reports of council activities included a broad range of topics that often became intermingled. The headline referred to whatever topic was deemed to be the most active or important in the mind of the reporter.

30. Council Minutes, 23 December 1907, p.125.

31. "The Power Agreement is Signed," *Calgary Herald*, 24 December 1907.

32. City Clerk's Papers, b.25.f194. Letter dated 3 September 1908. J.W. Campbell to Alderman A. Graves.

33. City Clerk's Papers, b.52.f419. Letter dated 11 January 1909. City Clerk to J.S. Dennis, CPR. It is clear from the 13 January 1909 reply from William Pearce that "water power" was being referred to and not a "water" supply stated in the 11 January 1909 letter.

34. City Clerk's Papers, b.52.f419. Letter dated 1 March 1909. Smith, Kerry, Chace to Mayor Jamieson.

35. Minutes of meeting dated 1 March 1909, between Joint Power Commission and representatives from the Calgary Power and Transmission Company and Board of Trade. Quotations are from these minutes. (Glenbow)

36. Council Minutes, 8 March 1909, p.271.

37. City Clerk's Papers, b.30.f226. Report of Joint Power Commission, 6 April,1909.

38. "Future Meeting to Deal with Power," *Calgary Herald*, 30 November 1909.

39. Hendry's report was compiled with the assistance of the eminent eastern Canadian engineer, C.H. Mitchell, who had previously prepared the initial reports on the Radnor, Horseshoe Falls and Kananaskis Falls sites of the Bow River for the Calgary Power and Transmission Company. Mitchell also acted for Smith, Kerry and Chace, the engineering consultants to that company. Hendry was chief engineer for the Dominion Water Power Branch of the Department of the Interior in Ottawa and his *Water Resources Paper No.2* was released as a substantial book accompanied by twenty-five superb topographical maps of the Bow River drainage basin, covering geology, water storage and possibly hydro power sites. The paper became the basis of all future power and irrigation developments on the Bow River drainage basin.

40. City Clerk's Papers, b.52 f:417,18,19. Correspondence between Patterson, Secretary, Calgary Board of Trade and Secretary of the Department of the Interior, Ottawa. These files comprise a complete document on the applications of both the city of Calgary and the Western Canada Power and Development Company for the Elbow Falls water rights.

41. City Clerk's Papers. Letter dated 1 September 1910. Jones and Pescod, Solicitors to the Honourable Frank Oliver.

42. "Can the City Use 4,000 Horsepower per Year?" *Calgary Herald*, 22 July 1910.

43. City Clerk's Papers. Letter dated 1 September 1910. McLeod to Oliver.

44. Council Minutes, 12 September 1910, p.218.

45. City Clerk's Papers. Telegram dated 13 September 1910. Jones to Oliver.

46. "The City Makes the Power Contract," *Calgary Herald*, 13 September 1910.

47. "Says City Engineer Misled on Power," *Calgary Herald*, 24 October 1910.

48. Ibid.

49. "Get Expert to Report," *Calgary Herald*, 25 October 1910.

50. Ibid.

51. Council Minutes, 24 October 1910, p.233.

52. City Clerk's Papers. Letter dated 3 February 1911, Assistant Secretary, Department of the Interior to J.W. Mitchell.

53. Public Archives of Canada, R.G. 89, V.128, File 1121. Letter dated 31 January 1914. F.H. Peters to E.F. Drake.

54. "City Applies for Water Power and Storage Right 35 Miles up Elbow River," *Calgary Herald*, 19 June 1923.

55. Z. Malhiot, "Seventy Years of Growth with Canada." The memoirs cover the author's activities from 1904 to 1917, including the personal account of his attempts to establish and finance the Bow River scheme. Much of Malhiot's memoirs cover the activities and events surrounding Calgary's social and cultural life during the first two decades of this century. (Glenbow)

56. Malhiot, p.450-51. The quote has been slightly edited to facilitate its reading.

57. Public Archives of Canada, RG89, Acc. 83-84/163, report M.C. Hendry to J.B. Challies.

58. House of Lords Registry Office, London. Beaverbrook Papers (hereafter referred to as HLRO. Beaverbrook Papers). Box A 65. Letter dated 9 October 1912. R.B. Bennett to Sir Max Aitken.

59. Ibid.

60. HLRO. Beaverbrook Papers, Box A 65. Letter dated 16 October 1912. Bennett to Aitken.

61. Ibid., p.594.

Chapter 6

TWO MARITIMERS CORRAL
THE BOW RIVER

No one up to 1909 had met with any degree of success in developing a pioneer hydro development on the upper reaches of the Bow River. The original Alexander and Budd proposition at Horseshoe Falls showed potential but even with the later transfer of the project into the hands of the consulting engineering firm of Smith, Kerry and Chace it still seemed unachievable because of the lack of financing. It was this state of affairs which prompted two New Brunswick natives, who saw potential business possibilities in Calgary, to commence their activities. William Maxwell (Max) Aitken and Richard Bedford Bennett began an enterprise which ensured that the Bow River would become a "Calgary Power Company, Limited" river, with the sole purpose of capturing the entire electricity demand of Calgary. It is the premise of this chapter that without the market potential of Calgary it is doubtful that the company (now TransAlta Utilities Corporation) could have succeeded as it did in becoming the largest single investor-owned electrical utility in Canada.

> As I was passing through the Kananaskis District, I saw what looked like a very fine power proposition within a hundred yards of the Railway track, and I think on the north side. Is this the Calgary power and transmission project? If not, I would think it worth your while to cover that district, with a view to ascertaining if there are any other likely power locations. [1]

So wrote Max Aitken, president of the Montreal Trust and Deposit Company in Montreal, to his brother, R.T.D. (Traven) Aitken, who lived in Calgary. A few days later, on 28 April 1909, Traven Aitken replied:

> With reference to Calgary Power and Transmission project, the Falls which you saw from the train are probably the Kananaskis Falls. They are situated about fifteen miles below Exshaw and I do not know of any other falls visible from the railway. Last summer I made an effort to run the Bow River from Exshaw down to

139

Calgary by canoe but owing to the lack of water at some points was unable to accomplish it. However, when the ice goes out and the weather becomes warmer I intend to follow the river down from Exshaw and see exactly what there is there in the shape of power location.

Max Aitken had made an early turn-of-the-century sojourn to Alberta at which time he had reaffirmed his friendship with Richard Bedford Bennett. Bennett had moved to Calgary from Chatham, New Brunswick in 1897 to join the law firm of Senator James Lougheed as a partner. He soon became a very successful corporate lawyer. Aitken was the son of an emigrant Scottish Presbyterian minister who, during the course of his ministry, had been transferred from his first parish in Maple, Ontario, a few miles north of Toronto, to Newcastle in New Brunswick. It was here that the young Aitken met Bennett, some nine years his senior, and began a life-long friendship. Bennett did his best to persuade Aitken to follow a career in law but Aitken's attempts at Dalhousie University and later, articling in Bennett's former law office in Chatham, failed. Max Aitken was interested only in pursuing business and, in particular, in making money. His success in business and financial circles in the Maritimes culminated in the formation of his own company, Royal Securities Corporation, Limited, out of which Aitken spawned many successful enterprises, making him both wealthy and an influential force in the nation.

From his Montreal headquarters, Aitken had a close working arrangement with Bennett in Calgary. Early in 1908, he wrote to Bennett with regard to some mortgages and in closing asked: "What about the Calgary situation? I should like to make a purchase of two plants and subsequently a consolidation. Why don't you take the situation up?"[2] There are two possibilities for the "two plants" referred to in Aitken's letter. There were two local cement companies, Western Canada Cement at Exshaw, and the Alberta Portland Cement Company in Calgary. In 1910 Aitken merged most of the independent cement producers in Canada into the Canada Cement Company so we know that he could have had some earlier interest in these plants. The other possibility was a merger of the Calgary Power and Transmission Company which had already embarked on the development of the Horseshoe Falls Hydro power site and the Calgary Water Power Company. Since no record remains to indicate any interest by Aitken in the old Calgary Water Power Company we can assume that his interest, as expressed to Bennett, was in the cement companies. However, even this encompassed electrical power since both cement plants required substantial quantities of electricity and, in fact, the Alberta Portland Cement Company in Calgary had already acquired some initial control over the water rights at the Radnor hydro-power site just downstream from Horseshoe Falls. Both Aitken and Bennett were well aware of the hydro-power potential of the Bow River. Both were also keenly aware of the business prospects presented by the growing community as indicated in Aitken's letter to his brother:

I think you might keep in touch with the Calgary Power and Transmission people and if you find that Smith is dropping the project, you might suggest that the Calgary people would do well to take it up with me. In fact, I was greatly impressed by the growth and prospects of the City of Calgary and I would be most favourably inclined to any project from that territory.[3]

This comment came one year after Aitken, through one of his newly-formed companies, Montreal Engineering, had attempted to .extract a franchise from Calgary for the operation of a street railway. Aitken was absolutely serious about the railway proposal and even dispatched his older brother, Traven, to Calgary to look after his interests. Negotiations with Calgary's city council were extremely difficult and by mid-summer of 1908 Max Aitken was starting to lose interest in the project. He wrote to his brother that, "In the event of this proposition falling through, which I presume is likely as the City will not grant us reasonable franchises, I am prepared to send you to Guatamala, providing you wish to go there."[4] It was not a case of Aitken sending his brother to Central America as a sort of "exile" but because the Aitken interests, through Royal Securities Corporation and Montreal Engineering, had acquired several potentially successful electrical and transportation utilities in Latin America. On 4 August Aitken wired Traven: "Regret exceedingly (but) cannot go outside business I know. If nothing doing better come (to) Montreal."[5] Traven replied in a lengthy letter, expressing his personal disappointment in the decision to forget the Calgary proposition: "You will remember that I took the matter up at your request. I am not in a position financially to carry on these negotiations and await the outcome. Your letter of the 24th (August) was the first information I had that you wished to discontinue the Calgary application."[6] He then proceeded to laud the potential of Calgary for business opportunities. Even though Traven appears to have accepted the finality of his brother's decision in regard to the street railway, he raised the matter of electrical power supply: "With regard to power, you do not need to buy out existing companies. You can get power at several points on the Bow River within a very reasonable distance of the City." The "existing companies" were the Calgary Power and Transmission Company which was still under the direct control of the Alexander and Budd Syndicate, and the Calgary Water Power Company of which Peter Prince had been founder. Traven continued:

You can sell 6,000 horsepower in the City and that is the full capacity of the Bow River at low water. You will have the City lighting-at least you will sell the power to the City-if you want it. The Cement works will take 1500 h.p. from you, P. Burns and Co. will take a large amount and a dozen other manufacturers will all take power from you. You want new business and it is here, and good business.

In a final attempt to convince Max to retain some business interest in Calgary he asked that Carl C. Giles, president of Montreal Engineering, a wholly owned subsidiary of Aitken's Montreal Trust and Deposit Company,[7] be sent to Calgary to survey the business possibilities. "If his (Giles) opinion does not bear me out then I will never trust to my own judgment again. I feel very strongly on this subject and would hate to see it pass out of your hands now," concluded Traven.[8] It is not known whether Giles came but certainly the impassioned plea of Traven must have had some effect on Max maintaining an interest in Calgary's business potential.

Max Aitken's reply was neither strongly for or against retaining an interest in Calgary. The stalemate in the negotiations with the city regarding the street railway led him to comment: "I think the Council is so socialistic that a satisfactory proposition cannot be obtained at this time."[9] However, some latent interest still remained regarding electrical power: "I do not believe that we can successfully undertake the development of the Calgary Power & Transmission Co.'s property on account of the contracts already entered into. Any other property must necessarily require a great deal of consideration." Clearly Max Aitken was aware of the development of Horseshoe Falls by the Calgary Power and Transmission Company and we can assume that he was equally aware of the financial problems that Alexander and Budd were having as the principals in that company. Five days later, on 8 September 1908, Traven finally agreed with his brother that the Calgary street railway proposition was in trouble. The council was elected because of their support of municipal ownership of a new street railway and while there was some public support for the Aitken proposal, the council would not move from its position. Traven believed that at the next municipal election, the incumbent council would be turfed out by newcomers who would support the Aitken proposal for a long-term franchise: "They (the council) are, however, a bunch of grafters of the meanest kind, and are holding off as long as possible."[10] In the same letter he also commented that, "In reference to power, the Transmission Co.'s plant cannot, I think, be developed at a profit, but there are water powers much nearer which can be. I do not think it would be advisable to go into them fully until assured of a franchise." A modified approach to a new city council had been conceived which they hoped would combine a street railway and power franchise.

Max Aitken gained a rather unexpected supporter for his franchise scheme when E.R. Wood, managing director of the Central Canada Loan and Savings Company in Toronto and also the president of the Alberta Portland Cement Company in Calgary, wrote to him on 26 September 1908. Wood had learned of Aitken's negotiations for a street railway and power franchise in Calgary and while he was not overly interested in the street railway he reminded Aitken that his company already controlled the Radnor power site downstream from the Horseshoe Falls. The falls, in turn, were controlled by the Calgary Power and Transmission Company. Aitken replied that he was not at all optimistic about the final outcome of his franchise negotiations. The franchise, he pointed out, included a provision for the tramway company also to be in the electric lighting business but that nothing had been done regarding power and light. "I think," concluded Aitken, "if the franchise is granted there will be opportunity for co-operation."[11]

Aitken immediately advised his brother of his encounter with Mr. Wood while asking to be updated on the current situation in Calgary with respect to the franchise negotiation, again expressing doubt as to the outcome. Traven replied on 21 October that he had discussed the power site at Radnor with J.W. Campbell, local manager of the Alberta Portland Cement Company, and was assured of that company's cooperation if the street railway franchise was terminated in Aitken's favour. He concluded, "The Council had a meeting last night and the S.R.F. (street railway franchise) was discussed. They talk of building a Street Railway themselves, but that is only a bluff."[12] In a handwritten postscript he added, "If the Transmission Company thought you would buy (electric power) from the Cement Company they would oppose the granting of a Street Ry franchise." But the city was not bluffing and by the summer of 1909 a municipally-owned street railway was inaugurated. Aitken was still left with the electrical power option but with two indigenous electrical utilities already operating within the city and with the franchise agreement of 1907 held by the Calgary Power and Transmission Company to supply hydro power into Calgary there did not appear to be any room for another private enterprise to prosper.

In Aitken's letter of 23 April 1909 to Traven describing his view of the Kananaskis Falls he had also advised him to keep in touch with the Calgary Power and Transmission Company inferring that Smith might be considering dropping the project. The second owners were equally unable to complete the Horseshoe Falls project and this was the signal for Aitken to spring into action.

On 29 September 1909, E.R. Wood wired J.W. Campbell. The telegram read in part, "Strictly private. In case we can make satisfactory arrangement with Smith to consolidate Radnor and Horseshoe powers which would you recommend should be developed first...considering probable contracts with Exshaw and Alberta Cement Companies?" Most significantly, Campbell was instructed to direct his reply to Royal Securities Corporation which, by this time, was back in Aitken's fold. It is obvious that Aitken and Wood, knowing that Smith's Horseshoe Falls project was in trouble financially, had given consideration to the consolidation of both power sites with Aitken providing the financing. What is also of interest here is the pending merger of the two independent cement companies in Calgary and Exshaw into the new Canada Cement consolidation for which Aitken was also the prime mover. J.W. Campbell was placed in an unenviable and compromising position because he was now privy to this new information while at the same time acting as a consultant to the city in contractual matters relating to the revised franchise agreement being sought by Smith and his Calgary Power and Transmission Company. On 30 September, J.W. Mitchell, the Toronto-based secretary of the Alberta Portland Cement Company, was advised by Wood to sign the documents of conveyance of the Radnor power site to National Securities Corporation, after which the signed copies were to be returned to Royal Securities Corporation in Montreal:

Arrangement has been entered into with the approval of the Directors of the Alberta Portland Cement Company by which the Radnor power is not to be conveyed to the Canada Cement Company, the latter company receiving the cash consideration mentioned in the conveyance in lieu of the power. A syndicate has been arranged to develop this and the Horseshoe Falls power, making contracts at satisfactory prices with both the Exshaw and Alberta companies for the supply to them of power for their respective plants.[13]

Aitken's plan to amalgamate the independent cement producers into the Canada Cement Company was now underway. The scheme included the development of the Radnor power site and Smith's troubled Horseshoe Falls site into a new syndicate for the sale of power to the two cement plants at Exshaw and Calgary and the City of Calgary by virtue of the franchise contract already existing with C.B. Smith's Calgary Power and Transmission Company. R.B. Bennett was targeted immediately by Aitken to handle his Calgary interests. Aitken wired Bennett on 6 October: "Legal matters pertaining to Canada Cement Company in Calgary placed in your hands. Papers going forward today." Earlier that day, Aitken had also wired Bennett regarding his plans for Radnor and Horseshoe Falls power. Because of its informative and enthusiastic content, the entire telegram is cited:

> Strictly private. I have joined with Kilbourn et al in Radnor power and Smith et al in Horseshoe Power. Present proposal is (to) develop Horseshoe power first. Hayward our General Manager at Stave Lake will accompany Smith to Calgary in two or three weeks and finally dispose of details. In meantime Smith has wired his Secretary to lay before you complete details of their legal position. Kilbourn has wired Campbell to join Smith's forces in securing amended franchise and contract with city. Will you kindly join Smith's forces in arranging this contract on terms satisfactory to Campbell. Get support of Dennis. If not attainable will try to use influence here. Stavert is writing Hogg asking him to assist. Everybody in Montreal aboard the band wagon. We expect you to act as Solicitor and Director of Company. My address Waldorf, New York, next three days. Have asked E.R. Wood to wire Burns.[14]

Bennett did not respond with the same degree of enthusiasm. He wired Aitken at the Waldorf Astoria on the following day: "Think hasty action inadvisable. Campbell acted (as) cities expert (in) Smith's negotiations."[15] Bennett was obviously concerned with the conflict of interest in which J.W. Campbell, as local manager of the Alberta Portland Cement Company, now found himself. Bennett was also well aware of the local political resistance he would likely encounter from the council because of the endless delays caused by the construction and financial difficulties of the Calgary Power and Transmission Company.

Aitken wasted no time in dispatching R.F. Hayward, general manager of Western Canada Power Company, Vancouver, to prepare a report on the feasibility of the developing the two sites. Two years earlier Aitken had acquired a major interest in the Vancouver-based company which was engaged in the development of the Stave Falls hydro plant, north of present Maple Ridge on the north shore of the lower mainland of British Columbia. Hayward's report to Aitken was very optimistic: "At the risk of repeating much that is well known, I will recite my reasons for believing that Calgary will, in the near future, require all the power that can be economically developed on the Bow River."[16] Hayward considered the city franchise with the Calgary Power and Transmission Company as "ambiguous in its terms and either in its present or in a modified form could never be satisfactory to the City or to the power company." He recommended a franchise for a twenty-five year period with the company having the right to recruit customers who had power requirements of ten horsepower and upwards. All matters relating to rates as well as undergrounding of power lines should be regulated by the Canadian Railway Commission. Power would be sold to the city for its lighting and railway systems on a sliding scale from $28.00 to $24.00 per horsepower per annum depending on the quantity contracted for but with a minimum of 2,000 horsepower. On the results of his evaluation of the technical data Hayward recommended that Horseshoe Falls be completed first, followed by the hydro site at Kananaskis Falls (for which Aitken did not have water rights) and finally, the Radnor site. Hayward also considered developing the Horseshoe and Kananaskis Falls sites into a single project but decided that the rock formation would not support a dam of the required height. Perhaps he was simply being prudent since he was aware of the effort already expended on the Horseshoe Falls site and knew that time was of the essence if a modified franchise was to be extracted from the city. In any event Hayward had already wired Aitken on 27 October 1909, more than one month before submission of his final report, to the effect that Smith's plans for the Horseshoe development be continued and that Bennett proceed immediately to get a "clear cut" contract from the city. Hayward also reported that he had seen the mayor who had indicated his personal support for the project. All that remained now was for Aitken and his associates to put the pieces together and form a new company to develop the water power sites with contracts to supply power to the Calgary and Exshaw cement plants and a new (or modified) franchise from the City of Calgary.

In May 1909 Cecil B.Smith had acquired complete control of the Calgary Power and Transmission Company through the acquisition of over 90 percent of the fully paid-up shares in the stock of that company and the assumption of the company's current liabilities which amounted to about $9,000. He was unable to refinance the Horseshoe Falls project on the general excuse that the terms of the franchise the company held with the city were too stringent. This, as we have already seen, was the signal for Aitken to move in on the troubled company. He had already arranged for the Alberta Portland Cement Company to convey its rights to the Radnor power site to the National Securities Corporation which was acting as an agent for the Royal Securities Corporation. The president of National Securities Corporation was the same Carl C. Giles who was president of Montreal Engineering.

On 4 October an agreement was executed between Cecil B. Smith, National Securities Corporation and the Royal Securities Corporation which effectively set the stage for the new company to emerge. Smith agreed to deposit his shares of the company with Royal Securities and, within a time not to exceed ninety days, to convey to Royal Securities "all of properties, rights, franchises and assets now owned" by the company. Royal Securities Corporation would assume the indebtedness of Smith's company amounting to $20,000 secured by thirty-year bonds. For this Smith received the sum of $45,000 to cover his personal indebtedness to the company while Smith, Kerry and Chace received a settlement of $5,680 to cover their indebtedness in the Calgary Power and Transmission Company. Further, Smith either by himself or with his partners, would remain as the engineer and prime contractor on the Horseshoe Falls project under contract to the new company. The responsibility of National Securities Corporation was to deliver the leases of water rights at the Radnor and Horseshoe Falls sites to Royal Securities Corporation. At the same time it would undertake to secure a contract with the Alberta Portland Cement Company for the new company to supply electric power to the Calgary plant for a period of fifteen years at $2.50 per horsepower month on terms similar to those contained in the contract already in force between the Calgary Power and Transmission Company and the Western Canada Cement and Coal Company. In return for the rights granted by Smith and the National Securities Corporation, the Royal Securities Corporation agreed to incorporate a new company under the provisions of the Companies Act of Canada with an authorized capital of $3,000,000 and an issue of $3,000,000 in 5 percent First Mortgage Gold Bonds of which not less than $1,250,000 would be issued.

All of the assets conveyed to Royal Securities by National Securities and Smith would be transferred to the new company upon which it would get a cash loan of $1,062,500 from Royal Securities at 10 percent in return for which Royal Securities would receive fully paid-up shares of the new company's aggregate stock in the amount of $1,750,000 and the entire $1,250,000 bond issue. National Securities Corporation received $35,000 to cover its expenses in obtaining the Radnor water rights. Upon delivery of the securities of the new company to Royal Securities Corporation, Smith received shares aggregating $300,000 and National Securities received $200,000, both at par value. The agreement was signed by Cecil B. Smith, representing the Calgary Power and Transmission Company, Carl C. Giles representing the National Securities Corporation and W.M. Aitken for the Royal Securities Corporation.

The new company, incorporated as the Calgary Power Company, Limited, held its first provisional directors and shareholders meeting on 15 November 1909 in Montreal. The $3,000,000 aggregate capital of the company was divided into 30,000 shares of $100.00 par value. At this meeting the contract between Royal Securities and the Calgary Power Company was approved. None of the provisional directors stayed beyond 4 January 1910 when the new directors took over. They included many familiar names: C.C. Giles, H.A. Lovett, W.H.

Hogg, W.M. Aitken, R.B. Bennett, C.B. Smith, H.S. Holt, and A.E. Cross. Aitken was elected as the first president with R.B. Bennett as vice-president. Smith was appointed managing director. By 31 March Aitken had resigned as president but remained a director. H.S. Holt of Royal Bank fame became president, followed by R.B. Bennett on 3 August 1911.[17] Smith soon fell into disrepute with the directors because they viewed his firm of consultants, Smith, Kerry and Chace, as incompetent after a series of delays and washouts took place at the Horseshoe Falls construction site. By the middle of 1910 Smith no longer appears in the directors' list. He did, however, retain his 2,558 shares in the Calgary Power Company.

The first challenge facing R.B. Bennett and C.B. Smith was to reaffirm the contract with the city which had been assigned to the Calgary Power Company out of the merger in Montreal. During the two weeks prior to bringing their formal proposals to council, Bennett and Aitken had worked out a strategy. Aitken wired Smith in Winnipeg and Bennett in Calgary authorizing them to contract with the city for 8,000 horsepower at $30.00 per annum for fifteen years. Bennett requested clarification of the basis of electrical demand, "It is, of course, apparent to you that it makes a great deal of difference whether the contract is made on a daily, monthly or yearly Peak basis."[18] Bennett was well aware of the different revenues which would accrue to the company depending upon the manner in which the peak demand was determined and he wanted Aitken to opt for an annual demand which would maximize revenues to the company. He also met with Mayor Jamieson before his first formal approach to the council and wrote to Aitken on 1 February 1910, "I had a talk with Mr. Jamieson...and he tells me privately that if Burns, Cross and others took a decided stand at the Council meeting for power in the manufacturing part of the City, a franchise will be granted."[19]

Aitken was still thinking solely in terms of extending the franchise agreement which the city had negotiated in 1907 with the Calgary Power and Transmission Company but Bennett was not convinced that this was the correct route to follow: "We are not any better off by having a franchise, and unless we get what we want I would advise you not to accept." Bennett believed that a better alternative was a simple wholesale power supply contract and as the negotiations dragged on throughout a large part of 1910, he increasingly supported this alternative. He understood that another utility operating beside the two already in operation would present a plethora of problems which the Calgary Power Company could do without. We must bear in mind that Bennett, who had acted earlier as legal counsel for Prince and the Calgary Water Power Company, had experience in this matter and he cautioned Aitken accordingly. Bennett also knew that the new company needed public support: "I think however that you should make arrangements for a vigorous newspaper campaign, and for a positive expression of opinion by the leading citizens of Calgary." In a later letter Bennett also briefed

Aitken on his contacts with the mayor and certain council members aimed at preparing the way for obtaining an easy contract with the city:

> I advised the Mayor that I would not appear before the City Council for business reasons, and he quite understood the situation, as did also the members of his Council with whom I had personal conversation.... I will have no difficulty in securing the attendance of a very influential delegation of power consumers at the City Council pressing for the granting of a franchise when the moment is opportune. I will organize the movement as though it came from the people and not from the Company.[20]

The first communication from the Calgary Power Company to the city council occurred on 10 February 1910 when it informed the council that it was the assignee of the contracts negotiated with the Calgary Power and Transmission Company during 1907 and virtually demanded that the time limits for power delivery under the terms of those earlier contracts be extended to September 1910. If the city should decide not to renew the contracts exactly as originally negotiated, the company would alternately entertain a twenty-year contract with the city, supplying 8,000 horsepower up to September 1912 and thereafter for the balance of the term at $30.00 per horsepower year. The option of a modified franchise was also included with the company being willing to purchase the city's entire electrical plant at a valuation to be fixed by arbitration and a price for lighting to consumers of eight cents per kilowatt hour "which will effect a direct saving to the citizens of a large and annually increasing amount."[21]

Council's response on 21 February was to appoint an ad hoc committee to consider the old agreements with Calgary Power and Transmission Company and the new proposal submitted by the Calgary Power Company. At the same meeting the aldermen approved a motion to appoint a further committee, chaired by Mayor Jamieson, to consider the question of the installion of a municipal hydro power plant. J.W. Campbell was immediately recalled by the committee to advise on the power question.[22] He submitted his recommendation to the ad hoc committee on 24 February with the council adopting it on 28 February. The counterproposal to Bennett and Smith was three-fold. First, the old franchise agreement would not be extended; second, subject to approval of the ratepayers, the contract amount would be 6,000 horsepower at $25.00 for fifteen years; and third, any contracts which the company already held with power consumers within the city limits were to be cancelled. The most surprising turn of events, however, was the committee's report which recommended a sum of $2,000 "for the purpose of making surveys of the Radnor and other sites, with a view of establishing a power plant for the City of Calgary."[23] Bennett's forecast of an easy victory for the Calgary Power Company was encountering obstacles which he had not anticipated.

The council's decision to consider municipal development of a hydro site on the Bow River had been precipitated by a Mr. W.H. Newsome of Calgary who had informed Mayor Jamieson of a hydro site capable of developing 3,000 to 5,000 horsepower near his ranch, about twelve miles west of Calgary in the Springbank district. Mayor Jamieson passed the information to City Engineer J.T. Child, requesting that he look into the matter and advise accordingly. Child replied that he was indeed aware of the Newsome hydro site but feared that the necessary civil works required to develop the power would result in extensive flooding "to the detriment of the ranchers along the river bottoms."[24] While this dialogue was going on between the mayor and Child, City Commissioner Graves requested that Child find out who held the assignment of water rights at the Radnor hydro site. Child replied that as far as he knew the water rights had already been applied for by Alberta Portland Cement Company. William Kennedy, a consulting engineer retained by the cement company, had seen Child in 1908 for information on the Radnor site and had "obtained all surveys necessary and made plans, etc., but as to what was done subsequently Mr. J.W. Campbell would be in a better position to inform us, he being Manager for the Alberta Portland Cement Co, at that time."[25] City Solicitor D.S. Moffatt was then directed to check further into the Radnor water rights. He reported that the cement company had filed for the rights as early as 1905 but the assignment had not been finalized because of pending revisions to the water power regulations in Ottawa.[26]

The city solicitor's letter also disclosed that J.M. Kilbourn was president of the Alberta Portland Cement Company, having succeeded E.R. Wood who, a year earlier, had allied himself with Aitken in the formation of the Calgary Power Company. Kilbourn also became a major shareholder of the Calgary Power Company.[27] The city solicitor then contacted M.S. McCarthy, M.P. in Ottawa who, in turn, discussed the Calgary city council proposal with Frank Oliver, Minister of the Interior. McCarthy's reply to the city solicitor expressed the opinion that the application of the Alberta Portland Cement Company would receive priority because of its early filing. The information was forwarded to Mayor Jamieson, and there is no record that the council pursued the matter any further.

C.B. Smith, the managing director of Calgary Power, took a hard line with Mayor Jamieson once the council decided to negotiate on a new contract rather than capitulating to the original proposals submitted by him and Bennett. He wrote to Mayor Jamieson from Winnipeg on the letterhead of Smith, Kerry and Chace, lecturing the mayor on the dangers of submitting the Calgary Power Company's proposal prematurely to a public referendum. He wanted the council to negotiate a contract agreeable to both parties and then send it to a public referendum if necessary. Furthermore, the recommendations made by J.W. Campbell and adopted by the council were, according to Smith, totally unaccept-able to the company. "I can assure you before hand," he said, "that such a contract, as you suggest, would not be entertained by the Company. As regards

Radnor—do not waste your money on this, as these water rights belong abso-lutely to the Calgary Power Company."[28] In a final warning to the mayor Smith concluded, "I trust that you will make haste slowly and give these matters further consideration before you finally strain the relationships between our Company and the City to a breaking point."

It was an arrogant letter which did not help negotiations. Mayor Jamieson replied in a short but curt letter. If the city could circumvent a referendum on the power matter the mayor agreed that it would be preferable: "The City is prepared to consider any reasonable proposition, but will not stand for any exorbitant prices. We expect and are quite willing to see the power company get a good fair return on the money invested and we think they should be satisfied with that."[29] Smith's name did not reappear during the remainder of the 1910 negotiation period.

The next formal offer by the Calgary Power Comapny was directed to City Clerk H.E. Gillis on 28 March 1910. This time the tone of Bennett's letter was very conciliatory: "Our Eastern as well as our Western Directors are much impressed with the possibilities of the growth and development of this City, and having large interests in this locality are anxious to assist in that development."[30] The quantity of power offered was scaled down from the original 8,000 horse-power to 4,000 with a price of $29.00 per horsepower per annum on an annual peak basis. The offer was entirely free of any reference to a franchise except that the company wished to retain the contract it had with the Alberta Portland Cement Company located in east Calgary. The company was anxious to promote the use of electrical power within the city and requested the city to agree not to re-sell power at a price exceeding $34.00 per horsepower to small consumers and $39.00 to large consumers.

The issue was now clearly defined. The Calgary Power Company was offering a contract for the wholesale supply of electricity to the city. Bennett wired Aitken on 2 April to the effect that the city council had practically agreed on a fifteen-year contract for 4,000 horsepower at $29.00 while allowing the power company to retain its right to service the local cement plant. The council, however, did have a major reservation: the proposed contract made no provision for an auxil-iary plant in the event of interruptions to the transmission line between Horseshoe Falls and Calgary. Bennett wrote to Aitken on 4 April outlining this new problem:

> A further difficulty arose in connection with what arrangements we were making to insure a continuous service. The City's present steam plant is practically out of business, and for the operation of not only the Street Railway plant but also for the operation of...their lighting system, the City will be entirely dependent upon us, and they, therefore, desire to know at the earliest possible moment what provision we propose to make in the way of constructing an auxiliary steam plant.[31]

Early aerial view of Horseshoe Falls Hydro Power Development.
Source: TransAlta Utilities Corp.

Interior view of Horseshoe Falls Power House c. 1920. Horizontal water turbines on
right are direct-coupled to alternating current generators on left.
Source: TransAlta Utilities Corp.

Aitken did not agree and on 18 April Bennett advised the council that the Calgary Power Company did not propose to construct an auxiliary steam plant. Instead Bennett talked about erecting two transmission lines to Calgary but in fact the second line was not installed until Calgary Power Company's second hydro plant at the Kananaskis Falls was developed in 1912. There is no doubt that this particular concern of council precipitated the decision to build the new steam plant in Victoria Park thus limiting very severely the quantity of power negotiated from Calgary Power Company. Bennett's comment to Aitken that the city's steam plant (Atlantic Avenue) was practically out of business is difficult to understand. If he meant that because it was working continuously at full capacity and additional capacity was urgently required in order for the city plant to continue to provide the service demanded then he was correct. Financially, however, the plant was providing the city with substantial surpluses of hard cash.

Sometime in early May the completion of the civil works at Horseshoe Falls was delayed by a serious washout. McCall knew that his plant would be unable to keep up with the growing electrical loads and that if some additional source of supply was not available by October the city would have to start refusing new business for its plant: "I think it would be better to let the Eau Claire [Calgary Water Power Company] take business from now on than for us to connect it up as we cannot possibly handle it with present equipment this fall."[32] McCall's timely intervention had an immediate effect. On 21 May Mayor Jamieson wrote to Bennett: "The Power Committee would like to meet you at the earliest possible date to try to come to some definite conclusion regarding power from your Company. We are now at the point where we must take active steps to supplement the present City plant failing an agreement with you."[33] By July Aitken was becoming impatient with the negotiations undertaken by Bennett and Smith four months earlier. He wired Bennett, "Is it possible for us to negotiate immediate contracts with one or two manufacturing concerns, this obviating necessity for city contract?"[34]

This was happening at exactly the same time that Dr. Ings and his Western Canada Power and Development Company were negotiating for a power supply contract with the city and this additional complication was not expediting affairs for any of the parties. The *Calgary Herald* summarized the problem facing the city fathers in an editorial on 22 July. The editor pointed out that since the Calgary Power Company was so uncompromising in its dealings with the city it deserved little public sympathy and while Dr. Ings' proposal deserved utmost consideration, it was flawed because of serious doubts about the water flows on the Elbow River. Because of this the city plan to expand its own power plant facilities was a prudent policy. The editorial concluded that, "The best way to get a reasonable arrangement with a power company is to be independent of it, and Calgary will save the cost of its auxiliary plant many times over in the freedom which it will give the City in making any power contract with an outside company."

The newspaper editorial prompted Bennett to write a personal note to Mayor Jamieson deploring the involvement of the newspapers: "I do not want to discuss the power question through the newspapers, but I think it must be apparent to you as a business man that the Company is not being fairly treated."[35] It was an odd complaint by Bennett who from the very beginning of the contract negotiation had planned with Aitken a covert strategy of influencing the council through newspaper campaigns and expressions of support from prominent citizens. Bennett offered to conclude a contract on a reasonable basis and he wanted to know soon so that the Calgary Power Company could complete some other arrangements. Mayor Jamieson replied that the city wanted "to do business with a power company if it can do so on a reasonable basis,"[36] and went on to delineate some items about which the city power committee had earlier requested additional information that had not been forthcoming. The mayor promised an early meeting of the committee to which Bennett would be invited in the hope that some arrangement could be finalized.

The Calgary aldermen were still not ready to accept the risk of surrendering the entire responsibility for a dependable power supply to another party, whether it be Calgary Power or Dr. Ings' Elbow River development scheme. On 1 August they approved third reading on a $125,000 by-law for the first stage of a new municipal steam plant to be located in Victoria Park. (The plant was to serve Calgary well and without it the city would have been in difficulty many times in those years when water levels were low on the Bow River and before water storage facilities were of sufficient size to be of use.) Despite the approval of the steam power plant, the need to contract for some additional power remained. Dr. Ings' proposal was further stalled as the city was also considering development of the same project. The Elbow River project was, however, plagued by the continuing dispute over the adequacy of the water flow, and the Calgary Power Company offer had the distinct advantage of its site being under development. The entire council visited the site at Bennett's invitation in early April and the coucillors knew very well that this development was the only tangible alternative for augmenting the city's growing power demands.

On 18 August 1910 the die was cast. The Power Committee presented two resolutions, both of which were accepted by the council. The first resolution consisted of two parts. Dr. Ings and his Elbow River syndicate would be asked for a listing of the personnel of their company and the city would contact the Department of the Interior in an effort to determine the status of Ings' application for water rights. The motion was clearly a red herring which would make it appear that the offer of the Western Canada Power and Development Company was still under consideration. The second resolution was more positive and indicated that the scales were now tipping in favour of the Calgary Power Company, Limited. Bennett was asked to submit a price for 2,000 horsepower on a one-year contract from the date on which the Company could deliver or until the time that a competing company was available to deliver power. Prices for additional 500 horsepower blocks as well as prices for the power beyond the proposed contract expiry date were also requested. The city was attempting to keep the door open for Ings' company in the remote event that it would be able to successfully develop a hydro-power site on the Elbow River. Bennett's reply to the resolution of the council was remarkable in that it acquiesced to all of the demands dictated by the city. It was a genuine gamble on Bennett's part. The 2,000 horsepower requested by the city would carry a price of $30.00 per horsepower year of continuous service, the demand to be billed on a monthly basis with a minimum monthly charge of 2,000 horsepower to apply. In other words, the minimum annual charge for power would be $60,000. Additional power would be supplied in 500 horsepower blocks with each block reducing in price by fifty cents per horsepower per annum up to a total of 10,000 horsepower when the price would reach $24.00. Bennett was also gambling that the Dr. Ings development would never get off the ground:

> In order that no question may arise as to ample time being afforded…a competing company to complete its undertaking, we are prepared to enter into the temporary contract to supply power until December 31,1912. This Company will meet any competition that may offer; not competition by quotation [an obvious reference to

Calgary Power Co. Ltd. East Calgary substation from which hydro power was delivered to Calgary c. 1920. The building still stands at the north end of the Highfield Industrial Subdivision.
Source: TransAlta Utilities Corp.

Dr. Ings' syndicate] but real competition of a company in a position to supply from actual development the power offered.[37]

Bennett also offered the services of an expert to canvass the city promoting power sales to prospective customers, expressing the hope that the city would do likewise. The company wanted no franchise: "It merely offers for sale to the City a commodity which it produces."[38] This new offer by the Calgary Power Company won the instant approval of the power committee who recommended its acceptance to the council on 9 September. Thus began an alliance between the City of Calgary and the Calgary Power Company which has endured to this day.

The contract went into effect on 12 September 1910 with the delivery of 2,000 horsepower to the east Calgary terminus of the transmission line from Horseshoe Falls on or before 1 April 1911 and would terminate on 31 December 1912 unless renewed as provided for in the contract. The city did not expect this initial contract to go beyond the specified termination date as is indicated by the inclusion of an article in the agreement providing that, "If at any time before the termination of this contract as herein provided any person, firm or corporation shall have electric energy actually ready to sell and deliver to the City at its boundaries, the City shall have the right to cancel this contract on giving one month's previous notice in writing to the company." Max Aitken was very concerned about this clause because he felt that it might be carried forward into future contract agreements. With this single reservation, Aitken offered Bennett his "sincere congratulations on the consummation of the Calgary Power contract, which I consider to be on a very satisfactory basis. I only regret that the quantity of power is not more than 2,000 or 3,000 horsepower, but this difficulty will be rectified by the increased consumption."[39] Bennett's reply was, surprisingly, in the form of a complaint, "It has been one of the most annoying and difficult matters that I have had to do with since I came here."[40] Not only did the first contract provide for only one-quarter of the power supply originally sought but future contracts were to be compromised by the existence of the new city-owned power plant at Victoria Park.

The company made its first delivery of power to Calgary on Sunday morning, 21 May 1911, three weeks behind schedule. The city never disputed the contract which the company held to supply power to the Calgary plant of the Canada Cement Company (formerly the Alberta Portland Cement Company). The company's other major customer was the Canada Cement plant at Exshaw. Eventually the cement plant in Calgary closed and the plant at Exshaw expanded its operation into one of the largest in Canada. The Calgary terminus of the original transmission line from Horseshoe Falls was the East Calgary Substation. The building still stands in its original state at the north end of the Highfield industrial subdivision near 11th Street S.E. overlooking the CNR railway line. The "poured-in-place" concrete substation building still mutely reflects the nature of the first industry it served. The old cement plant was located immediately north of the East Calgary Substation between the CNR tracks and present Ogden Road.

Bennett, now president of the Calgary Power Company, wrote to Aitken early in 1912 and advised him that the contract with the city had generated revenue of $42,828 for the previous year. The cement plant in Calgary produced $27,458 while the one at Exshaw grossed $15,233. It was a clear indication of how important the city contract was for the company and from those earliest years it made the continuity of contracts with the city its primary objective. It was a simple fact that neither party could do without the other although the city still retained some advantage in being able to either contract elsewhere or expand its own facilities for additional power requirements.

By the beginning of 1912 Bennett was anticipating the end of the temporary contract with Calgary. He wrote Aitken expressing his concern that a further contract with the city would be very difficult to negotiate because of the poor service given to the city as a result of frequent water failure on the Bow River. Bennett was also concerned about the very pessimistic view taken in Montreal of the company's financial performance, prompting him to reassure Aitken that even under the worst possible conditions, "we should be in a position to earn our fixed charges."[41] The Horseshoe Falls plant did not have much water storage behind its dam. The development in 1912 of the Kananaskis Falls site above Horseshoe and some storage facilities on Lake Minnewanka (largely at federal government expense with the company paying water rental) added additional water storage upon which both plants could rely when water flows were lower than normal. However, well into the 1920s the Victoria Park Power Plant was constantly called upon to augment the city's power supply and, in fact, the plant capacity was expanded substantially up to 1914.

The company was in the process of settling the damage claims brought against it by former Managing Director Smith. The company had dismissed Smith and his consulting company, Smith, Kerry and Chace, on the grounds of gross incompetence during the final construction of the Horseshoe Falls plant. The action was finally settled by a Court Order on 7 March 1913 that ordered the company to pay $20,000 to Smith, Kerry and Chace. Henceforth Montreal Engineering, a wholly owned subsidiary of Royal Securities Corporation, would become the prime supplier of engineering services to the Calgary Power Company. Bennett wrote to Aitken explaining his frustrations in settling Smith's claims: "He is most unreasonable and is, of course, the one most largely to blame for your having gone into the enterprise to the extent you did."[42] Bennett also criticized Smith for the manner in which he was manipulating his 2,500 shares of the company to his personal advantage on the London Stock Exchange: "I think it might be a good idea to have some of the gas crowd approach Smith and try to buy out his stock." Bennett continued with a personal complaint to the effect that he had not been treated very well with respect to the number of shares he held

(138 in all) when compared to Smith and other shareholders who had been in on the ground floor with him. Bennett confessed that he had been well paid for his legal services but "those who understand the inside workings of the City know that it required very great efforts on my part to get the matter finally closed out in the way in which I did and my influence with the Department of the Interior [Bennett was now a member of parliament representing the riding of Calgary East] has I think been exercised very much in the interests of the Company." If there was any doubt about Bennett's disenchantment with the company it was dispelled by his closing paragraph: "It occurs to me that when the storage dam is finished on Lake Minnewanka and our second transmission line is completed, it might not be a bad idea to try to sell the plant to the City by undertaking to deliver say one million dollars worth of the Common Stock for $750,000 fifty-year four percent debentures of the City."

The City of Calgary never knew how close it came to being the owner of the hydro plants on the Bow River. In any event, it did not take Bennett long to regain his confidence in the company and by the fall of 1912 he was again advising Aitken on various matters, the most important being whether the hydro plant could handle the anticipated demand for the coming winter months. He was beginning to sound exactly like Chief Engineer McCall who had expressed similar concerns about the municipal power plant only a year or so earlier. The second hydro plant at Kananaskis Falls would not be ready until 1913 but Bennett was hopeful that the second transmission line would soon be completed. A new manager, Mr. H.A. Moore, was to start soon with Calgary Power and then Bennett decided that his time could be better utilized to "manage this property as I should like (since)...divided management has brought about a condition that is anything but satisfactory to me and I should fancy to you, also."[43] Aitken was happy with Bennett's decision: "I do beg of you to take the full responsibility of the property;...I look to you as the responsible President of the Company and I would no more think of interfering with your decisions that I would think of interfering with the decisions of Mr. Jones in connection with the Cement Company."[44]

Almost single-handedly Bennett had been responsible for establishing the contractual arrangement between his company and the City of Calgary. It was a remarkable feat and the permanence of the arrangement is one of the few continuing reminders in Calgary of R.B. Bennett's impact upon the city. Bennett remained as president of the Calgary Power Company until 1921 but any direct intervention in matters relating to city contracts ceased after 1913 when he was signatory to the second contract. Direct intervention by Max Aitken into the affairs of the company decreased in late 1912 and ended completely when he sold Royal Securities Corporation to Nova Scotia financier I.W. Killam in 1919. R.B. Bennett's interests turned increasingly to national politics. He served in Arthur Meighen's Conservative governments of 1921 and 1926 as Minister of Justice and Attorney General, and Minister of Finance respectively. He became party leader of the Conservatives in 1927 and was swept into power as Prime Minister in 1930. He retired to England in 1938 where he was appointed to the House of Lords as Viscount Bennett. He died in 1947. Sir Max Aitken is remembered for his rise to fame in Britain as a newspaper baron and his elevation to the peerage as Lord Beaverbrook. His exploits with Winston Churchill as head of the Ministry of Aircraft Production during the Second World War are legendary. He died on 9 June 1964.

References

1. HLRO. Beaverbrook Papers, Series A, Box 65. Letter dated 23 April 1909. W.M. Aitken to R.T.D. Aitken.

2. HLRO. Beaverbrook Papers, Series A, Box 65. Letter dated 23 January 1908. W.M. Aitken to R.B. Bennett.

3. HLRO. Beaverbrook Papers, Series A, Box 65. Letter dated 23 April 1909. W.M. Aitken to R.T.D. Aitken.

4. HLRO. Beaverbrook Papers, Series G, Box 18. Letter dated 29 July 1908. W.M. Aitken to R.T.D. Aitken.

5. HLRO. Beaverbrook Papers, Series A, Box 19. Telegram dated 4 August 1908. W.M. Aitken to R.T.D. Aitken.

6. HLRO. Beaverbrook Papers, Series A, Box 19. Letter dated 28 August 1908. R.T.D. Aitken to W.M. Aitken. Additional quotes from same source.

7. For a short period beginning in late 1906, Max Aitken divested himself of his interests in Royal Securities Corporation and moved from Halifax to Montreal. There he acquired the Montreal Trust Company. We can assume that the name Montreal Trust and Deposit Company, appearing in 1908 correspondence to Aitken was synonymous. In 1908, Aitken sold the Trust Company to the Royal Bank and reacquired Royal Securities Corporation.

8. HLRO. Beaverbrook Papers. Letter dated 28 August 1908. R.T.D. Aitken to W.M. Aitken.

9. HLRO. Beaverbrook Papers. Letter dated 3 September 1908. W.M. Aitken to R.T.D. Aitken. Additional quote from same source.

10. HLRO. Beaverbrook Papers. Letter dated 8 September 1908. R.T.D. Aitken to W.M. Aitken. Additional quote from same source.

11. HLRO. Beaverbrook Papers, Series A, Box 29. Letter dated 2 October 1908. W.M. Aitken to E.R. Wood.

12. HLRO. Beaverbrook Papers, Series A, Box 29. Letters dated 20 October 1908. R.T.D. Aitken to W.M. Aitken.

13. HLRO. Beaverbrook Papers, Series A, Box 42. Letter dated 30 September 1909. E.R. Wood to J.W. Mitchell.

14. HLRO. Beaverbrook Papers, Series A, Box 42. Telegram dated 6 October 1909. W.M. Aitken to R.B. Bennett. J.M. Kilbourn is listed as a major shareholder in Calgary Power Company, Limited by 4 May 1911. Smith became the first managing director of Calgary Power. Dennis was probably Dennis Stairs, a prominent hydro power engineer with Montreal Engineering. Hogg, manager of the Bank of Montreal in Calgary, was a director of the new company after the first shareholders' meeting on 4 January 1910. E.R. Wood became a director on 5 May 1910 as well as a major shareholder.

15. HLRO. Beaverbrook Papers, Series A, Box 65. Telegram dated 7 October 1909. R.B. Bennett to W.M. Aitken.

16. Calgary Power Papers, b4.f17. Report dated 7 December 1909. "Calgary Power Development," R.F. Hayward to W.M. Aitken. Additional quotes from same source.

17. Calgary Power Papers, b1.f1. All references to early meeting of Board of Directors extracted from Minute Book No.1. The only Calgarians on the Board of Directors after January 1910 were R.B. Bennett and A.E. Cross, pioneer rancher and brewer.

18. HLRO. Beaverbrook Papers, Series A, Box 25. Letter dated 27 January 1910. R.B. Bennett to W.M. Aitken.

19. HLRO. Beaverbrook Papers, Series A, Box 25. Letter dated 1 February 1910. W.M. Aitken to R.B. Bennett. Additional quotes from same source.

20. HLRO. Beaverbrook Papers, Series A, Box 65. Letter dated 7 February 1910. R.B. Bennett to W.M. Aitken.

21. City Clerk's Papers, b40.f303. Letter from Calgary Power to city council, undated but confirmed by council minutes, p.55-6 as either 10 or 11 February 1910.

22. J.W. Campbell left the Alberta Portland Cement Company after it was merged into Canada Cement in 1910 but not before he had fallen into disfavour with Bennett and Aitken. He continued his activities in Calgary from his home on 14th Avenue S.E. as a consulting engineer from where his trail simply disappears.

23. Council Minutes, 28 February 1910, p.57.

24. City Clerk's Papers, b52.f419. Report dated 25 February 1910. J.T. Child, City Engineer.

25. City Clerk's Papers, b52,f419. Letter dated 24 February 1910. J.T. Child to City Commissioners.

26. City Clerk's Papers, b52.f419. Letter dated 1 March 1910. W.A. Cory to D.S. Moffatt. It is of interest that the mayor and council were unaware of the impending transfer of Radnor water rights to the Montreal syndicate. Even the local member of Parliament, J.W. McCarthy was not well informed on the matter.

27. Calgary Power Papers, b6.f45, By 4 May 1911, the major shareholders of Calgary Power Company, Limited were listed along with the number of shares held:

Aitken, W.M.	London, Eng.	976
Bennett, R.B.	Calgary	138
Clouston, Sir E.	Montreal	1250
Chace, W.G.	Winnipeg	443
Doble, A.R.	Montreal	250
Holt, H.S.	Montreal	551
James, P.F.	Montreal	275
Kilbourn, J.M.	Montreal	750
McConnell, J.W.	Montreal	525
Royal Securities	Montreal	3887
Smith, C.B.	Toronto	2558
Sperling and Company	London, Eng.	3890
Wood, E.R.	Toronto	1801

The largest shareholder, Royal Securities, was wholly owned by Aitken. Aitken disposed of Royal Securities in 1919 when he sold it to I.W. Killam, who had been one of his subordinates in that company. When he died in the mid 1950s, Killam was one of the wealthiest men in Canada as well as one of Canada's great philanthropists.

28. City Clerk's Papers, b52.f419. Letter dated 5 March 1910. C.B. Smith to Mayor R.R. Jamieson.

29. City Clerk's Papers, b52.f419. Letter dated 8 March 1910. Mayor R.R. Jamieson to C.B. Smith.

30. City Clerk's Papers, b52.f419. Letter dated 28 March 1910. R.B. Bennett to H.E. Gillis, City Clerk.

31. HLRO. Beaverbrook Papers, Series A, Box 65. Letter dated 4 April 1910. R.B. Bennett to W.M. Aitken.

32. City Clerk's Papers, b43.f331. Letter dated 19 May 1910. J.F. McCall to Mayor and Commissioners.

33. City Clerk's Papers, b43.f331. Letter dated 21 May 1910. Mayor R.R. Jamieson to R.B. Bennett.

34. HLRO. Beaverbrook Papers, Series A, Box 65. Telegram dated 4 July 1910. W.M. Aitken to Bennett.

35. Commissioners' Papers, b7.f36. Letter dated 26 July 1910. R.B. Bennett to Mayor R.R. Jamieson.

36. Commissioners' Papers, b7.f36. Letter dated 30 July 1910. Mayor R.R. Jamieson to R.B. Bennett.

37. City Clerk's Papers, b52.f419. Letter dated 29 August 1910. R.B. Bennett to W.D. Spence, City Clerk.

38. Ibid.

39. HLRO. Beaverbrook Papers, Series A, Box 65. Letter dated 16 September 1910. W.M. Aitken to R.B. Bennett.

40. HLRO. Beaverbrook Papers, Series A, Box 65. Letter dated 5 October 1910. R.B. Bennett to W.M. Aitken.

41. HLRO. Beaverbrook Papers, Series A, Box 65. Letter dated 16 February 1912. R.B. Bennett to Sir W.M. Aitken.

42. HLRO. Beaverbrook Papers, Series A, Box 65. Letter dated 16 February 1912. R.B. Bennett to Sir Max Aitken. Additional quotes from same source.

43. HLRO. Beaverbrook Papers. Letter dated 19 September 1912. R.B. Bennett to Sir Max Aitken, M.P.

44. HLRO. Beaverbrook Papers. Letter dated 2 October 1912. Sir Max Aitken to R.B. Bennett, K.C, M.P.

Chapter 7

AN UNEASY ALLIANCE

The relationship which developed between the City of Calgary and the Calgary Power Company after the signing of the first contract in 1910 evolved into a continuing admixture of cooperation and wariness which erupted at times into outright acrimony. The company was committed to a policy of gaining complete control of the electricity supply to Calgary and whatever action was needed to retain that objective was diligently pursued. During times of contract negotiation, the company always held the trump card. In fairness to the company it must be said that the city contributed largely to that advantage by never having, as S.J. Davies would remark in later years, "a horse to trade with."

As we have seen, the primary reason for Max Aitken's involvement with the electrical utility enterprise in Calgary was the promising outlook for the continued economic development of the area. When the company was ready to deliver power to Calgary in the spring of 1911, it came from a hydro plant having an installed capacity of 7500 horsepower developed from two water wheels of 3750 horsepower each. Conveniently, Calgary expanded the capacity of its steam-generated capability to 5000 horsepower. Both plants were brand new and both carried the highest possible fixed costs. The city, of course, embarked on the Victoria Park development largely because of its concern over continuity of service. In fact, the city's decision was correct, since the early years of power supply from the hydro plant were fraught with interruptions. There was no question that the unit cost of energy to the city was at its lowest when the company hydro plant was loaded to its capacity but during 1911-13 the electrical demand imposed by the city alone was such that the hydro plant, also under contract to the two cement plants at Exshaw and Calgary, could not supply the total combined load. So the steam plant in Victoria Park continued to operate not only as a "standby" plant but also to supply up to one-third of the city's annual electricity needs. James McCall reported at the end of 1913: "The steam plant was in operation during the year 18 hours per day for approximately nine months, and 24 hours per day for the remaining period."[1] While the city had contracted for the minimum supply of 2,000 horsepower in its initial 1910 contract, by the end of 1912 over 5,000 horsepower had been delivered although the price remained at $30.00 per horsepower.

The city did not enter into negotiations immediately upon expiry of the original electricity supply contract at the end of 1912. Commissioner A.G. Graves, R.A. Brown and James McCall were still of the opinion that the municipal power plant should be enlarged to take care of the city's electrical needs. They reasoned that if the city steam plant could be loaded to its designed capacity the improved load factor would make the cost of power only slightly greater than that obtained under contract and therefore the necessity for maintaining a substantial plant purely for "standby" or emergency service would be alleviated. Of course this argument was valid only if the power plant provided sufficient over-capacity to allow for operating contingencies such as when the single largest machine was out of service. R.A. Ross, consulting engineer from Montreal, was retained to advise on these matters including negotiating the terms of a further contract with Calgary Power Company Limited. The Ross Report, recommending a significant expansion to the Victoria Park Power Plant, was acted on by the city council and a further 5,000 kilowatt generator was installed in 1914. If the city electrical load had continued to grow as it had during the period leading up to the First World War, this expansion would have likely continued. As it happened the city's economy went into a serious slump and the load growth leveled off remaining relatively unchanged until 1924.

By mid May of 1913 R.A. Ross was negotiating in Montreal with the Calgary Power Company on a new contract for the city. He was insisting on a fairly substantial penalty clause for interruption of service and Commissioner Graves was advised that the company was objecting, claiming that such a clause would lead to financial ruin. Ross was not concerned with any further delay in signing a new contract: "we need not worry very much about results or be too anxious to give them everything they wish, now that the new machinery has been ordered."[2] The "new machinery" was the 5,000 kilowatt generator for the Victoria Park plant. On 22 May, H.A. Moore, local manager of the Calgary Power Company, explained in a detailed letter to Commissioner Graves why the company could not entertain the Ross demands. The company was reconstructing its transmission lines, adding another 6,000 horsepower of capacity at the Horseshoe Falls plant and a new development at Kananaskis Falls was underway.

All of these new additions and improvements, including additional water storage at Lake Minnewanka, plus a $4.00 reduction per horsepower over the price of the previous agreement were inducements which the city found hard to resist, and so on 15 September 1913 the city signed its second contract with the company, effective 1 December and running for a five-year period. The minimum amount of power provided for by the contract was 5,000 horsepower, priced at $26.00 per horsepower year for the first 5,000, reducing to $20.00 for all horsepower over 10,000. These prices were substantially lower than those of the 1910 contract. The contract also contained a renewal provision up to 1 December 1923 without any change in conditions or price and the company was, without doubt, banking on securing a greater degree of permanency in its contractual agreements with the city. This early "open-end" feature became standard in all future contracts. In later years when electrical loads reached much greater levels additional clauses were included forcing both parties to renegotiate after some predetermined level of power consumption had been reached irrespective of elapsed time.

The company and city officials often quarreled over how loads would be shared between the hydro plants and the city steam plant, all of which were required to maintain year-round continuity of service for Calgary consumers. Whether it was for this particular reason or because the water flows on the Bow River were unusually low during the spring and summer of 1915 or because of a major machine failure at one of the two hydro plants, a memorandum of agreement was signed by both parties on 1 June providing for the company to supply all the electrical power requirements of the city. The excess power over and above that provided for in the 1913 agreement would be provided up to 30 April 1916 by the Victoria Park Power Plant with the company paying for all operating costs during that period. In return, the city was required to pay a total of $190,000 for all of the power delivered by the company for the year, beginning on 1 May 1915 and ending 30 April 1916.

An analysis of the company proposal by R.A. Brown and J. McCall showed estimated savings to a maximum of $35,000 for the city over the one-year term of the agreement and it was executed accordingly.[3] At the expiry of the second contract in 1918, the city exercised its option and renewed the agreement for a further five-year period to 1 December 1923. The minimum quantity of power contracted was 7,500 horsepower, the amount deemed by R.A. Brown as the capacity of one transmission line between Calgary and the hydro plants. "It is not safe," Brown reported, "to figure continuous service in excess of the capacity of one line, which is approximately 7,500 H.P."[4] The city had also run a measured test on the cost of generating that portion of the city load in excess of 5,000 horsepower. The test was run over a seventeen hour period with careful measurement of the coal burned in the boilers and the electrical energy produced. It convinced both Brown and McCall that the least cost arrangement to the city was to purchase power from the Calgary Power Company at contract rates for a minimum of nineteen continuous hours each day and "for that portion of our load used for a lesser number of hours per day...generated cheaper by steam than by purchasing under the present contract."

It was the first serious attempt to operate both hydro and steam plants in such a manner as to produce the lowest overall cost of power with the steam plant being used to generate the power requirements of the city during the peak demand periods thereby reducing the cost of power demanded from the hydro plants. Using a thermal plant to supply peaking power was the complete reverse of the practice which followed when the Calgary Power Company acquired large thermal plants after 1950. The thermal plants were then base-loaded with the hydro plants being reserved wholly for the supply of peaking power, the difference in practice dictated by the large capacity of the thermal plants in relation to that of the hydro plants. In any event the city power plant could provide the entire electrical demand of the city beyond the minimum 7,500 horsepower contracted for from the Calgary Power Company, so there was no undue risk to the city's power supply.

The contract came up for renewal in 1923, and the council was largely in favour of the development of the Spray Lakes project if the provincial government gave strong support for this undertaking. The scheme was the brainchild of G.A. Gaherty who, as a young hydraulic engineer with the Montreal Engineering Company, had made extensive studies of the Bow River watershed shortly after World War I. The Spray Lakes project, located within the boundaries of Banff National Park, offered the advantages of substantial water storage which could be drawn down to the Bow River through a much higher hydraulic head with correspondingly larger power outputs than the low-head hydraulic plants already in place at the Horseshoe and Kananaskis sites. The additional water would also help to alleviate the often unreliable electrical outputs of those two plants. The council was very hopeful that the Spray Lakes project would receive the approval of the federal government and so was not amenable to the new proposal of the Calgary Power Company for a five-year contract with provision for a two-year extension to 1930. The aldermen viewed the company proposal as a seven-year contract and they balked. The company, however, argued that a five-year contract was necessary to simply recover the costs of a new transmission line to service the city's electrical demand. The additional two-year notice period would protect the company in the event of the city not renewing the contract.

The council finally decided in favour of a four-year agreement with a one-year notice of contract termination. However, because the price offered by the company was considered to be very attractive and since the offer was valid only until midnight of 6 August 1923, the day upon which the council was meeting to decide on the final disposition of the new contract, it was accepted for a five-year period without the controversial two-year extension clause which the company accepted. This resulted in a contract that had no formal provision for its termination. The new agreement received three readings on the same night. At the meeting notice of motion was given by Alderman F.J. White for a resolution favouring "the Provincial Government making immediate application to the Federal Government for priority right to survey the Spray Lakes project and development of same, should investigation warrant such action being taken."[5]

The 1923 contract represented a major departure from previous ones because the monthly horsepower demand was replaced by an undertaking to supply energy "up to sixty million (60,000,000) kilowatt hours per annum or such further amount as the City may require and the Company is willing to supply"[6] with the city agreeing to purchase at least 90 percent of its total annual energy requirements from the company except for those periods when less than three transmission lines were in operation. This provision seriously limited the ability of the city power plant to supply power but in 1926 a supplementary agreement was signed by the parties for the use of the power plant during periods of water shortage at the company's hydro plants. The supplementary agreement remained in force until the main agreement expired in 1928. During that period the city's power plant provided the additional power required by the company to maintain uninterrupted service to other major power consumers, notably the Canada Cement plant at Exshaw and the village of Cochrane. The company agreed to pay the city 1.65 cents per kilowatt hour for all such energy provided, compared to the one-half cent paid by the city to the company. In 1926 the city consumed almost 60 million kilowatt hours for which it paid the company the sum of $300,000. The recorded kilowatt demand was 15,000 which is equivalent to 20,000 horsepower. The resulting price computed on the old "horsepower per annum" basis was $15.00 compared to the $30.00 figure of the original 1910 contract, a reduction of 100 percent. Nevertheless, the steam plant was still needed in Calgary to secure a power supply to the company's consumers because of the unreliability of the Bow River.

There is little doubt that during the first thirteen years of the "uneasy alliance" between the Calgary Power Company and the city the company could not have successfully operated without the existence of the city power plant. Jack Sexton,[7] now retired from a long-time senior consulting engineering position with the Montreal Engineering Company, started his career with the Calgary Power Company in 1928. He was of the opinion that of all the rivers in North America that qualified for hydro-electric development, the Bow River was low on the list because of its undependable water flow. Peter Prince had already faced this problem in his attempts to produce water power at the Eau Claire site. Sexton also noted that the Calgary Power Company was barely covering its expenses in early years and during the presidency of R.B. Bennett the owners were discouraged about the company's future. At the lowest point of this discouraging and uncertain period, in 1924, G.A. "Geof" Gaherty became the managing director of the company. Under his leadership the fortunes of the Calgary Power Company changed dramatically. He became president in 1928.

Gaherty's reputation as an outstanding hydro-electric engineer and economist had already preceded him. During his career with Montreal Engineering, Gaherty had often reported to I.W. Killam, owner of Royal Securities Limited and a director of Montreal Engineering, on the potential of the Bow River if increased water storage facilities could be achieved. Gaherty, like the city, favoured the Spray Lakes scheme but realized the difficulties involved with a project situated entirely within the boundaries of Banff National Park. On Gaherty's advice Killam undertook to gain complete control of the Calgary Power Company by acquisition of nearly all of the common shares. Gaherty then recruited from Westinghouse Electric G.H. "Harry" Thompson who had acquired substantial experience in Alberta while working with the collieries in the Crowsnest Pass area. This outstanding pair of engineers and visionaries began to reshape the future of the Calgary Power Company on a broad Alberta base, and undoubtedly their combined efforts alone were responsible for assuring the future of the company. Gaherty's preference for the Spray Lakes project was temporarily shelved when he opted for the more politically acceptable water storage and hydro power site at the confluence of the Bow and Ghost rivers, about forty miles upstream from Calgary, and it was for the development of this site that Jack Sexton was initially recruited. When compared to the two earlier Horseshoe and Kananaskis hydro plants, the Ghost River development was a giant step forward with its planned initial capacity of 36,000 horsepower, expandable to an ultimate 54,000. Then, in 1925, the electrical growth of Calgary suddenly surged forward after ten years of stagnation. However, in order to ensure that this potential growth was available for the new hydro-electric development on the Ghost River, the company realized that it must both gain control of the city's power plant and negotiate a further contract with the city thus ensuring the project's financing. The 1928 contract was successful on both counts.

The first matter that required the attention of the city council as the 1923 contract drew to an end was the negotiation of a termination clause. This was done on 19 March 1928 by extending the contract to 31 July 1930.[8] In preparation for a future power supply the city council instructed R.A. Brown to call for a public tender with a closing date of 27 March 1928. This was the only time that the city called for a public bid on its power supply and in view of the fact that the only parties who could possibly bid were the Calgary Power Company and the city, we are forced to conclude that the move was prearranged by both company and city officials to indicate to the citizens that the parties were dealing with each other at "arm's length." In the specification for the power supply, the city indicated that it would consider "the leasing of its steam plant for use in the scheme of power production, at an annual rental equal in amount to the present fixed charges on the plant, namely ($95,000), Ninety-five Thousand Dollars."[9] City council was divided on the matter of leasing the Victoria Park Plant as was indicated by a motion from Alderman J.W. Russell, "That the Commissioners be requested to negotiate an agreement with the Calgary Power Co. Ltd., on the basis of the City retaining control of the steam plant."[10] The motion, however, was defeated. Both the Calgary Power Company and the city submitted their bids and the final analysis of the cost was overwhelmingly in favour of the company with savings to the city amounting to well over one-half million dollars over the ten-year life of the proposed contract. So the city executed the contract and leased the Victoria Park Power Plant to the Calgary Power Company for $75,000 per annum and forever lost its best bargaining card.

It is doubtful, however, that the city was really serious about expanding its own power generating facility. Cheaper hydro-power had won the day and it would remain so for the next quarter century until no further economic hydro-power development remained on the Bow River and steam power again returned to dominate electric power production in Alberta. Jack Sexton recalled that he was present at Calgary Power's head office in the old Toronto General Trust Building on 8th Avenue when the news arrived that a new contract had been signed. The financing of the Ghost River project was now assured and it precipitated a celebration which lasted into the small hours of the morning.

Calgary's energy requirement in 1929 was 75 million kilowatt hours with a maximum demand of 20,400 kilowatts or 27,300 horsepower. The new energy charge from the company was 0.74 cents per kilowatt hour, giving rise to a total annual cost of $555,000 or $20.33 per horsepower per annum. This was still lower than the original 1910 cost of $30.00 but substantially higher than the 1923 figure of $15.00. Clearly the charges under the 1928 contract included the new costs of financing the substantial capital investment which the company had already incurred in the Ghost River project which was completed in 1929.

The Great Depression hit the Calgary Power Company as severely as it did the city and, in fact, the company barely managed to survive as the Ghost project saddled it with additional capital financing costs with little additional revenue to offset those costs because power demand leveled off. While the 1928 contract did not terminate until 1940, certain events in 1937 forced the parties into substantial revisions in their contractual relationships which both parties deemed could be most advantageously settled by concluding a new agreement rather than revising the 1928 agreement. The main problem was the 1926 revision to the city charter granting permission to the city to expropriate the assets of the Calgary Water Power Company in 1938. If the city failed to purchase the assets, the permissive legislation would be invalidated. The old company had been a wholly-owned subsidiary of the Calgary Power Company since 1928 and both the company and the city were anxious to rid themselves of this small operating utility. Secondly, the disastrous Bushy Ridge brush fire of 1936 had given rise to the need for a new steel tower transmission line between the hydro plants and Calgary. The expense of this project that would primarily ensure Calgary's electrical supply required a revision of the rate charged to the city. Neither party was interested in recovering this expense by the application of a surcharge to the existing wholesale rate.

In the aftermath of the 1936 fire, the city commissioners seriously considered the expansion of the Victoria Park steam plant by the addition of a new 15,000 kilowatt turbo-alternator but Robert Mackay, now the superintendent of the Electric Light Department, finally ruled in favour of the steel transmission line option. Mackay knew that the $1,500,000 capital cost estimated for the extension of the Victoria Park Plant would never receive favourable consideration by a council already strapped with all of the problems of the depression. The new agreement was ratified by the council in July 1937 with a 15 percent reduction in the rate for energy and providing for the Calgary Power Company to continue its operation of the city's power plant until 1950 but without the annual rental of $75,000. The city also agreed to purchase the assets of the old Calgary Water Power Company, with the exception of the 1st Avenue W. steam power plant. The 1937 agreement was certainly a good one for the city with respect to the cost of power with the company counting on its future with excess capacity in the Ghost hydro plant and maintaining control over the municipal power plant. G.A. Gaherty had recorded in the company directors' minutes of 31 May 1928 that the acquisition of the shares of the old Calgary Water Power Company accompanied by their lease of the Victoria Park Power Plant and a new contract to supply power to the city would "result in our having full control of the power supply in the city of Calgary."[11] In 1937 and in subsequent years, the company remained staunchly committed to such a strategy.

In 1937 a new feature surfaced regarding the form of contracts between the city and the company with the result that no succeeding contract would ever run to termination. For example, in 1928, the contract called for the delivery of up to 128 million kilowatt hours of energy in any year of the contract which had an expiry date of 31 July 1940. However, as we have already seen, by 1937 other factors had intervened which made it seem advantageous to both parties to extend the 1928 contract to 31 July 1950, although the amount of energy deliverable under contract still remained at the 1928 level of 128 million units per annum. In fact the specified maximum amount was not reached until 1945 but this was in large part due to the intervention of the depression years. In later contracts, as electrical loads started to escalate at uncommonly high levels, the pattern which developed was for the company to negotiate for quantities of electrical energy as high as possible coupled with escape clauses against cost inflation forcing the parties to renegotiate on a new price before the contract expired. On the other hand, the city always tried to keep the delivery level at a lower figure so that it did not feel unduly "locked in" to the company for its power supply.

By late 1943 it became obvious that the contract limitation of 128 million kilowatt hours would soon be exceeded as electrical load growth after the end of the Second World War started to increase at pre-1930 levels. The Calgary Power Company was pressing the city to take over ownership of the old 1st Avenue power plant which had not been included in the 1938 sale of the Calgary Water Power Company assets. The company maintained that the reason it had not pressed the city to purchase the entire assets in 1938 was because the city had firmly maintained that it could not finance them. Then the war intervened and the Calgary Power Company decided to hold on to the old plant "due to growth in load in the city and the difficulty of obtaining generating equipment during the war."[12] Now that this danger had passed, the company expected the city to live up to the full terms of the 1926 city charter amendments requiring the purchase of all of the assets. To offset the cost of buying the remaining assets the company agreed to release the city from certain financing obligations regarding the costs of establishing a dual 66,000 volt line infeed and a new transformer station at the city's Number 1 Substation on 9th Avenue and 7th Street W.

Upon receipt of the company's new contract proposal the city retained R.A. Brown, who had resigned as general superintendent of the Electric Light Department in 1936, to advise on the company's proposals. The choice was a shrewd one considering the high esteem in which Brown was held. Brown's report of February 1944 to the city council began with considerable praise for the Calgary Power Company for averting a serious power shortage during the late war years due to their foresight in building the Lake Minnewanka Power Plant. The hydro plant to which Brown referred is a familiar landmark alongside the Trans-Canada Highway just east of the Banff townsite. It was developed within the boundaries of Banff National Park during the war to supply firm power to the Alberta Nitrogen Plant in southeast Calgary. The plant produced anhydrous ammonia which was essential in the production of vital wartime explosives. During these years this single plant had electrical energy requirements equal to that of the entire city of Calgary. Brown also confirmed the opinion of Robert Mackay that the proposals being offered by the company were good ones but in view of the rapidly increasing electrical requirements of the city he recommended a maximum annual energy amount of 160 million rather than the 150 million kilowatt hours proposed by the Calgary Power Company. Brown also expressed his concern over the fact that the city was becoming a captive customer of the company.

Nor was Calgary Alderman Frank Freeze prepared to surrender easily to the Calgary Power Company. "I am not wishing," he said, "to start any controversy but rather that we should consider carefully any further extension of what is presently a very long agreement and whether we wish to purchase certain assets which may be of doubtful value and whether we wish to place the City still more completely in the power of the Calgary Power Company."[13] Alderman Freeze followed his remarks with twenty-three questions all related to the draft contract. They were referred to R.A. Brown and the city solicitor for answers. These questions showed an amazing understanding of technical matters relating to the proposed new contract and of existing power interchange agreements between the company and the city of Edmonton, whose power plant was municipally-owned. The solicitor and Brown replied in some detail to each question and the tone of the answers showed their great respect for Alderman Freeze's incisive thinking. The replies were accepted by Alderman Freeze and filed but these questions were the last to be put forward independently by any alderman with respect to this and future contracts. These purchased power contracts were becoming by far the costliest ones that the city council would ever approve. We can excuse the aldermen for their apparent disinterest since they often found it difficult to comprehend the technical and economic aspects of producing electrical power and they were usually prepared to leave the decisions to their experts. Of course the cost of power was not a charge to property taxes. Thus the seventh purchased power contract between the city and the Calgary Power Company was signed without further incident on 20 March 1944 for a period deemed to begin on 1 August 1943 for a further ten-year period until 1953 with a 3 percent rate reduction from the previous contract.

The old Calgary Water Power Company power plant on 1st Avenue W. was unceremoniously scrapped. Several of the boilers were sold to Canadian Utilities Limited for reinstallation in its Drumheller plant. The 1,800 kilowatt turbo-generator set, the only useful machine remaining in the older plant, was relocated to the Victoria Park Power Plant. The old generators at Victoria Park were now obsolete. Their only value was to pump much needed but high-cost energy into the company's electrical grid during the development period of the modified Spray Lakes hydro project in the early 1950s and as soon as this project became viable the Victoria Park plant was scrapped.

Electrical load growth, except for a brief forward surge in 1940 and 1941, was relatively stable during the Second World War. The end of hostilities and the return of servicemen sparked a upturn in the national economy, and in Calgary the electrical load growth suddenly assumed a level unequaled since before World War I. The contracted energy amount of 160 million kilowatt hours per annum appeared as anything but pessimistic and within the space of five years it became obvious that the 1943 contract was obsolete. The maximum quantity of 160 million units was exceeded in 1948 and a new rate for purchased electricity would be needed. The contract did provide for rate adjustments after the contracted amount had been exceeded but the company did not request the city to renegotiate until December 1949 at which time the energy needs had reached 175 million kilowatt hours. The Calgary Power Company was also faced with new financing for its Spray Lakes project and so a revised contract was essential. The company proposed a new contract with all energy delivered to the city at three-quarters (0.75) of a cent per kilowatt hour. J.H. Wilson, the newly-appointed superintendent of the Electric Light Department, was in favour of leaving the rate for the first 160 million kilowatt hours at the old level of 0.64 cents with all additional energy at 1 cent. The company's rate proposal represented a 10 percent increase over the 1944 negotiated rate and that did not sit very well with some of the aldermen, in particular D.F. "Don" McIntosh. "With everything else the more you buy the less you pay," commented McIntosh.[14] However, there was not much that the council could do at this stage. Wilson's recommendations were accepted, including the appointment of outside consulting engineers to report on the company proposals and, more important, to provide estimates of the costs involved in building and operating a new city-owned power plant.

The prestigious local consulting firm of Haddin, Davis and Brown was retained to prepare a report on the power plant. They, in turn, engaged the services of Mr. Ed Kelly, the engineer who was responsible for the thermal power plants of Canadian Utilities Limited, a smaller private electrical utility operating out of Drumheller into northeastern Alberta. The Haddin, Davis and Brown report was completed in October 1950 and recommended a new city-owned steam plant of 110,000 kilowatt capacity. The costs for power generated by a city-owned plant were about the same in the initial years of operation as the rate being offered by the Calgary Power Company but as the plant was loaded to capacity the costs showed dramatic decreases. The plant was designed to assume the total city electrical load with the city maintaining its contractual arrangement with the Calgary Power Company up to the expiry of the existing contract in 1953 and paying a premium rate for all energy required beyond the contract amount of 160 million kilowatt hours. Superintendent Wilson was quick to point out that the loss of the city electrical load would be a crippling blow to the Calgary Power Company but not a "death blow." By 1950, the city's contract represented over one-quarter of the company's total revenues. The company was already committed to large capital expenditures in completing its Spray Lakes hydro project and upgrading its electrical transmission system between the Bow River hydro plants and Calgary from 66,000 volts, the voltage level which, with minor exceptions, had been used by the company since its beginnings, to 132,000 volts.

The company was not prepared to let the city's plans for a power plant go beyond the initial planning stage and immediately set about to frustrate them. Quite independently the company produced a report on its concept of a suitable power plant to meet the electrical requirements of the city. The design of this power plant was essentially the same as that proposed by the city's consultants except that the company's plant was moved ten miles outside the city thus requiring some additional transmission costs. Both plants were fueled by natural gas with the company using a slightly more pessimistic forecast for future natural gas prices. The company plant bore higher construction costs and its 120,000 kilowatt size was estimated at $18,000,000 compared to the city consultant's estimates of just over $12,000,000, for a capacity of 110,000 kilowatts. The major difference was the method of financing. The city consultant used a "capital recovery" formula requiring that any bonds issued in the open market be "callable," whereas the company assumed the entire indebtedness being discharged using a "sinking fund," a method that is more costly over the life of the bond issue. Higher interest rates were used by the company: 3 7/8 percent for a twenty-five year period against 3 3/4 percent by the city for twenty years. Based on the company's report, the city's energy requirement for 1955 was forecast as 293 million kilowatt hours at a cost of 0.944 cents per kilowatt hour compared to the estimate of 0.715 cents out of the city consultant's plant on a forecast 1955 energy output of 235 million kilowatt hours. The price differential was of significant magnitude to cast doubt on the city's report. Considering the vested interests of each party there were obviously areas where preconditions needed to be rationalized because both reports were spawned by reputable engineering consortiums. The counter report by the Calgary Power Company was entirely honest by its standard of preconditions but for political purposes, at least, the damage had been done.

Council met as a Committee of the Whole in a special meeting on 7 December 1950 to consider the power contract. Mayor Don Mackay outlined to his fellow aldermen the choices they would need to consider. There was the Haddin, Davis and Brown report recommending construction of a $12,000,000 power plant supported by superintendent Wilson. Acceptance of this plan would be followed by cancellation of all contracts with the Calgary Power Company, with a termination date of 31 July 1953, and with payment to the company of one cent per kilowatt hour for all excess energy over 128 million kilowatt-hours per annum up to the termination date. The other choice was to continue a further ten-year contract with the company for the delivery of up to 300 million kilowatt hours per annum at a unit price of 0.75 cents. A large number of the councillors were favourably disposed to the recommendation for a new city-owned plant but others, such as Alderman N.D. McDermid, were staunchly opposed to government involvement in business, completely ignoring the fact that the city had already done so. Logically McDermid should have followed this argument with a motion that the city sell its electrical distribution plant to the Calgary Power Company. He wanted the council to consider another company that would be willing to build a plant and sell power at a lower price than the Calgary Power Company. Such an idea had been debated over half a century earlier when the council decided to extend a franchise to Peter Prince to operate in direct competition with the original Calgary Electric Lighting Company. The Calgary Power Company was asked if it would be prepared to debate the rate of 0.75 cents per kilowatt hour before the Board of Public Utility Commissioners but the company solicitor, E.J. Chambers K.C., replied rather, that "no useful purpose could be served by publicly debating the Company position."[15] The discussions went on with the only decision being to refer the entire matter back to the proper city officials for further negotiation with the company and with instructions to report back on the following evening.

Exactly what transpired the following day as the parties continued to negotiate is unknown. But the author, having joined the Electric Light Department the previous year, attended the council meeting on the evening of 8 December 1950 and remembers what happened. Calgary's council chamber was located on the third floor of the old sandstone city hall. The dais at the eastend accommodated the mayor, city solicitor and commissioners who faced the semicircle of the aldermen's individual desks. The city clerk and his assistants occupied the area between the two groups. A bar behind the aldermanic desks isolated the public who came to view the proceedings. On the right of the chamber, in front of the bar, was an open area furnished with a large round oak table around which the city staff, usually department heads, sat during regular council meetings. On this particular evening the city staff, including Superintendent Wilson and E. Kelly, representing the city's consultants, sat in the public area. The Calgary Power entourage included President G.A. Gaherty, E.J. Chambers, and several others who were invited to sit at the round table normally reserved for city staff. The formal commissioners' report to the council recommended verbatim acceptance of the contract proposal with the rider that 1955 would be soon enough to consider a power development by the city. A few token questions were asked of company representatives but the city staff, including Wilson and Kelly, were ignored. The motion to accept a new ten-year contract with the Calgary Power Company was adopted with two dissenting votes from Aldermen P.N.R. Morrison and D.F. McIntosh, who were part of the longstanding labour-oriented trio, Alderman E.B. Watson being absent. It all happened so quickly that Ed Kelly, the consultant who had prepared much of the city's report, became so upset that he had to be physically restrained. The city council had spent good hard cash for a report and in the final act had confined it to the waste basket without so much as a question. It was a bitter pill for Kelly to swallow and his pride was deeply hurt. The 1955 date for a reconsideration of a city-owned power plant was likely included to simply recognize the efforts of both Wilson and Kelly.

It has always been the opinion of the author that Calgary missed its "golden opportunity" when it accepted the 1950 contract without a struggle. As it happened, the forecasts of load growth by both the city and the company were so conservative as to border on the ridiculous. The Haddin, Davis and Brown report had forecast the energy requirement of the city in 1963 at 325 million kilowatt hours, whereas the actual consumption in that year was nearly three times that amount. The forecast of the Calgary Power Company was not much better. The forecasts had been made on a 7 1/4 percent annual growth but by 1952, the growth rate had shifted to a 12 percent level. The power plant proposed in 1950 would have been loaded to its capacity three years after its proposed commissioning. The secret for any electrical generating plant wishing to achieve low-cost energy is to get it loaded to capacity as quickly as possible. The only possible doubt there could have been with respect to a city plant was the future price of natural gas but even if that price had doubled over the ten year period the effect would still have been fairly small on the cost of electrical energy over the period. By any count the plant, if it had been developed, would have been nothing less than a municipal "gold mine." The main factor in 1950 was the effect of the possible loss of the city electrical load to the Calgary Power Company at a time when it was embarking on major new developments. Without doubt that was the reason for the efforts, both overtly and covertly, of the Calgary Power Company to defeat the proposed city plant. The city, on its own initiative, would never again be able to demonstrate the overwhelming advantages of its reentry into the generation of electricity.

It is ironic that this unusually rapid load growth would also mitigate against any future plans for civic power plant ownership. This was a fact of which the Calgary Power Company was well aware, and after 1950 it was a factor that virtually guaranteed its retention of the city's total electrical requirement.

The Spray Lakes project was the last major hydro development on the Bow River. Some additional hydro sites such as Radnor and Shepard remained but they were now insignificant in relation to the rate of electrical load growth both in Calgary and Alberta and did not rate much consideration for development. The smaller Bearspaw hydro plant west of Bowness Park was added during the late 1950s but its primary function was ice control to alleviate winter flooding of the Bow River in Calgary. G.A. Gaherty, president of the Calgary Power Company, was a hydro-power disciple. When it came to thermal generation of power, it was general knowledge that he had myopic vision despite his brilliance as an engineer. Nevertheless, there was no hydro-power alternative left for the company, and in 1956 it had commissioned its first thermal plant at Lake Wabamum, about forty miles west of Edmonton. Ample cooling water and the adjacent availability of large quantities of easily recovered strip-mined coal made the site one to be envied by any thermal power plant engineer. One can be certain that the 0.9 cent per kilowatt hour energy which only six years earlier had been predicted for a gas-fired city-owned power plant had no application to Wabamum where the initial two 66,000 kilowatt generators were supplied by steam produced from natural gas. The units which followed were fueled with what was probably some of the lowest cost coal in North America.

The power supply contracted to the city in 1950 provided for the usual three-year extension of the preceding contract followed by a further ten-year period to 31 July 1963, making it essentially a thirteen-year term. The contract provided for energy delivery up to 300 million kilowatt hours in any year with a demand limit of 75,000 kilowatts. This was the first time since 1923 that reference to power demand had surfaced in the agreements and it was obvious that the company was preparing the way for future agreements which would incorporate a "two-part" rate with separate prices for demand and energy. The city, after the 300 million kilowatt hour limit was reached, could add 80 million additional kilowatt hours and 20,000 kilowatts of demand each year without incurring any penalty on price. The company maintained the right to notify the city not later than 1 August 1958 on terms for a further agreement. This "telescoping" form of agreement was now a standard contract feature and assured that no contract would run its entire limit to expiry. While the provision seriously limited the city with respect to any future plans it might wish to develop to generate part or all of its power needs, it did have the advantage of an assured and continuous electricity supply, critical to any growing city.

Lest the reader have the impression that relations between the city and the Calgary Power Company were always adversarial, it should be mentioned that

the association was, except perhaps during periods of contract negotiations, relatively harmonious. After 1944 both parties recognized that as the city grew in size certain facilities which had hitherto been installed by the company in the process of supplying electricity under terms of earlier contracts were clearly part of the expanding city electrical network and should logically belong to the city. Most contract agreements from this time included supplementary agreements for sale of those company assets. The 1950 agreement, for example, recognized that all power should be delivered at 13,200 volts, and so the 4,000 volt facilities which the company had earlier installed at the city's Number I Substation at the corner of 9th Avenue and 7th Street W. were sold to the city. Later as Calgary exploded into a major Canadian metropolis it became increasingly necessary to purchase power at higher voltage levels and the supply voltage moved in stages up to 132,000 volts supplied from company bulk terminal stations around the perimeter of the city. The physical expansion of the city often made it advantageous to both parties to have substantial rural distribution areas annexed to the city so that growth was orderly and without duplication of distribution facilities. The parties co-operated fully in matters relating to the promotion of electricity in the residential, commercial and industrial markets.

By 1958 the city electrical load had grown from 40,000 kilowatts in 1950 to over 121,000 kilowatts and while there was ample provision in the contract for load growth in excess of that amount, the parties were obliged to renegotiate before 31 July 1959 on the terms for which additional electrical power would be supplied. Harvey Wilson, his memory still fresh with the stinging rebuke he had received when the 1950 contract had been approved by the city council, quickly recommended the appointment of outside consultants to again look at the economics of a city-owned power plant. A prominent consulting company from Niagara Falls, Ontario was commissioned to make the report and a draft copy was available by late summer of 1958. This time the consultants were instructed to prepare their report on the basis of either the city generating its entire electrical requirement, or more moderately, an alternative whereby the city would generate only that part of its total electrical requirements in excess of 300 million kilowatt hours each year up to 1963 when the city-owned plant would assume the full city electrical load. In this manner it was hoped that the capacity which the Calgary Power Company had committed to the full term of the contract would be utilized and then normal load growth on the remainder of the company's service area would sustain any additional capacity required by the company. The report assumed that for the ten-year period 1963-73 the plant would be fired with natural gas, or if necessary, by coal from Drumheller.

The draft report came to the attention of S.J. (Stan) Davies, the technical member of the city's Gas Committee. The Gas Committee was a formal group set up to represent the interests of Calgary natural gas consumers particularly when the local gas utility made its regular applications to the Public Utilities Board for rate increases, or when other matters which might have adverse effects on the cost of natural gas to Calgary consumers. Davies owned and operated a natural gas utility in the Turner Valley district and was recognized as an experienced professional. Davies supported the use of natural gas as the favoured fuel for a city-owned power plant and wrote a series of letters to the city commissioners in 1959 defending his position.[16] On the matter of the proposed plant location, Davies took umbrage with the consultants' report. The report had gone to some lengths to show that it was cheaper to move coal from Drumheller to Calgary by rail than to locate the plant at Drumheller and transmitting electricity for the ninety or so miles. Davies contended that the eastern consultants were not familiar with the characteristics of western plains coals and that they had seriously underestimated the quantities of coal which would be required in Calgary. Using Davies' figures, it would be far more economical to locate the plant at Drumheller even if natural gas was used as the preferred fuel. There was also another fatal flaw in the report. The eastern consultants had assumed that a supply of the type of coal upon which they based their report was readily available whereas, in fact, it was in fairly short supply. These factors finally laid the report to rest but the report did serve to guide the city in its negotiation with the Calgary Power Company.

Contract negotiations continued and resulted in a new "two part" rate offer of $1.37 per kilowatt of annual load demand and 0.4 cents per kilowatt hour for all energy. Previous contracts had been based on a horsepower per annum charge with no cost attached to the energy consumed. After 1923 the company changed to a straight energy charge per kilowatt hour. The rate now being offered was a combination of charges for both power and energy. This "two-part" rate was not uncommon since the city already billed its large power consumers in this manner. This change in rate structure reflected the fact that much of the company's electricity was now being generated at its Wabamum plant using fossil fuel and these costs bore a substantial relationship to the cost of energy produced. The kilowatt demand charge, on the other hand, related entirely to the fixed or capital costs of the power plants, whether thermal or hydro. The new rate represented a total cost to the city of slightly over 0.75 cents per kilowatt hour. This was essentially the old 1950 contract rate but the added incentive was now available for the city to improve its annual load factor. For example, if it were possible to improve the load factor to 100 percent the unit cost would reduce to 0.50 cents per kilowatt hour. Compared to the cost of power forecast in the consultant's report, there was no price advantage to the city over what was being offered by the company. A new contract was signed on 31 August 1959 for a maximum demand of 300,000 kilowatts with the price on both demand and energy firm for the first 240,000 kilowatts.

From the mid 1950s Alberta was engaged in the process of exporting large quantities of both crude oil and natural gas to the United States energy market. By today's standards the energy was cheap, the market insatiable, and Alberta seemed to have inexhaustible supplies of both oil and gas. Davies, the city's gas consultant, viewed exports with some degree of alarm because Canada had no control over the end use of the exports once they left the country, and uses of natural gas which were considered proper in the United States were often frowned on as being inappropriate for Alberta. By the end of the 1950s the Oil and Gas Conservation Board, which regulated exports, was beginning to favour the use of coal rather than natural gas for electricity generation. In 1959 the Alberta and Southern Gas Company, a wholly-owned subsidiary of Pacific Gas and Electric of San Francisco, had applied for a permit to export over 4 trillion cubic feet of gas over a twenty-five year period to Northern California for purposes which included the generation of electricity. The city of Calgary made a submission to the Oil and Gas Conservation Board at the time of the public hearings on the Alberta and Southern application to the effect that if the same gas could be burned in California for electric power production, it must also be a suitable use in Alberta. The city also argued that it was cheaper to generate electricity in Calgary by natural gas than the combined cost of electricity generated by gas at the Calgary Power Company's Wabamum plant, plus the transmission costs to Calgary. The Board tacitly agreed to the city request by setting aside 400 billion cubic feet of natural gas as part of the reserves of the province for generation of electrical power at Calgary but it was only one-third of the amount the city had applied for. The city pursued the matter with the National Energy Board in Ottawa but the result remained unchanged.

It was unfortunate that Calgary did not see fit to seriously follow through on the acquisition of the rights to a major Alberta supply of fuel even if it was only that amount of gas which the Conservation Board had decided was appropriate for the purpose of generating electricity. Davies had always supported such a move and was not being facetious when he maintained, on many occasions, that for the city to be serious about generating its own power it must have a "horse to trade with." That "horse" would have been of infinite value even in the usual process of negotiating a purchased power contract with Calgary Power. However, that reserve of natural gas set aside by the Oil and Gas Conservation Board became the "bait" which attracted another company in early 1962.

On 27 February 1962 a company called Dynamic Power Corporation submitted a proposal to the city council to supply bulk power to the city. The principals in the scheme were two brothers, Frank and Clive Brown, who were directly involved in a consortium of small oil companies in Alberta known as Dynamic Petroleum. The proposal by Dynamic touched off a year of talks and proposals. There was no doubt about the seriousness of the promoters but detailed analyses by the city and its experts concluded that the new company could not produce an end result which was any better than that of Calgary Power Limited. Furthermore, when all of the local and provincial taxes were added to the federal income tax, it was obvious that Calgary was in a much better position to undertake on its own the type of proposal submitted by Dynamic.[17] Of critical concern to the city were questions relating to the lack of detail by Dynamic Power Corporation about the type of fuel it proposed to use and its price over the twenty-five year term of its proposal since the gas reserve set down by the Conservation Board was certainly not adequate for the entire period. The company thereupon withdrew its offer and was not heard from again until 1964.

Coincidental with the proposal from Dynamic Power Corporation was the finalizing of the Columbia River Treaty between Canada and the United States. The treaty was signed after many years of often heated debate between British Columbia, Ottawa and the United States. The treaty was simple in concept. Canada would provide enormous water storage basins on the Canadian side of the Columbia River, particularly the Big Bend reservoir which would be created by a huge earth-fill dam at Mica Creek, and the Arrow Lakes which would store more water by means of a rather less spectacular dam at Castlegar, B.C. This huge storage basin would stabilize the water flow on the American portion of the Columbia River. The net result would be a large increase in electrical power and energy from existing dams on the lower American reaches of the Columbia. Under the treaty, one half of that additional electrical energy was to be delivered back to British Columbia, near Trail.

Members of the Calgary's Electric Light Department, with their consultant, Professor J.A. Harle, head of the electrical engineering department at the University of Alberta, decided to see whether it was economic to "wheel" some of that treaty power back to Calgary. Because of the distances involved (the power had to come from as far away as Portland, Oregon) and the difficulties in designing a stable transmission line for the size of the electrical load involved, the idea had to be abandoned. At the same time Premier W.A.C. Bennett announced that British Columbia could not use the power since the Canadian demand was not great enough. He persuaded Ottawa that a better deal would be to sell the downstream electricity benefit to the United States for a lump sum payment calculated on the present worth of that power. British Columbia received a sum of around one-quarter billion dollars. Professor Harle was of the opinion that Calgary should also make a strong bid for power from Mica Creek. The recently nationalized British Columbia Hydro and Power Authority planned to machine Mica Creek for hydro power at some future date since it had a potential output of some 1 million horsepower with a good load factor. He argued that Calgary was the closest metropolitan area to Mica Creek and transmission was not nearly so critical as with the original "down stream" benefits scheme. The plan was to tie into the British Columbia Hydro transmission system which was to go south from Mica Creek through the Windermere Valley to Cranbrook, B.C. Calgary would build and operate transmission lines due west from the city connecting near Fairmont, B.C.

There was little doubt that B.C. Hydro was interested in such a project. Premier W.A.C. Bennett had already announced that he was prepared to market surplus power from Mica Creek as far south as California and hence there would be no particular objection to looking at Calgary as a market possibility. The idea failed because Mica Creek would not be machined until late 1973 and the contracted amount of 300,000 kilowatts from Calgary Power would be exceeded in 1966. Today these interconnections between British Columbia and Alberta have taken place albeit not in exactly the same way as the city envisioned in 1963.

When discussions with Dynamic Power Corporation broke off in 1963 the outstanding unresolved question related to the fuel supply with which Dynamic had planned to meet the needs of its proposed thermal generating plant. It was with some surprise that the company, in late 1964, publicly announced its interest in a large coal deposit centred around the hamlet of Ardley, east of Red Deer, Alberta. The company's new proposal was that Calgary and Edmonton should share in a joint venture at Ardley by building a thermal power plant which would utilize strip-mined coal supplied by Dynamic. Initially the scheme had consider-able appeal to both Calgary and Edmonton, the latter having already embarked on an extensive geological survey to prove up the coal potential of the Genesee district, west of Edmonton, in which it had acquired an interest. The idea was considered by the engineering staff of both cities and there was considerable agreement on the advantages of such a scheme provided the existing electrical transmission grid in the province (owned largely by Calgary Power) could be utilized for delivery of power between the cities through payment of a "wheeling charge" to cover costs.

By autumn of 1964 the results of the studies had reached the attention of the mayors and aldermen of both cities with the scheme widening in scope when the city of Red Deer sought to become a party to the project. Red Deer, like Calgary, was also "locked in" to Calgary Power as its sole wholesale electricity supplier. Red Deer had earlier attempted to obtain a hearing before the Public Utilities Board about what it considered to be an excessive rate charged by Calgary Power. However, the hearing was aborted when the Board decided that it had no jurisdiction to hear the case since Calgary Power operated under a federal charter. Since Red Deer's electrical load was small in comparison to the major cities there was great advantage to them being a part of a larger municipal undertaking. The scheme acquired the name of "Tri-City" and but for purely political factors may well have succeeded.

At the same time the "Tri-City" scheme was being considered, Calgary Power was actively negotiating for a new contract with Calgary because the 240,000 kilowatts of maximum electrical demand specified in the 1959 contract had been reached during the winter of 1965. A price remained to be established for the residual 60,000 kilowatts or, as in previous years, an amended contract for the entire electricity requirement. The city, anxious to see the outcome of Tri-City, dragged its feet. It was probably the longest negotiating period since R.B. Bennett's first contract in 1910. Calgary's mayor, Grant MacEwan, cooled to the proposal when he learned that the cost of power to Calgary out of the jointly-owned plant at Ardley would be higher than for Edmonton. The higher cost was because Calgary could only load the plant with its excess power requirements over the amount of 300,000 kilowatts, which was under contract to Calgary Power, while Edmonton had the advantage of being able to transfer all of its base load to the Ardley plant, retaining its existing gas-fired plant in Edmonton for peaking power from a plant which was relatively free of fixed costs. This was not, however, the only factor leading to the death of the scheme. Time was running out for Edmonton and its council instructed the administration to prepare a report on the city's immediate power needs considering a coal-fired plant at Genesee, the Tri-City scheme, or a new local natural gas-fired plant. Edmonton finally opted for the last alternative since it had the lowest capital costs and the end cost of power was only slightly more than that from the Tri-City scheme. With the withdrawal of Edmonton the Tri-City scheme collapsed and Calgary was now left with two alternatives. It could sign another contract with Calgary Power or it could make one last attempt to generate the excess requirement of power locally using natural gas. The city produced an updated analysis of the second alternative and in late 1965 submitted it to a Vancouver consultant for a second opinion. While the consultant endorsed the city report, his conclusions were not encouraging.

Any remaining prospects Calgary may have had for the generation of some power was quickly dampened by the new attitudes of the provincial Social Credit government. The city gas and power committee, chaired by Alderman Jack Davis, himself a prominent local consulting engineer, met with the Minister of Mines and Resources, in September 1966. Contrary to the positive attitude with which the minister had viewed the Tri-City scheme only a year earlier, he was now very negative about the city generating power using natural gas. The province would not consider financing a city-owned plant through its wholly-owned Municipal Finance Corporation, requiring the city to finance on the open market at higher costs. Furthermore, the province was considering a major revision of the "Power Commission Act" and its body of fairly redundant regulations. The new revisions would view provincial power needs on a "single system" basis and require that generating units be sized for that purpose rather than for local needs. The Minister also viewed the use of natural gas for generation of electricity as inappropriate preferring it as an export commodity, with coal being utilized for power generation. While the minister did not disapprove of the city alternative of a gas-fired thermal plant, he left no doubt regarding the difficulties which any move in that direction would encounter.

The final advantage that municipal generation held over private companies such as Calgary Power Limited was also about to disappear. Municipal utilities were exempt from the payment of federal income tax. These taxes levied on private electrical utilities were not unsubstantial and were always viewed by the private utilities as discriminatory particularly since Alberta was the only remaining

Canadian bastion of large private electrical utilities. The private utilities, both gas and electric, were successful in lobbying the federal government to remove the effect of the income tax by refunding it to the province from which it was generated. Alberta followed with its own legislation ordering these amounts to be refunded directly to the consumer as a discount on electricity or natural gas bills with the added reminder to the consumer that the discount was due to the benevolence of the provincial government.

It is not surprising that the 1965 report prepared by the city electrical department (now called the "City of Calgary Electric System") concluded that "generation by the City of Calgary of its own electrical requirements using natural gas is feasible but extremely marginal when compared to the recent rate offer from Calgary Power Ltd."[18] A further extension of the 1959 Agreement between the city and Calgary Power Limited was approved by the city council on 14 October 1966. The contract would run for a minimum of ten years beyond 31 August 1970, with that ten-year period being the notice of termination if given by either party. The amount of power under contract was increased from 300,000 to 550,000 kilowatts. It was the best contract the city would ever negotiate with the company. The demand charge was set at $1.35 per month per kilowatt of load demand, declining in each successive year until the figure of $1.18 was reached and holding until 31 August 1972 at which time the rate was open for review by either party. All energy would be sold at 0.35 cents per kilowatt hour. Assuming a 50 percent annual load factor the average cost per kilowatt hour purchased was 0.685 cents in 1967 decreasing to 0.619 cents by 1972. These amounts did not include the rebate from the provincial government. There can be no doubt that the exhaustive efforts on the part of the city, from 1963 to 1965, to identify alternate sources of electricity supply came very close to meeting S.J. Davies' definition of a "horse" with which to trade. But the future was clouding over with the threat of escalating inflation and it would not be long before its effects would be felt.

The negotiated prices for electrical demand and energy in the 1966 amendment to the 1959 contract were firm until 1 September 1972. By the end of 1970, however, the company had started to complain that it was losing money on the city contract. By 1972 the city electrical energy requirement amounted to 30 percent of the company's total energy sales whereas the revenue derived from those sales amounted to only 21 percent of the company's total revenue. This alone was not an accurate indication of whether or not the company was losing money on city business since not all electrical energy is sold at the same rate. It would be safe to say that the city contract was probably of marginal value to the company in view of the accelerating inflationary trends of the period. Early in 1972 the company announced that it was going to alter its corporate charter to allow regulation by the Alberta Public Utilities Board. The decision to get under the umbrella of the Public Utilities Board was indeed a shrewd one. From a political and public relations viewpoint the company would now be seen as a truly Albertan corporate entity. It also guaranteed the financial future of the company at the small penalty of making a full disclosure of its affairs in a public arena. A new rate for electrical power and energy supplied to Calgary beyond 1 September 1972 was proposed which was a return to the rate of the 1959 contract: $1.37 per kilowatt of annual demand and 0.40 cents per kilowatt hour for all energy. The rate proposed represented a 15 percent increase with the company agreeing to support this rate before the Public Utilities Board as an appropriate one based on ''cost of service'' studies which they had prepared for their submission to the Board.

The idea of ''regulation'' of monopolies by the state is common to North America, particularly to the United States where monopolies are viewed with a fair degree of alarm because of their perceived interference with the process of a ''free and competitive'' marketplace. The idea has never gained much acceptance in Europe where, for example, corporate monopolies are viewed more benignly. In Alberta the proceedings of a regulatory hearing follow a fairly standard format. The Commissioners of the Public Utilities Board sit as a quasi-judicial panel whose decisions are final and from which there can be no appeal. The hearing is structured to cover two general areas of concern.

''Phase One'' of the hearing is devoted entirely to the determination of the total revenue the company should be permitted to generate to cover all of its legitimate costs, including the amount it should earn for its investors from that part of the ''rate base'' (the net value of all of its assets dedicated to public service) which belongs to the common shareholders as equity. The theory is that investors will not leave their capital in the company or invest new equity capital unless the ''rate of return'' is sufficiently high enough to maintain their continued interest. All of these cost factors and particularly those associated with investor-return or investor-confidence in the financial marketplace are very complex matters and there are no nice convenient standards against which they can be objectively examined. Experts are called to substantiate the views of the company or those of the interveners, and since the matters under consideration are so technical, an expert can usually be found to defend any reasonable position accepted as a precondition by the parties. The hearings may be lengthy and the Board, assumed to be unbiased, must make the final decision as to who has the best case. From the author's experience, the decisions of the Board in ''Phase One'' weigh heavily in favour of the applicant company.

''Phase Two'' of the hearing is convened after the total revenue requirements have been determined and relates to where the revenue will come from. During ''Phase One'' the interveners have a tendency to be supportive of each other since they all have a combined vested interest in keeping the company's revenue requirement as low as possible. In ''Phase Two'' proceedings, when the costs are allocated between various classes of consumers, the interveners tend to become adversarial as each supports his own vested interests. The revenue to be generated by each "consumer group" is determined by the company in studies which attempt, with varying degrees of success, to allocate the assets of the company required to provide service to each group. By the time all of the witnesses have given testimony and been cross-examined by the other parties, the hearings can become very lengthy. "Phase Two" hearings of an earlier hearing may often overlap with "Phase One" of a later hearing, resulting in a seemingly neverending process. In fact, rate hearings regarding applications by Calgary Power Limited have run continuously since 1972. The costs of such hearings are substantial and normally the Board directs the party filing the application to absorb such costs. However, these costs also become a legitimate cost to the company and are eventually recovered from its consumers.

The question, of course, is whether the regulatory process really looks after the interests of the consumer. The average consumer, unless he is either knowledgeable or naive, has little hope of making his case before such a technical group. Occasionally a single consumer will appear before the Board and, while he always receives a courteous reception, his evidence, often emotional or subjective, is generally viewed as an interesting diversion from the often boring mainstream proceedings. The ultimate cynical view is that the proceedings are nothing more than self-serving, guaranteeing the financial future of the applicant. We cannot help but harken back to the early years of electrical power in Calgary when crude competition was expected to be the ultimate protection for the consumer. The truth of the matter is that all the parties to one of these hearings are victims of the economic and operating technology which is characteristic of the whole enterprise. The Board, if it can merely be an effective arbitrator to all of these complex equations, has done its job. We would all feel easier about the perceived effectiveness of the process if it did not occur with such regularity. Perhaps the well known axiom "familiarity breeds contempt" is apropos.

While the city had negotiated in 1972 for a firm price for its power for a period of five years, this was only illusionary. In fact the city had lost its single strong negotiating position of being the company's largest customer and was now at the mercy of the regulatory process. The only strong position the city had when arguing its case before the Public Utilities Board was the concept of "value of service" which had long been recognized as a valid factor in rate-making theory. Simply stated it says that some classes of customers are more valuable than others. The City of Calgary, because of its position as the largest single "locked-in" customer of the company, both in electrical usage and revenue, rated more "value" than some transient customer with bad load characteristics. Because of this "value of service" factor, Calgary was usually assigned a cost ratio of less than 100 percent of the company assets presumed to be used to supply that electrical requirement but in recent hearings even this factor is being viewed with less sympathy.

While the imposition of the regulatory process on Calgary Power Limited marked the end of over sixty years of face-to-face negotiating between city and company, it also marked the beginning of an unprecedented period of economic inflation and electrical load growth. The rapid increase in electrical loads required the injection of equally large capital investments to service the additional load. The electrical loads in the province during the 1970s were of such a scale that in order to achieve the maximum level of cost efficiency in the production of electricity machines of ever-larger capacity were added.

This is the philosophy of ''economics of scale'' and it carries with it some fairly significant risks since it can take several years to get these giant machines into full production. If, during that period, load growth stops or is seriously curtailed, the machines will sit idle while their large fixed costs continue. The regulatory process has traditionally allowed these interim costs of construction to be treated as an expense but more recently applicants have been seeking the authority to imbed those costs into the ''rate base'' as they are incurred. Whatever the final outcome on this point the end result will always be increasing costs for the consumer. In 1972 the cost of electricity to the residential consumer in Calgary for 700 kilowatt hours of electrical usage was $10.85. By 1983 the cost for the identical usage had escalated to $40.80, an increase of nearly 400 percent over a ten-year period, or approximately a 20 percent compounded increase in each of those years. At the present time, even with the severe economic recession, there appears to be no relief in sight.

In Alberta there are three major producers of electrical energy: two private or investor-owned utilities, TransAlta Utilities Corporation (Calgary Power Limited) and Alberta Power Limited; and the municipally-owned Edmonton plant. Medicine Hat also has its own plant, but the smaller Alberta city is so isolated from the major electrical networks that there has never been any serious move to integrate it into the broader Alberta grid. This is much to the advantage of the citizens of that city who still enjoy the cheapest power rates in the province. Of the three major producers, the ratios of combined demand and energy are divided roughly between TransAlta at 64 percent, Alberta Power at 15 percent, and Edmonton City at 21 percent. TransAlta and Alberta Power produce from coal-fired plants while Edmonton still utilizes natural gas at much higher cost, although it plans to convert to coal. All three producers have been able to make use of large capacity machines, and recent operating agreements between the two private companies have allowed Alberta Power to install machines larger than it could use if it operated in isolation. Even with these modifications the power from TransAlta plants bears the lowest overall costs while Edmonton's are the highest because of the use of natural gas. This means that the residential and farm customers of TransAlta enjoy lower rates than the same customer groups of Alberta Power and these particular customer groups are the most politically vociferous.

During all of the rate hearings before the Public Utilities Board in the 1970s, the most vocal of the interveners were the Rural Electrification Associations which represent most of the farming population of Alberta. In fact the farm groups in Alberta were at one time fairly supportive of publicly-owned power. A decade of continuous Public Utilities Board hearings has made these politically sensitive groups even more aware of the existence of the non-homogeneous power system in Alberta. The government of Alberta made its move to placate these groups on 30 November 1981 when it introduced Bill 92, the "Electric Energy Marketing Act." The plan was simple enough in its concept. All of the power produced by the three major power producers would be "pooled" at some fictitious interface then purchased for an instant by the Electric Energy Marketing Agency when the costs would be averaged and the power resold to each generating authority for resale to the "downstream" customer. The argument used was that since approximately 80 percent of the cost of power was imbedded in the generation of the electricity the "pooling" and averaging of those costs would provide the required equalization of power costs to most Albertans. It was a hybrid alternative to having a single power utility in Alberta. The net result to Calgary was dramatic cost increases. The last vestige of advantage to TransAlta consumers was now wiped out and it is not without significance that the latest contract agreement between the city and TransAlta Utilities contains no mention of price because it is now fully determined by agencies of the provincial government. So much for free enterprise!

Since the formation of the Electric Energy Marketing Agency the regulatory process in Alberta has become even more complex. Nothing has been simplified and additional costs have been loaded on top of already excessive regulatory costs. One can spend a lifetime wondering about the rationale of our elected representatives. That electricity might cost more in one area of the province than another should really be of little consequence if the costs of providing that commodity are in fact higher. Certainly this logic applies to most other commodities where pricing is rarely uniform. If the provincial government really wanted a single electric utility operating in the province, why did it not use its private-sector bias to induce the formation of one integrated privately-owned utility which when combined with the regulatory process, would solve the problem? One wonders just what the lip service which the Alberta government pays to private ownership really means, when on one hand it decries public ownership of electric utilities and on the other maintains firm ownership and control of Alberta's largest public utility, Alberta Government Telephones.

The power supply agreement of 1984 contains no reference to price but includes a letter of understanding that TransAlta would consider the city of Calgary as a participant in any future generating plant in the vicinity of the city on the basis of "sharing in the fully distributed costs and benefits of the plant."[19] At best there is little chance for such a scheme particularly now that provincial regulatory agencies exercise such a heavy hand in all deliberations relating to the planning and operating of major power facilities. It is unlikely that they will allow another party to further complicate an already complex situation.

The almost eight decades of relationship between TransAlta Utilities Corporation and the City of Calgary has been a unique model in Canada. It is unfortunate, in the author's opinion, that the company chose to abandon its former name of Calgary Power Limited for its new corporate name TransAlta. The reason advanced for changing "from Calgary Power Limited to TransAlta Utilities Corporation, in order to overcome confusion with the City of Calgary Electric System and to reflect a broadening of scope"[20] of the company's operations, seems a rather shallow one considering the obvious reality that the company owes much of its overwhelming success in Alberta to its long relationship with the City of Calgary.

Nevertheless, the "uneasy alliance" reflects a certain characteristic of Calgary where entrepreneurship, from the beginning, has been highly prized without suppressing the need that citizens find to be collectively involved with appropriate municipal enterprises. Both the city and the company can look back with justifiable pride on their accomplishments. We can only hope that the future holds the same promise.

References

1. City of Calgary. *Annual Report 1914*. Consolidated Report of Power Department.

2. City Clerk's Papers, b.79,f632. Letter dated 21 May 1913. R.A. Ross to Commissioner A.G. Graves.

3. Council minutes, 31 May 1915, p. 463-64. Letter dated 17 May 1915. Brown/McCall to Commissioner Graves.

4. Council minutes, 17 June 1918. Letter dated 31 May 1918. R.A. Brown to Mayor and Commissioners.

5. Council minutes, 6 August 1923, p.319.

6. City Clerk's Record Office. Memorandum of Agreement, dated 6 August 1923 between City of Calgary and Calgary Power Company, Limited.

7. Jack Sexton wrote a history of Montreal Engineering in 1982 under the title *Monenco, The First 75 Years*.

8. Council Minutes, 19 March 1928, p.92.

9. Calgary Power Papers. "Instructions to Bidders and Specifications for Electric Power Supply," dated 6 January 1928.

10. Council Minutes, 14 May 1928, p.238.

11. Calgary Power Papers, b2.f4. Board of Directors Minutes, 30 May 1928, p. 19-20, (status: author).

12. Council Minutes, p.634-36. Letter dated 30 October 1943. H B. Sherman Manager, Calgary Power Company Limited to Mayor.

13. Council Minutes, 20 March 1944, p.146. Both the questions of Alderman Freeze and the replies of Brown and City Solicitor Collinge are contained in the same minutes.

14. "City Health Service Will Be Examined," *Calgary Herald*, 23 January, 1950. McIntosh was one of the members of the famous trio of McIntosh, Morrison and Watson who gained prominence in the late 1940s as labour representatives on council.

15. Ibid.

16. City of Calgary. Electric System Archives. Collection of papers and reports leading up to 1959 City of Calgary submission to Oil and Gas Conservation Board, not catalogued but notably 1959 letters, S.J. Davies, P.Eng. to City Commissioners dated 27 May, 29 June, 5 July, 3 August, 3 September, 1 October.

17. City of Calgary. Electric System Archives. "Report on Proposals Submitted by Dynamic Power Corporation," dated 23 April 1963.

18. City of Calgary. Electric System Archives. Report, dated 14 February 1966, "Future Power Requirements-City of Calgary Electric System."

19. City Clerk's Records, 1984. Power Supply Agreement between the City of Calgary and TransAlta Utilities Corporation.

20. TransAlta Utilities Corporation. *Annual Report 1981*.

Pole-setting crew in action c. 1930.
Source: Electric System Archives

Chapter 8

THE BROWN/MACKAY DYNASTY

In this chapter we will pick up the theme of chapter four which covered the early years of the municipally-owned electrical utility and focus it on the people and events which surrounded two remarkable men. One was a dedicated but rather dour Scotsman with an insatiable capacity for work named Robert Mackay, and the other was a breezy, gregarious Irish-Scottish genius, named Robert Arthur Brown. Together these two men, with their unique talents, would consolidate the infant municipal enterprise into a permanent institution. The joint activities of these two individuals spanned almost exactly the period between the two World Wars. We should also keep in mind that during this period Calgary remained relatively unchanged although the population grew by some 25,000 souls. Unlike the first decade of this century when Calgary underwent its first great boom cycle, the period between the wars was one characterized by relative stability. The major exception being, of course, the decade of the Great Depression of the 1930s.

In 1907, Charles O'Brien came up from the ranks of Calgary's Fire Department to become the electrical superintendent replacing Lionel White who seems to have left Calgary to seek his fortunes elsewhere. Coexisting with White and O'Brien was another rugged Scotsman, J.F. (Jimmy) McCall, who had been retained by the city in 1905 to superintend the first municipal power plant on Atlantic (9th) Avenue. It is true that in 1928 when the Victoria Park Power Plant was leased to the Calgary Power Company Jimmy McCall became an employee of that company rather than the City of Calgary but that quirk of fate in no way detracts from his continuous superintendence of the only power plants owned and operated by the city. McCall went into relative obscurity after the 1928 lease of the Victoria Park Power Plant to the Calgary Power Company but prior to this time his knowledge and experience was constantly sought by R.A. Brown. The administrative ties that O'Brien had with the Fire Department were broken a few

191

months after he became electrical superintendent and the electrical inspection activity was transferred to him. He then held the joint title of City Electrician and Chief Wiring Inspector. Provision was also made for O'Brien to delegate the wiring inspection duties to another employee when it was deemed necessary. All of these changes were recommended in the 6 May 1907 report of the Light Committee of Council. On 28 January 1908, following the Light Committee's recommendation, Mr. H. Hinde was appointed as Calgary's first electric wiring inspector and meter reader with a detailed job description. This appointment marked the beginning of the Calgary's Electrical Inspection Branch which has remained intact as an administrative activity of the city's electrical utility. Where Hinde came from is not certain but we can suppose it was, like O'Brien, out of the Fire Department because prior to this time the department had been the responsible agent for the primitive electric wiring inspection service in Calgary.

The earliest record of Robert Mackay is found in a letter dated 28 February 1908, addressed to the mayor and aldermen. Mackay was a cornet player in the 15th Light Horse Military Band which had its regimental headquarters in Calgary. He also acted as the band manager and his letter contained a detailed and glowing report of a recent tour of Britain which the band had made the previous year. Dr. MacKenzie Rogan, conductor of the British Coldstream Guards' Band, had publicly commended the quality of the Calgary Band, inspiring Robert Mackay to write:

> Previous to these remarks the Calgary Band had taken part in a Grand Military Tattoo under the direction of Dr. Rogan, and before leaving the stand he compli-mented the Canadian Band on their playing, stating that it gave him much pleasure to have such a body of musicians playing under his baton. He also said that it agreeably surprised him to hear such a Band from Canada, especially as they came from Western Canada, he never anticipated it possible for a band of this standard to be organized in Western Canada, where conditions were entirely different from the British Isles.[1]

It was an interesting report and may have had no small influence on the engagement of Mackay as a civic employee in the Electric Light Department on 6 April 1908, at a salary of $75.00 monthly. The nature of the job was not spelled out in any detail. Mackay's daughter, the noted Calgary artist Marion Nichol, remembered her father working variously as a lineman, meter reader and office technician preparing jobs for issue to field crews. While still in his teens, he had worked as a leather craftsman with the pioneer Calgary business of Riley and McCormick. In the late 1880s Mackay's family had immigrated directly to Calgary from Thurso, on the most northerly coast of Scotland, setting up their family home on the corner of 3rd Avenue and 2nd Street E. Mackay was very much a self-educated man who by the end of 1914 had completed a correspon-dence course in electrical engineering. He served as a volunteer fireman and regularly ran in the Herald Road Race. He also was responsible for the introduc-tion of women's curling clubs to Calgary.

By 1909, Mackay was listed in the city's budget estimates as a meter reader which placed him under the direct supervision of Chief Wiring Inspector H. Hinde. On 15 April 1910 City Electrician O'Brien recommended to the city commissioners that Mackay be promoted to the position of wiring inspector: "Mr. Mackay has been in my department for a number of years, and according to the work he has done I am fully satisfied he is capable of filling the position of Wiring Inspector."[2] It is not at all clear from existing records whether Mackay was replacing Hinde at this time but by the end of 1911 he was filing his own annual report on the operations of the Wiring Inspection Department, indicating beyond any doubt that he had become its head. In his first report he lodged a complaint regarding the office facilities out of which he had to operate. "I would suggest," he wrote, "that offices be provided for this Department on the top floor opposite and on the same style as the School Board Offices. This would give us a chance to conduct our business as it should be done, without interfering with the Electric Light Department."[3] By 1912, his staff consisted of four assistant wiring inspectors, G. Noble, G. Notley, J.H. Ross and J. Doherty. Both Noble and Notley became chief wiring inspectors in later years while J.H. Ross became an alderman and a leading technical school educator in Calgary. Robert Mackay had progressed a long way in four years.

R.A. Brown was born in 1886 at Point Levis, Quebec, one of a family of ten children. He began his career in the infant electrical industry with the Quebec Light, Heat and Power Company and, by the early years of this century, had moved to the Westinghouse Electric Company in Pittsburg and later St. Louis. Like Robert Mackay, he was also a self-educated man and his career in the electrical field prior to coming to Calgary was one of continued successes. He was a constant reader and an avid student who kept himself in tune with the latest in his chosen field of electrical technology. For a while he worked as a laboratory assistant to Dr. Charles P. Steinmetz[4] at the General Electric Company in Schenectady, New York. Just what attracted Brown to Western Canada is unknown but, by 1906, he was associated with the Northwest Electrical Company in Calgary, leaving the following year to superintend the construction of the city of Nelson, B.C.'s hydro plant at Bonnington Falls, west of that city. By the time he returned to Calgary in 1911 to assume his duties as city electrician, he was already a seasoned and experienced veteran and was to become one of the greatest assets that both Calgary and later the province of Alberta ever acquired.

City Commissioner Graves must have had some contact with Brown during his earlier 1906 sojourn in Calgary and been impressed enough with Brown that he would contact with him when a problem arose in Calgary. Graves wrote to Brown in 1910 regarding wages being paid to linemen in Nelson. Brown replied, "This will acknowledge receipt of your letter of Oct. 3rd in which I note you are having some little trouble with your linemen as to wages and working hours...I hope that the information contained herein is that which you require and if I can

CALGARIANS IN CARICATURE

R. A. BROWN

Electricity, so little known but a few years ago, has become one of the features of every city in the country, but few have developed it to a higher pitch of municipal efficiency than Calgary, and a great deal of that efficiency is due to the efforts of R. A. Brown, Calgary's city electrician. Mr. Brown was born in Montreal and educated there, taking up work with the old Royal Electric company, which has since been merged into the Montreal Light, Heat and Power company. After spending about 6 years in the electrical business in Montreal, he went to Pittsburg in 1901 and joined the Westinghouse Company, going later to Chicago with the Western Electric company. He then went to the world's fair grounds at St. Louis, and installed the electrical apparatus for the big fair, and while with the Westinghouse and the Western Electric concerns he installed electric plants from New York to New Orleans.

From the St. Louis fair Mr. Brown came to Winnipeg and installed the plant in the C. P. R. Royal Alexandra hotel, and then came to Calgary. In 1907 he installed the hydro-electric plant on the Kootenay river for the town of Nelson. Returning to Calgary he started as city electrician in December, 1911, and his work here since taking that position has been of such prominence as to need no comment.

Mr. Brown is a member of the Masonic fraternity and an Oddfellow. He is also somewhat of a baseball fiend, and takes an interest in all clean sports.

Calgary News-Telegram caricature of R.A. Brown, July 13, 1913.
Source: Glenbow Archives

be of further service to you in this connection please command me."[5] Little did Brown know how soon he was to be commanded.

Charles O'Brien fell into disrepute as city electrician with the city commissioners and, by late autumn of 1911, the city was looking for a replacement. H.E. Kensit, an electrical engineer with the consulting engineering firm of Smith, Kerry and Chace, was offered the position. His company was engaged in Calgary with the hydro-electric project at Horseshoe Falls for their clients, the Alexander and Budd Syndicate. Kensit turned the position down after apparently expressing an early interest in the job. The commissioners reported to the council on 2 November 1911 that they were advertising for applicants for the position but it would appear that Commissioner Graves wasted little time in contacting Brown in Nelson. At the next council meeting eleven days later, the commissioners recommended R.A. Brown for the position. Brown sent his acceptance on 21 November 1911.

Brown's first annual report to the mayor and commissioners was a masterpiece of information and communication. It consisted of thirteen pages of wide-ranging material, covering organization, management techniques, cost accounting, works in progress, statistics and Calgary's present and future power supplies. It was written to communicate to laymen since Brown never allowed his superior technical knowledge to confuse his intended readers. It provides a basic insight into the nature of this remarkable man. He was not egocentric and always included both his superiors and his subordinates whenever praise or commendation was deserved. While military-style authoritarianism was generally the order of the day in employer/employee relations, it was not so with R.A. Brown. The first work undertaken in 1912 was that of reorganizing the officers who were put in charge of each important branch of the department and made entirely responsible for the proper carrying out of all work under their jurisdiction. Delegation of authority and teamwork was the hallmark of Brown's management style. He identified the problems which resulted from his first contract with the Calgary Power Company and elaborated upon them at some length in his report. The city must not, he maintained, be at the whim of the company in respect to future power supplies. He outlined the alternatives available to the city from natural gas and coal: "It is evident that the task of choosing the best of the above methods of power generating for Calgary to adopt is a very complex one and the Commissioners are to be commended on using good business judgment when they decided to secure the services of an eminent electrical expert to deal with this question."[6] The eminent expert was R.A. Ross, consulting engineer from Montreal. Brown had convinced the commissioners of the need for the consultant but he gave them full credit for exercising good business acumen. "R.A." or "Bob" as he was called, was also looking to the future: "The laying out of a program such as just mentioned will put the City in the position that all monies appropriated for electric light and power purposes will be expended on nothing but what will work into and form part of the ultimate plant to which the City of Calgary will look to for its future supply of electrical energy.''

In 1912, most communications or reports to the city council were concluded in the pattern of Robert Mackay's annual report: ''Trusting this report meets with your approval; it is respectfully submitted, I am Yours obediently, Robert Mackay, Wiring Inspector.'' The closing remarks in Brown's annual report for 1912 constitute a remarkable contrast:

> I wish to take this opportunity of thanking the Mayor, Commissioners and City Council for the royal support which they at all times willingly rendered, and particularly to thank Commissioner Graves for his active support and strong personal efforts in the interests of the Department. I also wish to thank the staff for the faithful and energetic way in which they carried out the work entrusted to their care. Respectfully submitted, R.A. Brown, City Electrician.

A little bit of ''Irish blarney'' perhaps but everything that followed in Brown's career with the city was also laced with sincerity. Mr. Don Little, who joined the city in 1928 as a junior clerk in the Light Department, retiring as commercial services manager in 1970, recalled, with a great affection, his first working day. Brown came out of his office and introduced himself to the new employee with the offer of a ''Life Saver'' from a roll he carried in his coat pocket. This was long before the time of the now-accepted coffee break and Don Little became, by that simple act of friendliness, a lifelong admirer of R.A. Brown.

Brown recognized early in his new career that it was simply not enough for his Electric Light Department to sell electricity without ensuring that the customers were obtaining maximum value for their energy dollar. ''We decided,'' he said, ''to secure the services of one or two good technically educated men to assist in the work of advising our present and prospective power customers...it being our belief that we should sell utility rather than power.''[7] Unfortunately, it is not possible to determine with any assurance who these ''technically educated men'' were but the 1913 estimates for the Wiring Inspection Office shows the addition of the four inspectors, Noble, Notley, Ross and Doherty. Of these, the first three were known to be qualified technicians. It is entirely likely that these new inspectors shared the duties of wiring inspector and advisor to power customers. Later in the year Robert Mackay, Chief Wiring Inspector, was given additional responsibilities. Brown recorded that:

> Mr. Robert Mackay was also added to the technical staff of the department in the capacity of superintendent; his duties being to superintend all maintenance and construction work, and to take full charge during my absence. Mr. Mackay has proved a very valuable man to the Department...a good engineer...able to handle men and to carry out work in an efficient manner.[8]

While the distinction between Mackay's duties as chief wiring inspector and superintendent were not clearly defined, Mackay wrote in his annual report, ''I might add that the majority of my time is spent in connection with duties in the Electric Light Department.''[9]

Brown introduced Calgary to the use of electric battery-powered vehicles in 1913 when his cost analysis of gasoline versus electric-powered vehicles weighed heavily in favour of the latter. Seven trucks ranging in capacity from one to five tons were purchased and placed in service wherever long heavy hauls of materials were required. Concluded Brown, ''a good electric truck and battery, properly maintained and intelligently cared for, is the most economical and satisfactory modern delivery unit of today.''[10] Brown's application of electric vehicles in Calgary won him instant notoriety and he became somewhat of a North American authority on the subject. The author remembers the odd whirring, clicking sound of these vehicles which still lumbered about Calgary in the late 1920s. Unfortunately, they had one major disadvantage and that was their slowness. They were powered by nickel/iron alkaline batteries which were almost indestructible and as late as 1950 some of these original batteries were still operating switchgear in several of Calgary's electrical substations. The electric trucks could compete with horse-drawn vehicles but as gasoline-powered trucks improved, the day of the electric vehicle ended.

One of R.A. Brown's battery-powered trucks dressed for Christmas
promotion of electric appliances c. 1920.
Source: Electric System Archives

Tragedy struck on Monday, 16 March 1914. Two linemen from the Electric Light Department were electrocuted while working on secondary voltage service wires on 17th Avenue and 5th Street E., across from the Victoria Park Exhibition grounds. The cause of the accident was a secondary wire which had been left in contact with a series streetlighting arc circuit on the same pole. Evidently while the linemen were working on the secondary wires, the series circuit was somehow energized and the high voltage electrocuted them. Three street railway linemen were identified as being the last to work on the fatal pole and they were immediately the ones susupected of carelessness. The linemen were suspended and the city council appointed an ad hoc committee comprised of Aldermen H.W. Riley, H. Addshead and D.R. Crichton to investigate the accident. At the same council meeting on 31 March 1914, R.A. Brown was asked by Alderman E.H. Crandell about automatic safety apparatus which could have prevented the accident. "Superintendent Brown," the *Herald* reported, "at this point arose to reply and his technical language, although given in the utmost sincerity, aroused a burst of laughter."[11] Brown proceeded to give a lengthy technical explanation of why the accident happened and how the suggestion of Alderman Crandell would have made no difference even if such a device had been available and installed:

> As Mr. Brown proceeded with this explanation, a dazed look spread over the aldermanic faces. There was a brief moment of silence when he (Brown) finished and then Alderman Frost, the council's official jester, stated self-complacently: 'That's right'. A burst of laughter greeted this remark, in which even the Mayor joined. Mr. Brown, somewhat surprised, came forward again and explained apologetically that he meant no disrespect...but it was a difficult matter to explain to anyone not familiar with such work.[12]

The committee decided that a visit to the accident site would be workable and two of them, Aldermen Riley and Crichton, decided that they should climb the pole to see at close hand the actual point of contact. Newsmen followed this daring pair to the 17th Avenue site, and reported that, "The Aldermen climbed the tall stick under the tutelage of Superintendent R.A. Brown...who pointed out to each one the exact spot where the cross occurred, with surrounding circumstances." One newsman remarked that should the aldermen slip the city would need two by-elections, to which Brown laconically replied, "Slipped...they couldn't. I'll bet there are finger prints in the iron cross pieces where they were holding on."[13] The committee brought down an entirely inconclusive report on the accident. It could find no evidence that the problem had been caused by any one of the three street railway linemen. The linemen were reinstated but not before the council ruled that in future "all wires erected by the Fire Department, Street Railway Department or the Police Department on poles on which electric lighting wires are strung be placed by men working with the Electric Light Department."[14]

While it is unfortunate that this tragedy provoked some humor, we must understand that safe operating practices in 1914 were very primitive. Linemen

City officials investigating site of the electrocution of two linemen in March 1914 at
17th Ave. and 5th St. E. Aldermen H.W. Riley and D. Crichton on pole with
R.A. Brown and City Commissioner Graves on ground at right.
Source: Electric System Archives

considered that leather gloves alone were adequate protection from electric shock
and they largely escaped electrocution or burns because the primary distribution
circuits were ungrounded, offering some degree of inherent safety. Rubber gloves
and other protective devices were only beginning to gain acceptance and industrial accidents were not viewed with the same degree of seriousness as they are
today.

The economy of Calgary began to decline seriously in 1914. The great boom
years of the first part of the century had come to an end and, except for a brief
revival immediately following World War I, did not return with the same vigor
until the mid 1950s. For the Electric Light Department it was a period devoted to
innovation rather than expansion. The Victoria Park Power Plant had reached its
maximum expansion and the 12,000 volt bulk supply to Calgary's electricity
needs was solidly in place. The extent of that network was graphically indicated
in a schematic drawing approved by R.A. Brown in 1914. The 12,000 volt
network remained relatively unchanged until the early 1950s and served all of
Calgary's electrical needs, illustrating dramatically how little the city grew physically between the period of the two world wars.

Salary increases for civic department officials had come fairly regularly during the boom period but by 1914 restraint was the order of the day. The local press reported that only two civic department heads were likely to be considered for salary increases and they were City Clerk J.M. Miller and R.A. Brown. Brown's annual salary was $3,200. In view of the "'phenomenal success' of the Electric Light and Power Department in achieving substantial profits while reducing...the price of current to domestic consumers and the municipal street railway (to) the lowest in the history of the city," the *Herald* supported an increase in the stipend because "the Superintendent has been working literally night and day during the time he has been in the city's employ and for this work receives a salary which a third assistant for a private corporation of similar capitalization might receive."[15] However, by 1915 even R.A. Brown could not escape the city's need to economize and his salary, along with a general reduction throughout the civic service, was reduced by 20 percent from $3,700 to $2,960 annually.

The Electric Light Department now numbered seventy-two employees and listed them for the first time, either by name or position, in the current budget estimates accompanied by their monthly salaries. Robert Mackay was still shown filling the dual function of "Assistant Superintendent and Wiring Inspector." Brown is called the "Electrical Engineer" but more correctly should have been called "Superintendent and Electrical Engineer." The name of Donald S. Brown appears in this list for the first time. He was a brother of R.A. Brown and had left Montreal where he had been employed as a meter technician to seek his fortunes on the west coast. However upon his arrival in Calgary to visit his brother he was persuaded to stay for a higher salary than the one being offered in Vancouver. Don Brown eventually became the supervisor of meters in the Electric Light Department, retired in 1957 and died in 1983. A very quiet and introverted person, he was the complete antithesis of his breezy brother.

Another name appearing for the first time was that of J.N. Lightbody, a graduate electrical engineer from Wisconsin, who started as a draftsman and soon became the designated electrical engineer of the department, although he never eclipsed Brown or Mackay. He remained with the department into the early years of World War II but was always in the background as a shadowy, enigmatic figure. R.A. Brown once described him as a brilliant but shy man.

The power department still survived as a separate entity with Jim McCall as superintendent. The plant had reached its maximum capacity and forty-one employees were listed on its payroll. In addition to operating the steam plant, the Power Department also provided the operators at each of the four main substations serviced from the 12,000 volt primary network. It was an odd staffing arrangement since the electrical substations were assets of the Electric Light Department, and that department was responsible for their maintenance. By the end of 1915 some aldermen were pressing the commissioners for the amalgamation of Brown's Electric Light Department and McCall's Power Department.

Group picture of outside electrical workers waiting their entry
into the 1926 Stampede Parade.
Source: Electric System Archives

1 Malcolm Hornby	*9 Kay Wilson*	*16 Bill Mayell*	*23 Unidentified*
2 Mont Wilson	*10 Bill Gibson*	*17 Unidentified*	*24 John Forsberg*
3 Charlie McCarthy	*11 Bill Gilbert*	*18 Ted Guinn*	*25 Frank Bell*
4 Ashley Van Camp	*12 Milton McDougal*	*19 Harling Boy (Tom)?*	*26 Reg. Brighton/*
5 Dad Picken (Joe)	*13 Whitey Roebeck*	*20 Harling Boy (Vic)*	*Brydon?*
6 Howard Hepburn	*14 Bill Picken*	*21 George Tyler*	*27 Walt Gillingham*
7 Unidentified	*15 Jack Stevenson*	*22 Bill Lison*	*28 Tom Harling*
8 Norm Thompson			

Regretfully, the names of the unidentified people have not been discovered.

A horsedrawn water pipe thawing outfit c. 1916. Designed by J.N. Lightbody,
the Electric Light Department resident engineer.
Source: Electric System Archives

Brown and McCall appeared to work well together. All matters which related to the Calgary Power Company's contract for supply of hydro power were coopted and reports dealing with those contracts were often signed by both men. Commissioner Graves replied to the question of amalgamation by saying that he was satisfied with the present arrangement but that as soon as "it would appear best to make a change in the present system, I shall not hesitate to make such a recommendation."[16]

World War I was in its second year and the citizens of Calgary were no less loyal to the cause of the British Empire than was any other part of Canada. Owing to their predominantly British origins they might even have enjoyed an edge. Council passed a motion on 19 May 1915 instructing the heads of all departments "to dismiss from the City's service all enemy aliens who may have been naturalized since August 1st.,1914, or who may not be naturalized, this being the time in which the Empire has been at war." In other words, if an employee of German extraction had become a naturalized Canadian on 2 August 1914, he was fired. If that action was not bad enough, the council also followed it with a decree that no men could be employed by the city if they were under forty years of age because anyone of that age who was fit to work for the city was also fit for the Canadian army. Since this was a matter already in hand by federal authorities, it appears almost vindictive on the part of the council but such was often the case with extreme patriotism. Since R.A. Brown was just thirty at this

Number 3 Substation built on 16 Ave. N. section of "Ring Main" in 1912.
Source: Electric System Archives

time, we can assume that his position was classified as essential and so he escaped World War I service. His brother Donald, however, served for three years in the trenches as did a great many of the Light and Power Department employees, some of whom never returned. Because of the war and the exodus of men to serve in the trenches Calgary stagnated so much that only a handful of pre-war employees were needed to maintain an acceptable service level to the end of the war. Council also entertained motions to raise the cost of domestic and commercial electricity in order to pay the property taxes of enlisted married men who owned property but none of these measures were implemented.

Four electrical substations were connected to the 12,000 volt "ring main" which surrounded the city. The primary purpose of these stations was to reduce to 2300 volts the voltage used for the local distribution of electricity in the areas surrounding each substation. These stations also supplied electricity to operate series streetlighting circuits and in the case of Numbers 1, 2 and 3 Substations, direct current for the street railway. Number 3 Substation, located on the southeast corner of 17th Avenue and 1st Street N.W., was the site chosen for additional direct current capacity to supply power to street railway extensions in the north. A combined Brown/McCall report considered all of the pros and cons of either providing new heavy copper feeders from Number 1 Substation located in the downtown core to the north of Calgary, or adding the additional capacity at Number 3 Substation. The latter won by a large margin and an additional 1,000 kilowatt direct current motor-generator set was installed there in 1920. It was the last large rotating direct current machine purchased by the Electric Light Department. In 1927, Number 3 Substation again became the site of the installion of the first 600 kilowatt mercury-arc rectifier for direct current supply. Number 3 Substation still stands on its original site although the original red brick building, with its huge leaded glass windows, was renovated in the late 1950s.

By 1920, the net worth of the assets of the Electric Light Department including the power plant at Victoria Park, was $2,900,000. This had been financed primarily by the city borrowing by-laws, specifically in the name of the electrical utility. Repayment of the debt was through the use of sinking funds, the cost of which was a direct charge to the light and power departments. Depreciation accounts were also used, presumably to provide for replacement of assets or to finance new additions. The departments were also responsible for their respective debenture interest charges. Surplus funds were either diverted into the city's general revenue accounts for relief of taxation or, on occasion, toward the financing of new extensions. The total revenue requirement to cover these capitalization and operating costs was generated from the rates charged to consumers of electricity.

Interior view of electrical underground manhole c. 1918. This downtown underground system became the nucleus of the secondary network system in 1936.
Source: Electric System Archives

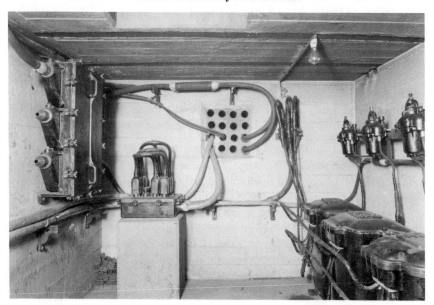

Inflation was one of the consequences of the First World War and early in 1919 Brown reported to the council that, "Since the beginning of the war, the price of copper, lamps, carbon and electrical apparatus generally has increased on an average of 76%, and labour has increased approximately 30%."[17] During the war, most maintenance had been suspended as had appropriate rate increases, prompting Brown to comment, "Such a policy cannot be carried on indefinitely without materially impairing the general efficiency of the Department." So the rates were increased to generate an additional $55,000 of revenue yearly. The city had undertaken a rather massive program of installing underground conduits and had passed money by-laws to an aggregate value of $300,000 to cover the cost. Because the conduits had to be in place before the city paved the streets much of the conduit system would remain only partially used for many years. However, the city's general accounts had continued to support the annual fixed charges of the conduit system, covering interest, depreciation and sinking fund which amounted to about $20,000, and this was offset somewhat by annual rental fees to the Electric Light, Street Railway, Police and Fire departments, amounting to $5,000. In 1920 the city council decided to make the full costs of the conduit system a charge to the Electric Light Department. This was the first major move taken to separate fully the financing of the electrical utility from that of the general requirements of the city. In the same year the first general rules were formulated to define those expenditures for either new extensions or the replacement of older facilities which would qualify for payment out of accumulated depreciation funds.[18]

In the summer of 1920 Commissioner Graves ended his report to council on the financial health of the Electric Light Department by remarking that "the policy of investing annual surpluses in improvements to plant and equipment results in a very material benefit to the present day users of the utility and, to my mind, is the only sound and safe method of operation."[19] The year was also significant for R.A. Brown because he was appointed superintendent of the Municipal Street Railway Department following the resignation of Thomas McCauley who returned to the Maritimes to manage the New Brunswick Light and Power Company. Because of his foresight Brown was able to shift the burden of the Electric Light Department almost wholly to the shoulders of Robert Mackay with whom he had elected to share the responsibility of management some eight years earlier. Brown, now general superintendent of both Street Railway and Electric Light departments, threw himself wholeheartedly into the business of public transportation. It was to become a series of great successes and frustrating failures for him. However, his decision to leave the responsibility of the Electric Light Department to Mackay was one he would never regret. Despite his totally different management style, Mackay proved entirely adequate for the tasks ahead.

The council meeting of 11 July 1921 was an important one for the Electric Light Department. At that meeting the council endorsed the finance committee report recommending the continuation of Commissioner Graves' policy of utilizing annual utility surpluses as a contribution to capital expenditures, thereby reducing the need to obtain debt capital: "In its first year of operation this new system of financing has proven entirely satisfactory and your Committee would recommend that the same procedure as in operation last year be continued for this year; the amount of such contribution, however, not to exceed the amount of the surplus from revenue account."[20] This policy worked to the advantage of the Electric Light Department to such an extent that by the end of 1953 the department was entirely free of debt while offering rates for service which were among the lowest in western Canada.

In 1921 a new phenomenon appeared in Calgary with the advent of the domestic electric cooking range. It was dependable, efficient and priced competitively. By the end of the year eighty of the new ranges had been installed in the city. The electrical consumption of these ranges was accounted for by electricity meters installed separately from those used to measure lighting consumption. The awkward method of utilizing two meters within a single domestic residence to measure energy did not change until residential combination rates were introduced in 1928. Commissioner Angus Smith was persuaded by R.A. Brown to

Early electric range promotion in Calgary Herald, June 26, 1923.
Source: Glenbow Archives

recommend to the council that the Electric Light Department actively promote the use of electric cooking and water heating. The basis of the recommendation was that the city purchased power from the Calgary Power Company at a price which was determined by the annual peak demand with the city having to control the maximum demand on the hydro system by operating its own Victoria Park Power Plant which always had extra capacity available. Since the city plant had to be "under steam" for most of the time whether it produced power or not, it was deemed to be good business to place additional loading on the municipal plant at incremental cost. Furthermore, tests had confirmed that the electrical cooking load occurred "off-peak" for nearly 86 percent of the time it was used.

The various range manufacturers displayed their wares in the basement level of the city hall where the Light Department had its headquarters and where all customer accounts were collected. Electric water heating was also promoted but those consumers who decided to use both cooking and water heating were required to install an additional "double-throw" switch on the metered heating service to prevent the cooking and water-heating electrical loads from occurring simultaneously. The price of the energy for such a service was reduced substantially from 3 cents to 2 cents for each kilowatt hour consumed. Since the user had to pay an additional $40.00 (a sizeable amount in 1922) to have his wiring altered to accommodate the use of electricity for both water heating and cooking, that part of the program was not successful. We can easily imagine how many dual users neglected to transfer the "double throw" switch from the electric cooking position to the electric water heating position and were thereby infuriated when their morning bath water was ice cold! So while the electric range gained in popularity, water heating in Calgary remained solidly within the market domain of the natural gas utility. By the end of 1922, the number of electric ranges installed had risen to over 300 despite extremely low natural gas prices.

By 1924 the city was again in an economic decline and the amalgamation of many civic departments was recommended by the commissioner, among which was the consolidation of the Power and Light departments under R.A. Brown. Jimmy McCall, who by now had been with the city for nearly a quarter century, was "given the opportunity to remain in the service in such capacity as the rearrangement would indicate he can be of the best service to the City."[21] He remained with the power plant as a city employee until 1928 when the Victoria Park plant was leased to the Calgary Power Company and he became an employee of that company. Considering the past achievements of this rugged Scotsman, the demotion of 1924 must have had a very negative effect. The economic realities of life always produce their casualties but, as consolation, McCall still had his beloved power plant to look after.

The Bowness Improvement Company, a real estate development enterprise originally promoted in 1911 by John Hextall, had been operating a small electric distribution utility to supply the residents of the new area of Bowness, a few miles west of Calgary. The company operated a small plant on the Bow River near the CPR mainline bridge where it crossed the Bow River just below Bowness Park. In 1926 the company shut down its system. The city purchased most of it thus annexing the Bow River valley area west of the city limits to the service area of the Electric Light Department. This was followed in mid 1928 by the city negotiating with the Lacombe Home to take over its private line at no cost on the understanding that the Electric Light Department would assume all of the maintenance charges. In turn the city offered electrical service to all those customers who could be easily reached from the line running south to Midnapore. R.A. Brown reported that, "The revenue at present being received is $1,350.00 per year. We anticipate that during the next year the revenue can be increased to $2,350.00, and the prospects are that the average city growth will maintain so far as this line is concerned."[22] The demand for service extensions to the rural areas surrounding Calgary was to result in the city acquiring a distribution area substantially larger than that contained within the city limits. This would eventually require formal definition by the Public Utilities Board.

From 1926 to the start of the depression years another surge in load growth from 12,000 to 20,000 kilowatts almost doubled the power demand of the city. In 1926 the Victoria Park Plant was again supplying one-half of the entire electrical load due to an extremely low water year on the Bow River. Because of this there was renewed interest on the part of some aldermen in taking another look at the expansion of the city's generating facilities rather than committing the city to further contracts with the Calgary Power Company. The interest, however, was dampened by the knowledge that the company was developing a new hydro-power project at the Ghost River site. In 1927 the gross revenue of the Electric Light Department was just short of $1,000,000 and after all expenses, including sinking fund, depreciation, interest and taxes had been paid a net surplus of $75,000 remained. A.G. Graves, city commissioner, reported to the council: "Last year's operations I regard as by far the most satisfactory that the Utilities have had for at least five years. The substantial increase in business gives evidence of an improved condition in our City, and I look forward with hope for the continued prosperity of the Public Utility Departments."[23]

To meet the growing electricity demands the first major plant expansions in over fifteen years were undertaken. The main downtown substation Number 1 at 9th Avenue and 7th Street W. received a building extension on its east side to accommodate switchgear for new distribution circuits. The "portable" substation placed in service in 1929 was equipped with a new mercury-arc rectifier for street railway service. The "portable sub" consisted of a railway flatcar covered by a corrugated sheet steel enclosure. It was moved regularly between a location half-way to Bowness along the Bowness street railway line and on the Ogden street railway line near the Bonnybrook Bridge. In the summer it provided the additional power needed to handle increased passenger traffic to Bowness Park and during the remainder of the year it augmented the aging motor-generator sets

No. 1 Substation at 9th Ave. and 7th St. W. in 1929. The outdoor switchyard terminated two Calgary Power Company 66 kV lines.
Source: Electric System Archives

No. 1 Substation interior c. 1929. Motor generator sets supplied power for the street railway. One in foreground being overhauled. Sets were scrapped in 1954.
Source: Electric System Archives

in Number 2 Substation, located near to the CPR Ogden Shops. It was publicized in many technical journals and won R.A. Brown another round of accolades for his ingenuity. The "portable" remained in service until the mid 1960s when it was scrapped.

Two new "state-of-the-art" substations were planned and placed into service. Number 4 Substation which until this time had been located in a frame construction barn-like building on the south side of 34th Avenue S.W., between 14th and 15th streets, was relocated to the northwest corner of 34th Avenue and 14th Street S.W. It was a Spanish-type masonry building which has remained unchanged to the present day although additions have been added. It contained the very latest in metalclad switchgear and was equipped with the first supervisory controls enabling it to be operated remotely by the operator in Number 1 Substation. Another new installation, Number 5 Substation, was erected on 9th Avenue between the city hall and the police headquarters building. It was a modern two-storey building of red brick and housed indoor water-cooled transformers for local electrical distribution as well as a new 1200 kilowatt mercury-arc rectifier for street railway supply. Later it would also become a major supply point for the

No. 4 Substation built in 1928 at corner of 14th St. and 34th Ave. S.W. It was the first fully automated installation.
Source: Electric System Archives

new secondary network system in downtown Calgary. Like its new companion Number 5 Substation was also equipped for remote operation. These installations marked the first venture into the relatively unknown area of automation and were harbingers of future developments.

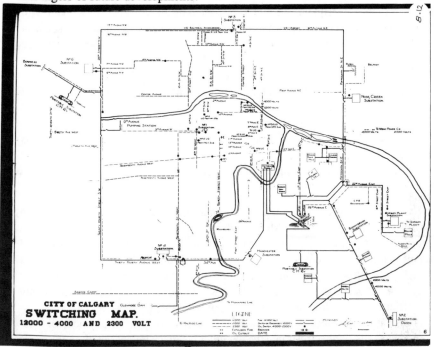

Electrical network switching map c. 1930. The "Ring Main" of 1911 is still a prominent feature.
Source: Electric System Archives

The mantle of the Great Depression did not settle over Calgary or, for that matter, the province of Alberta as quickly or dramatically as it did in those areas of North America which were highly industrialized. However, by 1932, its effects were slowly eroding the Calgary economy and a new set of problems besieged the Electric Light Department. The first problem to require attention was that of the employment of unnaturalized aliens. This issue was raised in the name of unemployment relief rather than patriotism as had been the case during the war. The Electric Light Department reported that it had three American-born employees on staff. One was J.M. ''Joe'' Rudolph, who by this time had been a tradesman employee for nineteen years but had not become a British subject (there were no Canadian citizens in those days) because ''of certain monetary interest he has in an estate in Indiana and (he) was afraid he would lose same if he took out citizenship papers in Canada."[24] However, that problem had been recently settled and Rudolph was in the process of being naturalized. Rudolph advanced to the position of assistant superintendent, a position he held until his retirement in 1956. He was one of the more colourful characters to grace the Electric Light Department and highly respected by all who knew or worked with him. His son, John Rudolph, a carbon copy of his father in appearance, became a well-known operator in the Alberta oil patch during the 1960s. Another employee who came under close examination was J.M.C. "Jimmy" Lightbody, who was described as "married and a taxpayer, employed by the City for sixteen years" who only recently applied for naturalization. Lightbody was the lone department electrical engineer. A shy retiring person he left no obvious legacy other than old drawings with his name appended. The third American "alien" was Charles C. Madson who had apparently made no effort towards naturalization since his service record was only of three years duration. Charlie, like the others, survived this silliness and put in a long service career as a truck driver until he retired in the late 1950s.

It was not long before people and organizations began to have difficulty in paying their electricity bills. All through the early years of the Great Depression the city council was flooded with requests to forgive overdue accounts or extend the period for repayment, and above all, not to eliminate the 15 percent discount which was allowed for prompt payment of accounts. For Mackay a leading indicator of the success of his department was the level of bad debts. Both he and his office manager, John Maberly, were obsessed by this view. While the generous discount allowance was a powerful incentive for prompt payment of customer accounts, it also frustrated the defaulter when the loss of the discount made the unpaid amount even more onerous. The defaulter was pursued with almost vigilante fervour until the bill was either discharged or the electricity service was discontinued. The activity to reduce the bad debt level to less that 1/10 of 1 percent of annual gross billings was in itself a fairly costly procedure. Don Little always remarked of the period that, "We were great 'counters of pencils' but we never figured out what it cost to count them." This strict attention to bad debts was an obvious expression of Mackay's Scottish thriftiness and he defended his position vigorously and successfully throughout his years in office. Lest the reader succumb to the impression that Mackay was unsympathetic to the plight of depression victims, we need to place the problem into context. It was quite possible during these difficult years for a family to obtain its entire monthly electricity needs for $1.77 and very frugal users could at least get enough light for as little as 85 cents each month. But even these amounts became difficult for many people.

Local school boards, small business enterprises, rooming house operators, landlords, service organizations and charitable groups all descended upon the council for forgiveness of utility bills. Organizations such as the YMCA, engaged in feeding and sheltering unemployed men, generally received the compassionate attention of the council which paid the outstanding bills out of its meager general revenue accounts. But wisely those costs were not passed along to the operating utility nor did the city council attempt unduly to "raid" the surpluses of the utility in those years in which they occurred. The city took its share by its policy of taxing the gross revenues of the utility and maintaining a "contribution" to general fund revenues of the city but even these amounts were not increased over what they had been in the immediate predepression years. It was a policy that paid off handsomely by enabling the utility to become nearly debt-free by the end of the Depression.

A particularly vicious attack was mounted against the rate policy of the Electric Light Department in May of 1934 by a local pressure group going under the austere title of "Landlords and Home Owners Protective Association." This group packed some political clout and its submission to the council precipitated an interesting chain of events. To highly skilled and intelligent men like Brown and Mackay, the resolution made them bristle with anger but whatever their actual feelings, they responded with an objectivity that kept the council off-guard for a year and a half. The resolution, in part, charged the Electric Light Department with devising rate schedules to purposely "extort an unequitable toll out of poor citizens of Calgary...while inhibiting the use of electricity because of high rates."[25] The practice of disallowing discounts after the due date was described as a "wicked contrivance to torture poor people." Their solution was for the city council to cut the domestic light rate by 50 percent "to conform with rates in other cities." A tabulation of rate "comparisons" with other Canadian and American cities was also included. Council, because of the political influence wielded by this protest group, did not take long to vote unanimously "in favour of a complete survey of the whole municipal electric light operation."[26] As a first step the resolution from the Protective Association was referred to Superintendent Mackay for study.

Mackay's report two weeks later was a masterpiece of rebuttal.[27] He prefaced his report with a short history of electricity rates from 1907 to the latest revisions of 1928. He showed dramatically how electricity rates had been steadily reduced in Calgary. This was followed by tabulations of the surpluses of the Electric Light Department and the amount of the contributions, taxes and rentals paid from 1918 to 1933. The figures showed that over that period twice as much money had gone to city general funds as had accumulated to the utility's benefit. This, of course, directly benefited the landlords in the form of tax relief. Mackay then went into a discussion of the local market conditions in which his utility had to meet competition, mainly from very cheap natural gas, followed by a simple explanation of the theory of rate-making: "It is a fact that the only reason that we can sell kilowatt hours for lighting purposes at 5 cents per kilowatt hour is because we sell a lot of kilowatt hours for power at 1 cent per kilowatt hour."[28] He explained how the combined lighting and heating rate for domestic use was an "incentive" rate to encourage "off-peak" use of electricity in the home by the utilization of more diverse uses of electricity other than lighting, which in turn could qualify for a lower rate. He quoted papers and outside authorities in support of his stand. For his "coup de grace" Mackay selected five typical electricity users, including domestic, commercial and power classes, with typical energy and power demands and canvassed all of the cites quoted in the original resolution from the Protective Association. The returns were carefully tabulated and the result showed that Calgary was indeed higher in typical costs than such eastern cities as Toronto and Ottawa but was significantly lower in its energy charges than the majority of the cities selected by the Protective Association. Mackay concluded:

> The amount of $8.50 as quoted by Mr. MacPherson evidently refers to an account of 200 kilowatt hours monthly consumption at 5 cents per kilowatt hour, less 15% discount. We do not know of a domestic service in this city that has such a consumption and paying the 5 cent rate. We have many domestic services that consume 200 kilowatt hours and over monthly but they are on the Combination Rate.[29]

The Mackay report, together with the original resolution from the Protective Association, was referred to an ad hoc committee chaired by Alderman J.H. Ross, who had been an electrical wiring inspector under Mackay. The committee expanded its terms of reference to include utility merchandising and policy in regard to utility finances. The committee's interim report in early July 1934 confirmed that Mackay's report on rates was unassailable. They commented, "Progress only in consideration of this matter is reported meantime." (In fact throughout the next eighteen months the committee failed to attack Mackay's report successfully on any point and by early 1936 the matter had reached a stalemate). The 9 July 1934 meeting of the committee resulted in a recommendation that "the Supt. of the Electric Light Department be afforded an opportunity of visiting various points to be decided upon by the City Commissioners with a view to acquiring first-hand authentic information"[30] with regard to the various matters contained in the committee's terms of reference. The recommendation sparked some controversy at the next council meeting with Alderman W.A. Lincoln asking, "Does this mean a trip all over North America?"[31] Council approved of the exploratory trip by only one vote and Mackay traveled a large part of North America east to Montreal and south to Chicago. In all he visited sixteen major Canadian and American cities and his report to the committee on 24 September 1934 caused it to comment that "some time will have to be given to the consideration of the large volume of information contained before any definite recommendation can be forwarded to your Council."[32]

Although Mackay addressed all of the matters connected with his trip, he was most enthusiastic about his discovery in several major eastern American cities of newly installed "secondary network" systems for the distribution of electricity in areas of concentrated electrical loads. From these systems both single phase (lighting) and polyphase (power) services were provided from a single customer service and were coupled with an extremely high level of reliability. Mackay saw the advantages of applying this system to Calgary's downtown area where the existing assets of the Calgary Water Power Company would shortly be acquired by the city, and he made immediate plans for its introduction. In a 1934 letter to the commissioners Mackay outlined his plan: "we should commence to shape our distribution system in the downtown business area so that a complete network system would be operative in about four years."[33] A year later he was reporting on the beginnings of a secondary network in the centre of the city: "The block between 7th and 8th Avenues, 2nd and 3rd Streets East was changed over to the system in September 1935."[34]

While all this attention was focused on the future of electrical supply into the downtown core, another major project which had been initiated in the earliest years of the Depression was nearing completion. Much of the original overhead distribution system, dating back to 1905, was in need of replacement. Early wood poles were not generally treated against decay and they were too short for joint-use by both electric and telephone utilities, a common and accepted practice by 1933. As these lines were replaced the original 2,300 volt primary circuits were changed to 4,000 volts. This did not require any change of copper conductors but nearly doubled the electrical capacity of the lines. All that was required was to securely "ground" the distribution system and alter the connections of the substation power transformers which supplied the distribution feeders. A primary voltage distribution system which had its neutral point solidly grounded provided a much safer system for the electricity user but it did present new dangers for the linemen who had been accustomed to "ungrounded" primary systems. As a result the working practices of tradesmen received more attention and the electrical utility industry became a pioneer in the active implementation and diligent enforcement of safe working environments for its tradesmen. By 8 February 1934 Mackay could report that, "Our replacement programme was carried through last year and our 4000 volt cutover has been completed and distribution losses continue to decrease and our regulation has been considerably improved."[35] An interesting companion innovation, which can be attributed to either Brown or Mackay, was the use of a pre-cast concrete "well" to surround the butt end of all the new poles installed from 1928 to 1933. This well was filled with creosote at the time of installation, and then sealed at ground level with an asphalt pitch. The idea was that the "wells" would be periodically replenished with the wood preservative. The reservoirs were, in fact, never refilled but many hundreds of these poles are still providing good service after almost sixty years with their "concrete rings" still intact and showing at ground level.[36]

In 1933, Mackay predicted: "we have reached the bottom of the depression and from now on conditions in general are going to be on the mend."[37] This was perhaps overly optimistic, considering that the Depression continued unabated until the commencement of World War II but after 1934 a slow annual growth in

Typical distribution pole line constructed during the late 1920s and still in use. The poles in this view all have concrete wells surrounding the treated butt buried in the ground.
Source: Bilodeau/Preston Commercial Photographers

electrical load of about 2 percent did start to appear. Mackay decided that it was the right time for the Electric Light Department to commence planning for a customer service bureau ''to advise users of electric light on the proper type, location, intensity and the use of electric light fixtures and bulbs.''[38] The National Electrical Industry in North America had introduced a program called ''Better Light, Better Sight'' and Mackay was convinced of its benefits not only to the consumer but for the electricity sales of the utility:

This campaign is being sponsored not only by those interested in the electric industry, but oculists or eye physicians, optometrists and opticians, paints and varnish manufacturers, household furnishing manufacturers, health and school authorities are taking an active interest in the preserving of the eye-sight movement.[39]

The new bureau, while given approval by the city council at the end of 1935, did not get under way until the summer of 1937 when three home economists, Kathleen Kirkland, Mary Davidson and Dorothy Dickinson, were selected and sent away for specialized training in the art of lighting and illumination.

The efforts of this specialized team were overwhelmingly accepted by the general public as both domestic and commercial users of electricity began to modernize their lighting practices. Unfortunately the program ran into the Second World War years when the availability of materials was severely restricted and by war's end, the staff of three had been reduced to Kay Kirkland, who by this time had expanded her services to more general homemaking activities and had become known as the "Home Service" girl. She remained with the Electric Light Department up to the time of her marriage in 1962. Mary Davidson married A.W. (Bert) Howard who became general manager of Calgary Power Limited and then president and chairman of the Board of Directors of TransAlta Utilities Corporation.

Fluorescent lamps, introduced in 1939, were available in commercial quantities after the war and this led to a renaissance in the art of lighting. Most approaches to commercial users to light their premises with fluorescent lighting were successful but Don Little often related the story of the crusty proprietor of the old Princess Drug Store, near the city hall and "skid row." Since many of the store's clientele had the habit of helping themselves to whatever they could manage to get away with, the idea of improving the lighting in the store was seen by the owner as an incentive for his "customers" to choose what they wanted to steal. There was "no sale" here!

R.A. Brown, in spite of the responsibilities of managing the Electric Light Department and municipal railway, maintained his interest as a consultant. He had been a principal in the formation of the United Electrical and Engineering Company of which he was president. The company had been instrumental in bringing the benefits of electricity to many Alberta towns including Bassano, Gleichen, Strathmore, Cluny, Rockyford, Olds and Okotoks, through the installation of local power plants. Most of these small rural town plants were eventually absorbed into the facilities of the Calgary Power Company as that company expanded its distribution network in southern Alberta just prior to World War II. Brown's interest in the petroleum developments of Alberta was what won him his greatest achievement. While Turner Valley, south of Calgary, was not the first Canadian area to produce petroleum products, it quickly became the centre of interest after the famous Dingman Number 1 well produced natural gas and naptha in large quantities in 1914.

Much has been written about those early discoveries and the frenzy the early "boom" years of the infant petroleum industry brought to Calgary. According to Graham McIvor, Brown's personal secretary for many years, the probability of "R.A." having been in attendance when Dingman Number 1 came into production is possible but not absolutely verifiable. For many years after the discovery in Turner Valley, the product produced was either natural gas, much of which was "flared" as a waste product, or "wet gas," condensate, or naptha as it was variously called. Some of the condensate was of a high enough gravity that it could be used as a fuel for internal combustion engines and some was pipelined to a refinery in Calgary for further processing. But crude oil it was not and it became one of R.A. Brown's obsessions to believe that crude was available in commercial quantities in the Turner Valley field.

Albert Bishop, who joined the Electric Light Department as a draftsman-clerk in 1935, remembers the plan Brown developed for finding crude oil in Turner Valley before the days of sophisticated seismic technology. The condensates or napthas produced by the various wells had differing degrees of specific gravity. Brown kept a plot of all the wells and their gravities and joined together wells of equal density thereby creating a "density contour" map. He surmised that at the centre of the contour linking the wells of highest gravities was the place to drill a well to a much greater depth than had hitherto been considered, or even believed possible. By this time Brown was deeply involved with the petroleum industry as a director of a company and in land deals which would play a dominant role in the expansion of Home Oil Company into a major Canadian-owned petroleum operation.[40] Brown could not gain serious support for his crude oil theory so he decided to take the plunge on his own. The story is that he mortgaged everything he owned to raise the required capital to initiate his venture. Brown knew that trying to finance his venture through the sale of "penny" shares would not work. The scandals which had attached themselves to earlier oil booms financed in this manner by unscrupulous promoters were still fresh in the minds of those who had been burned. Brown elected instead to offer "royalty shares" with a fixed percentage return to the investor based on the proceeds from the sale of the crude oil if and when it came into production. Bishop recalled that he, along with many other Electric Light Department employees, were offered these shares for a $500.00 investment. It seems like such a small amount by today's reckoning but these were the depression years and for most people $500.00 represented a major part of the annual salary. So although the offer was there none of Brown's contemporaries in the city were prepared to take the gamble. The rest is history. The well, Turner Valley Discovery Number I, was drilled to the unprecedented depth of nearly 7,000 feet when it "blew in" on 1 June 1936 and ushered western Canada into the modern petroleum era. The Madison limestone formation had been penetrated for the first time and Alberta would never be the same again. This, the greatest of Brown's many outstanding achievements, set the stage for his retirement from the City of Calgary.

On 20 October 1936, R.A. Brown submitted his resignation to the mayor and city commissioners. He had been with the city for exactly twenty-five years:

> In tendering this resignation I am reminded of the heavy debt of gratitude that I owe to the elected and appointed officials of the City, the staff of my Departments and in particular Mr. Robert Mackay, Superintendent of the Electric Light Department and Mr. Charles Comba, Assistant Superintendent of the Street Railway Department, for the loyal and unswerving support given me at all times.[41]

Brown praised the city administration for its policy of financing Electric Light Department extensions from revenue rather than through an increase of the capital debt. "The adoption of this policy," he wrote, "has resulted in a low capitalization, a minimum of fixed charges, and a large revenue as compared with the bonded indebtedness." The city council passed a resolution viewing, with regret, the resignation of "R. A. Brown and wishes to convey to him its most sincere gratitude and appreciation for the many excellent services rendered this City by him during the past twenty-five years as a City official."[42]

The resignation of R.A. Brown was tendered to be effective on 30 November 1936. Just eleven days before the entire Jumping Pound area west of Calgary and south of Cochrane had been devastated by a prairie fire which had been fanned by extremely high winds over a tinder-dry area. It was the famous Bushy-Ridge fire and its equal has not been seen since. The damage in the fire-swept area was catastrophic. While Calgary suffered from a pall of smoke and dust, the major loss to the city was its entire electricity supply because all four of the wooden pole transmission lines from the Bow River hydro plants to Calgary were either burned or blown down. Brown described the breakdown as a "terrible and unprecedented situation."[43] Never before had Calgary's electricity supply been in such jeopardy. Immediate relief was obtained by starting up the Victoria Park Power Plant but during the three hours it required to get the plant operational the entire city was without electrical service of any sort. The old plant was not able to handle the electrical loads being imposed upon it and had difficulty in keeping pace. Only the commercial core of the city could be supplied with electricity. The rest of the city went without until the following day when the Calgary Power Company crews succeeded in obtaining an interconnection with the East Kootenay Power Company in the Crowsnest area of southern Alberta. Meanwhile, all of the employees of the Electric Light Department were put into round-the-clock service building and maintaining a sandbag and boulder dam across the Elbow River above the Victoria Park Power Plant to capture all of the very small water flow for diversion to the plant's condensers and feed-water pumps. Mackay remarked, characteristically, about the incident that, "When times are trying that is the time to find out the mettle of your crew."[44] The final outcome of the Bushy-Ridge fire was the erection of the first steel tower transmission line between Calgary and the Ghost Hydro plant, a distance of about fifty miles. In his annual report for 1936 Mackay wrote, "we have taken up with the Calgary

Power Company the possibility of having them change one of their lines from wooden poles to steel structures, (and) we are of the opinion if one of these lines had been on steel poles we would not have been placed in the predicament we found ourselves in on November 19th, 1936.''[45] So the long era of the Brown/Mackay dynasty came to an end, but Brown's interest in and loyalty to Calgary did not terminate until his untimely death in 1948 at the age of sixty-two.

With the resignation of R.A. Brown, the city council abolished the position of general superintendent of electrical utilities and separated the Electric Light and Street Railway departments, each with its own superintendent. Robert Mackay was appointed superintendent of the Electric Light and Power Department effective December 1936, at a monthly salary of $310.00. In addition he remained in charge of the municipal airport and civic garage. He was an absolute authoritarian with his staff, even with his closest associates. Unlike Brown, he did not delegate authority easily and any sort of emergency, however minor, almost guaranteed his personal intervention and supervision. While he was highly respected by both peer and subordinate alike because of his abilities and experience, most people felt that working under him was a fearsome experience. In his memoirs Charles Dyson, a longtime lineman now retired, wrote, ''Bob Mackay worked from a meter reader to Superintendent of Electric Light and was a very smart and capable man who said what he meant and meant what he said.''[46]

Between 1927 and 1939 the total electrical load had grown by 10 percent on demand for power and 20 percent for energy. The higher rate of growth for energy usage represented only an average annual growth of 1 1/4 percent with the demand much less. In fact the growth in both demand and energy was negative for 1932-34 and in 1933 large layoffs of electrical tradesmen, particularly linemen, had occurred. In a letter addressed to the city council on 5 May 1937, Mackay named eight linemen who had been separated in ''the big lay-off of 1933'' because of lack of work. Mackay assured A.L. ''Griff'' Griffiths, who had earlier complained to the council because of the lay-off, that as soon as times improved he would rehire him. ''Mr. Griffiths is a good construction lineman and a willing worker,'' conceded Mackay.[47] Griffiths did indeed return to full employment and the tough little Welshman, who was a favourite with all, became a supervising foreman, a position he held until his retirement in 1962.

The author's only personal encounter with Bob Mackay occurred in the summer of 1947 when, as a university student, I was looking for a summer job. I was dispatched to Mackay's office where I had to wait for some time before he deigned to see me. During that time I made the acquaintance of a person who would become a most important influence in my future development. She was Gladys Belbin, personal secretary to Mackay since the 1930s. She continued in that capacity for the three department heads who would follow Mackay, including myself. She was highly respected by everyone, unexcelled as a public relations agent, and knew every facet of the operation of the Electric Light and Power

***Stampede parade float c. 1930. Centre figure is Gladys Belbin who served as
departmental secretary from 1929 to 1964.
Source: Electric System Archives***

Department. Miss Belbin ushered me into a rather austere room where this
large-framed man was bent over a rolltop desk located behind his regular working desk. After a minute or two he broke away from whatever was so intently
engaging his attention, and turning around, accosted me with the sternest pair of
steel-blue eyes, and without the slightest sign of recognition. Obviously someone
had phoned ahead to brief him of my imminent arrival for his first words were,
"So you want a job, do you?" After I had assured him that indeed I was in need
of a summer job, Mackay simply stared at me for what must have been another
two minutes. The intenseness of those eyes, coupled with no visible expression,
was a most unnerving experience that I have never forgotten. After what seemed
to be an eternity, he reached for his phone and his secretary was advised to bring
"Albert" to the office, whereupon I was surprised by the appearance of one of
my university classmates, Albert Bishop. It seemed that Bishop needed another
willing hand in completing a survey and re-mapping the Electric Light Department distribution system and so my initial encounter with that department began.
It was to last for the next thirty-one years. Mackay retired in 1948 but I did not
have occasion to meet him again until 1967 when he made one of his rare outside
appearances at a centennial year old-timer's reunion. By this time he was nearly
blind, although still as erect and stern as I had remembered him. When informed
that the bad-debt ratio for the Electric Light Department was still as low as in the
days of his reign, the stern expression suddenly vanished into a broad smile of

satisfaction. Marion Nichol, Mackay's daughter, remarked that in private life her father was a very kind man who suffered from intense shyness. Indeed Mackay had, from the beginning, supported his daughter's desire to become an artist, sending her to Europe to study under the finest tutors, and this seems the antithesis of the man who, to his contemporaries, appeared so very severe.

Most of the activity of the Electric Light Department between 1936 and 1940 consisted of refurbishing much of the old distribution facilities. It was not only necessary to maintain the quality of the service provided but it meant the retention of a minimum number of skilled tradesmen during the difficult depression years. The successful operation of any enterprise, and particularly one in which the product being marketed is one which the public tends to view as a perpetual right, requires people with skills and experience. This was a factor that Peter Prince recognized, making his enterprise publicly acceptable while that of his earliest competitor failed. Mackay used his remaining tradesmen to full advantage, taking up any slack by rotating them between the overhead line rebuilding program and the new underground secondary network system gradually evolving in the downtown commercial district.

In 1937 the first three-phase submersible network transformers had been installed and the first "network protectors" were purchased. These devices enabled the low voltage winding of the transformers to be solidly interconnected, providing a degree of electrical service continuity hitherto unknown. By the end of 1939, secondary network service had been extended to all users of electrical power in the downtown core between 6th and 9th avenues from 4th Street W. to 3rd Street E. The installed capacity was 4,000 kilovolt amperes (KVA) with a demand of just over 3,000. It was the first secondary network system installed in western Canada and the third in Canada, having been preceded by Toronto and Hamilton. It represented the crowning technical achievement of Mackay's tenure as superintendent. In his 1939 annual report to council, Mackay remarked that, "The network system is working out very satisfactory and our load is increasing....While the full benefit of this system will not be reached until 1954, we are now securing results that are beneficial and reducing our distribution costs and in addition giving us a guarantee of continuity of service in the downtown area."

The last major development of the Depression Decade was the move of two city utilities, electric light and waterworks, to a new location on 6th Avenue W., between Centre Street and 1st Street W. The Electric Light Department had maintained administrative quarters in the basement of the old city hall since it opened in 1911. In an effort to ease unemployment the federal government in 1939 enacted the Municipal Improvements Assistance Act under which it would contribute 50 percent of the labour costs of approved municipal projects and finance the remainder of the cost at an interest rate of 2 percent. It did not take long for the city council to act and by April 1939 contracts were awarded for the erection of the new building. It was, at that time, the largest single building

Utilities building of 1939. The clock and decorative wall fixtures were never added because of cost constraints. It was sold to Alberta Government Telephones in 1958.
Source: Electric System Archives

project in downtown Calgary and it had the honour of being the first fully air-conditioned office building in the city. In Mackay's words:

> We started to move into the new building on Friday, December 1st, and by 2 o'clock Saturday morning, December 2nd, all equipment and furniture were in place ready for business.... The building was open for public inspection on Saturday, December 2nd from 2 p.m. to 5 p.m. About 5000 people took advantage of this invitation and they seemed to be very much impressed by the building and the modern machinery used in our many various operations necessary to produce a service account and to keep records and amass valuable distribution figures in order to keep control.[48]

The new Utilities Building served as the focal point of the civic utilities until 1957 when it became too small and entirely inadequate for the needs of a city on the eve of its second major expansion cycle. It was sold to Alberta Government Telephones who still maintain it as a commercial marketing outlet.

By 1938 there were positive signs that the worst of the Depression was coming to an end. The new Currie Military Barracks in southwest Calgary were completed in 1937, and the British American Refinery in east Calgary was completed in 1939, each adding significant electrical loads. The amalgamation

Main floor view of utilities building c. 1939.
Source: Electric System Archives

of all of the Calgary Water Power Company services into the city utility added to the load growth and an air of optimism prevailed. "The use of electric current in the home, factory, office and store is becoming more popular and more dependence is being placed on electric service to provide comfort, ease and economy," reported Mackay as he summarized his 1938 report to city council. World War II overshadowed this recovery and almost overnight the dreadful mantle of the Great Depression years vanished only to be replaced by the uncertainties of what this equally dreadful new circumstance might produce.

The reality of the Second World War meant the addition of new electrical loads which were war-related. Enlarged training facilities for the Canadian Army at Mewata Park and Currie Barracks, coupled with four major Royal Canadian Air Force facilities consisting of two Service Flying Training Schools, a Wireless School and the Equipment and Repair Depot in east Calgary, brought immediate and substantial electricity demands. The CPR Ogden Repair Shops were converted into facilities for the manufacture of naval guns and were in operation around the clock. The old Manitoba Rolling Mills in east Calgary, which had barely operated since the onset of the Great Depression, was reactivated for steel production. Between 1939 and 1942, a 50 percent increase in both electrical demand and energy took place. After 1942 the growth levelled off and did not show any significant increase until 1947. Mackay's immediate response to the war was concern over material shortages and rising prices, and within one month

***Electric Light Department administration office on second floor of
new utilities building c. 1939.***
Source: Electric System Archives

of the declaration of war he was busy stockpiling copper wire and distribution
transformers.

Another concern was the possibility of sabotage. Power plant and substation
windows were heavily screened, doors reinforced and kept securely locked,
floodlights erected and visits by other than utility employees forbidden. At the
very beginning of the war guards were actually posted at the major points of
electricity supply but by the end of 1939 Mackay commented, ''We found later it
was not necessary to maintain guards, it was felt that all suspects had by that time
been apprehended and placed in internment camps.''[49] Council again expressed
concern over security in late 1940. Some aldermen felt that citizens should start
stockpiling candles or coal oil lamps in case electricity supplies were sabotaged.
Bob Mackay was now unimpressed, pointing out that through the interconnection system of the Calgary Power Company, the city had access to power supplies
from East Kootenay, Lethbridge and Edmonton, all of which were additional to
the hydro plants on the Bow River and the Victoria Park Power Plant. Mackay
assured the aldermen:

> I don't think that any of our substations will be subjected to destruction as the
> elimination of almost any of our substations would be only a nuisance.... The
> supplying of foodstuffs in the shape of meats and hams, etc., is one of our greatest
> endeavours and we believe their plants could be crippled more effectively than by
> just cutting off electric service.[50]

Electric Light truck decorated for 1940 Victory Bond Parade.
Source: Electric System Archives

At this stage of the war there was every anticipation that the hostilities in Europe would not last long: "We hope and anticipate the war will not be of long duration and the outcome will be decisively in the favour of Great Britain and her allies; then we can with reasonable confidence look forward to a big increase in business in the near future."[51] Mackay's musing reflected the general attitude prevailing in the early days, but as time passed it dawned on everyone that this would not be a skirmish of short duration.

The Electric Light Department numbered about 100 permanent employees in 1942. The office staff, including all those who were involved in meter reading and billing and collection of customer accounts, numbered fifty-six. The remainder were tradesmen and their associated foremen and labourers engaged in the construction and maintenance requirements of the physical plant.[52] While most of those employees serving in administrative positions were too old to enlist by the end of 1941, enlistments from the younger members of the staff were becoming a regular event and by 1942 Mackay reported that "all eligible men have now joined up." In the office women were being hired to fill vacant jobs and they were found to be more than adequate replacements. In the male-dominated work world of 1942, it must have been with some chagrin that Mackay wrote, "We find these girls are doing a splendid job." In other areas Mackay was reluctant to refill positions, especially those of tradesmen, when the incumbents left for war.

He was concerned over their reinstatement into their jobs when the war ended and while he had the option of bringing in young men who were not old enough to enlist to serve apprenticeships he refused because of the "possibility of us having two or three men for each job available." Later, some apprenticeships were reluctantly established, but even after these men served their four-year apprenticeships, Mackay still refused to promote them to journeymen because of his concern about not having enough jobs open for returning tradesmen veterans. In the end it all turned out to the advantage of both groups. All returning veterans got their old jobs back and there was enough demand for additional tradesmen to support the promotion of the "four-year" apprentices to full journeymen.

An interesting bit of Electric Light Department family trivia cropped up in late 1940 when Mackay replied to a council request for a list of employees who were "related by blood or marriage to any heads of Departments, Foremen or Elected Officials of the City of Calgary."[53] Two brothers, W.S. "Scotty" Read and J.R. "Jack" Read, foremen in the meter repair and construction divisions respectively, were married to sisters of R. Mackay, making them brothers-in-law to the superintendent. The brothers had married Mackay's sisters on the same day, 23 August 1940. Also mentioned were two Wilson brothers, K.B. "Kay" and H.M. "Mont", who worked as foremen in the Trouble and Construction divisions respectively. The Wilson brothers had learned their trade as apprentices in the Electric Light Department, starting in 1922, and served long and distinguished careers until their retirement in the early years following the war. "Mont" Wilson, in particular, was remembered because of his huge frame which seemed to completely fill the cab of any truck in which he rode, and his habit of rarely speaking. He had a unique way of communicating his orders by pointing his fingers in various ways. J.E. "Tommy" Elliott who would, in the postwar years, become the supervisor of underground construction, was the son of J.R. Elliott and both father and son worked together as tradesmen.

In another relationship by marriage, J.N. "Joe" Rudolph, who became assistant superintendent of the Electric Light Department toward the end of the war, and W. "Bill" Schopp, a foreman in the meter room, had married sisters thereby becoming brothers-in-law. They had married some years after becoming employees of the department. W.A. "Bill" Northover, the longtime stoic accountant for the department, had two sisters, one of whom married J.E. "John" Maberly, office manager responsible for the billing and collection of electric light customer accounts, and the other who married J. Barnes, manager of the Calgary General Hospital which was also owned and operated by the city. Finally, there were two brothers, G.A. "George" and H.J. "Bert" Tyler, who were employed in the Trouble and Meter divisions respectively. George was not as well known as Bert who became the supervisor of meters, retiring shortly after the war ended and living a full and robust life well into nonagenarian years. Mackay ended his report with an apology: "We would like to point out that at many times during the past 30 years it was almost impossible to get men who could do our class of work in the Electric Light Department and we found it necessary to pick up capable workmen regardless of their relationship with any other employee or Official in the employ of the City.''[54]

The difficult years of the Second World War were coming to an end in 1945 when Mackay reported that thirty-three members of his staff had enlisted in the armed services out of a total personnel establishment of just over 100: ''We are handicapped on being short in our Engineering staff. We have been in this position for nearly two years, but we purposely kept from bringing in engineers to our staff in order to give some of our younger men who had enlisted in the Services a chance at these positions.''[55] Curiously, Mackay never mentioned anything in his annual reports about the death of J.N. Lightbody who had been the department electrical engineer for nearly a quarter of a century. The end of the war brought Mackay to the realization that he could not wait to fill Lightbody's vacant position and so he hired J.H. ''Harvey'' Wilson, the second outside professional engineer since R.A. Brown was retained by Commissioner Graves in 1911.

During the war the utility's physical plant remained almost static due in large part to the extreme difficulty in obtaining the necessary materials. Those expansions which did take place, notably to the downtown core secondary network, were undertaken under the watchful eye of the appropriate federal government rationing boards. As the war neared its end in 1945, a new substation was planned to replace a temporary installation which had been in place for many years on 24th Street N.W. at about 5th Avenue, and in the logical progression of numbering was designated as Number 6 Substation. Mackay conceived a new idea for eliminating the cost of a substation building. The high and low voltage outdoor metal-enclosed switchgear would sit on top of an elevated reinforced concrete slab which would form the roof of a basement in which control panels, batteries and washroom facilities would be housed. The substation, with only minor changes, is still operating and, together with the secondary network, remains as a reminder of the ingenuity of Robert Mackay. Another first occurred in 1946 with the purchase of a 5,000 kVA 3-phase power transformer, the largest to this time, for installation at Number 4 Substation.

In the years immediately preceding the war Mackay had often complained to the city commissioners about the lack of communication with the operating field crews and expressed the hope that this would be soon remedied by the use of a two-way radio system which was very much in its infancy. In 1947 the first commercial application in Calgary of the new frequency-modulated (FM) mobile radio was completed as eight units were installed in various Electric Light Department operating vehicles. While Mackay had to wait for nearly a decade, he finally had the communication network he wanted in the form of the best and most reliable system available.

The rural distribution network surrounding the city limits had become quite extensive by the end of the war and it was discovered that permission to operate such lines beyond the limits of the city was required from the Public Utilities Board. In some handwritten notes accountant A.W. "Bill" Northover described the history of the beginning of line extensions beyond the city limits. The first line was extended to the Country Club adjacent to 50th Avenue South in 1912, but ownership remained with the club. Then in 1915 the federal government paid for a line extension into the Sarcee Military Training Camp south of 50th Avenue at 37th Street S.W. The Lacombe Home line to Midnapore followed in 1921, with the city regaining ownership in 1927. Bowness followed with the acquisition of the assets in 1921, further extending the "rural" service area westwards. The Shepard line extension to service the RCAF Wireless School at the beginning of the war was extended further south in 1948 to the Bow River to service all of the farmers in that area with the first major rural electrification scheme. The extent of this project probably focused the attention of the Public Utilities Board on the fact that its permission had not been sought as was required by legislation. After a year of meetings, interviews and correspondence between Mackay and officials of the Public Utilities Board, a Board Order was granted, consolidating the area into which the Electric Light Department could extend its electrical service and the rates which could be charged.[56]

On 1 June 1948 Robert Mackay wrote to the mayor and commissioners of his intention to retire on 31 July, after forty years of continuous service to the city. The only candidates for his job were J.M. Rudolph, Assistant Superintendent, and J.H. Wilson, the newly hired electrical engineer. Joe Rudolph did not wish to be considered and elected to serve out his remaining years as assistant superintendent. The mantle fell to Wilson whom Mackay viewed with a fair amount of animosity. In consideration of the education and experience Wilson brought to his job, Mackay recommended him as his replacement: "Mr. Wilson has the technical training, experience and executive ability to take over the duties of the position now held by me and I would so recommend to you."[57] The Brown/Mackay dynasty which began in 1908 was finally over. Robert MacKay died at the age of eighty-nine on 27 February 1970. V.A. Newhall, who was the city commissioner when Mackay retired said simply, "I know of no finer administrator in the West." It was a fitting epitaph.

References

1. City Clerk's Papers. Letter dated 18 February 1908. R. Mackay to Mayor and Aldermen.

2. City Clerk's Papers. Letter dated 15 April 1910. C.A. O'Brien to City Commissioners.

3. City of Calgary. *Annual Report* 1911.

4. Dr. Steimetz was a pioneer in alternating current theory and development.

5. City Clerk's Papers, b4.f19. Letter dated 5 October 1910. R.A. Brown to A.G. Graves.

6. City of Calgary (Consolidated) *Annual Report* 1912. "City Electricians' Report for 1912." Additional quotation from the same report.

7. City of Calgary (Consolidated) *Annual Report* 1913. "Report of the City Electrician."

8. Ibid.

9. City of Calgary (Consolidated) *Annual Report* 1913. "Report of Wiring Inspector."

10. City of Calgary (Consolidated) *Annual Report* 1913. "Electric Vehicle Department."

11. "Cases to be Probed by Special Committee," *Calgary Herald*, 31 March 1914.

12. "Aldermen Climb Light Poles to Probe Accident," *Calgary Herald*, 3 April 1914.

13. Ibid.

14. Council Minutes, 30 March 1914, p.193. Extract from Commissioners' Report.

15. "Some Department Heads Likely to Get Increases," *Calgary Herald*, 7 April 1914.

16. Council Minutes, 22 November 1915, p. 813.

17. Council Minutes, 25 April 1919, p.243.

18. Council Minutes, 14 June 1920, p.443-448.

19. Council Minutes, 28 July 1920, p.494.

20. Council Minutes, 11 July 1921, p.415.

21. Council Minutes, 26 February 1924, p.70.

22. Council Minutes, 26 June 1928, p. 305.

23. Council Minutes, 4 March 1927, p.92.

24. Council Minutes, 14 March 1932, p. 156.

25. Council Minutes, 28 May 1934, p.542.

26. "Survey of Light Department Rates Planned," *Calgary Herald*, 29 May 1934.

27. Council Minutes, 25 June 1934, p. 661-667. Mackay's report is a model of the sort of submission that would go before a modern regulatory authority. It contained all of the necessary elements and arguments that would appeal to a regulatory body: "The primary object of a rate structure is to derive a certain total amount of revenue necessary to pay all fixed charges, taxes, labour and material and to get this revenue in the simplest and most equitable manner, allocating charges according to the class of service rendered, due consideration being given to other competitive methods of service."

28. "Survey of Light Department Rates Planned," *Calgary Herald*, 29 May 1934.

29. Ibid.

30. Council Minutes, 9 July 1934, p. 725.

31. *Calgary Herald*, 10 July 1934.

32. Council Minutes, 12 November 1934, p.1148.

33. City Clerk's Papers, b.337.f835. Letter dated 26 September 1934. Mackay to Mayor and Commissioners.

34. Electric Light Department. *Annual Report* 1935.

35. Electric Light Department. *Annual Report* 1933. The term "regulation" is a technical term to describe the permissible limits of voltage drop from normal under conditions of varying electrical demands.

36. Poles from the 1930s onward were almost always "butt" treated to prevent rot in that portion of the pole below ground level. However, since the poles were climbed by linemen using "spurs" the damage caused by constant climbing could soon cause decay above ground level. During the 1950s it became common practice to "pressure treat" poles along their entire length and with the advent of man-lift devices in the 1960s, the need to climb poles using spurs was greatly reduced. Pressure-treated poles installed today should last 100 years or more and this is another reason for the increasing wider use of underground distribution facilities.

37. Electric Light Department. *Annual Report* 1933, dated 8 February 1934.

38. Council Minutes, 12 November 1935. Report from R. Mackay to Commissioner T.B. Riley. p.900.

39. Ibid.

40. In his book, *Troublemaker*, James H. Gray has written a fascinating account of R.A. Brown's early exploits in the Turner Valley Oil patch.

41. Council Minutes, 9 November 1936, p.1005.

42. Council Minutes, 23 November 1936. p.1030.

43. "Calgary Power Service Normal Following Break Caused by Fire, Storm," *Calgary Herald*, 20 November 1936.

44. Electric Light Department. *Annual Report* 1936.

45. Ibid.

46. City of Calgary. Electric System Archives. Memoirs of C.J. Dyson, used by permission.

47. Council Minutes, 25 May 1937, p.441.

48. Electric Light Department. *Annual Report* 1938.

49. Electric Light Department. *Annual Report* 1939.

50. Council Minutes, 12 February 1941. p.99.

51. Electric Light Department. *Annual Report* 1940.

52. In his annual report for 1940, Mackay took time to list by name the "personnel of the administrative staff of the Electric Light, Heat and Power System." They were:

Assistant Superintendent: George Notley
Superintendent, Underground Division: E.D. Guinn
Engineer: J.N. Lightbody
Office Manager: J.E. Maberley
Accountant: N. McGlashen
Cost Accountant: A.W. Northover
Superintendent, Operating Division: E.R. Malcolm
Distribution Engineer: J.M. Rudolph
Superintendent, Meter Division: H.I. Tyler
Superintendent, Maintenance Division: A. Weeks

The author knew all of the above except Lightbody, who died during the war, and Weeks who had been replaced by A. Neiman. At time of writing only one has survived, N. McGlashen, who at latest report is living in a nursing home in Edmonton, Alberta.

53. Council Minutes, 12 November 1940. p.658.

54. Ibid.

55. Electric Light Department. *Annual Report* 1945.

56. Public Utilities Board, Alberta, Board Order No.11278, 22 March 1948. Map filed with Board.

57. Council Minutes, 8 June 1948, p.597.

Chapter 9

A DECADE OF TRANSITION

The appointment of J.H. (Harvey) Wilson as the superintendent of the Electric Light, Heat and Power Department in the summer of 1948 marked a significant change in both the management style and the growth pattern of the utility. From then until his resignation on 31 March 1960 the demand for electrical power increased from 38,000 to 140,000 kilowatts. It was also the period when, with few exceptions, all of those who had established lengthy service records under the Brown/Mackay dynasty retired, leaving room for increased staff to meet the needs of Calgary's growth. Many of the new staff were young professionals who had acquired post-secondary education at either universities or technical schools as a benefit derived from their war service status. This crop of relatively young intruders brought no bias from prior job relationships but were often viewed with suspicion by their more experienced counterparts. For the most part, however, the transition was accepted in the spirit of friendly rivalry.

Harvey Wilson was himself an intruder. He had appeared on the scene in 1946 as a complete stranger and was instantly at loggerheads with Robert Mackay. However, the two men grudgingly tolerated each other up to the time of Mackay's retirement when Mackay recommended that Wilson succeed him as superintendent. Mackay could not have made a better choice in view of the tremendous changes which were to take place in the decade after 1948 and for which Wilson's unique talents were well suited.

The author's first encounter with Harvey Wilson occurred in the summer of 1947. A small group of student engineers were hired to make a comprehensive field survey of the electrical distribution system from which new office records would be prepared. In the course of this project we were assigned to a room on the second floor of the Utilities Building. The room had as it basic furnishing a long flat table at which three people could work together preparing maps from field survey records. One day a rather paunchy man sauntered unannounced into

233

No. 6 Substation, 1948. Mackay's last project after 40 continuous years of service.
Location, 24th St. at 5th Ave. N.W.
Source: Electric System Archives.

the room, and sat down in a chair which he tipped back by resting his feet on the table. The soles of his shoes had holes and the man presented an altogether threadbare appearance. He was, however, a most pleasant and gregarious person. This was Wilson. He had just finished having a "big row" with Mackay over details of plans that Wilson was preparing for the new Number 6 Substation which was to be the crowning achievement of Mackay's career. Wilson's technical background was impeccable and he wanted certain details altered in the plan. Mackay, being the authoritarian that he was, did not take long to tell Wilson what he thought of his ideas and Wilson did not hesitate to press his point in return. Mackay had never been accustomed to having his subordinates argue with him so the altercations between the two were quite common, much to the amusement of the small staff located immediately outside Mackay's office. Wilson, however, would calm down very quickly after these encounters, usually by telling stories from his seemingly inexhaustible past experiences. As young student engineers we were immensely impressed with this congenial fellow and always looked forward to his unscheduled visits and stories.

Wilson was born in 1900 in Qu'Appelle, Saskatchewan. His father was engaged in a general contracting business in that historic town, just east of Regina on the CPR main line. It is not known how the Wilson family came to be in that part of the Canadian prairies but a daughter, Mrs. Tom Pinder, remembered that the family had come from Ontario. Wilson trained himself as a telegrapher and worked parttime for the CPR in Qu'Appelle, earning enough money to enroll in the Faculty of Applied Science at the University of British Columbia in 1920. He finished his undergraduate studies at the universities of Saskatchewan and Manitoba, graduating from the latter in 1925. Work was scarce in Canada so he went to Chicago where he worked for the Byllesby Engineering and Management Corporation, the owners and operators of power companies in many American states. He met his future wife, Merne, in Chicago where she was training to be a professional singer. She had come from Calgary, her family having homesteaded at Elnora near Red Deer. After their marriage in Calgary, the Wilsons returned to Chicago but because of the lack of employment moved to Arvida, Quebec, where Harvey joined the Aluminum Company of Canada. He gained invaluable hydro-power plant experience from his association with Dr. F.A. Gaby, chief engineer of the Ontario Hydro Electric Power Commission in designing a new power plant at Seven Rapids on the Upper Ottawa River. In 1938 Wilson moved to Baie Comeau, Quebec, where he was appointed electrical superintendent of the hydro plant and electrical distribution facilities of the large paper mill owned by Colonel McCormack, of *Chicago Tribune* newspaper fame.

In view of the recent election of Brian Mulroney as Prime Minister of Canada, it is of interest that Mulroney's father worked directly under Harvey Wilson as a plant electrician in the paper mill. In fact, the Mulroneys and Wilsons were neighbours and young Brian, as a frequent visitor, is remembered by Wilson's daughter as a very nice, well-behaved boy.

Wilson's tenure with the paper mill extended into the early years of the Second World War, by which time his wife Merne had become the editor of the paper plant's "in house" newspaper. She was a strong supporter of Great Britain and the monarchy and voiced no uncertain criticism of Colonel McCormack and the anti-British stand he heralded through the *Chicago Tribune*. While Wilson did not lose his position with the paper mill because of his wife's editorial activities, it was rumoured that word of these activities reached the ear of McCormack himself. Toward the end of the war Wilson and a friend, Bill Rounding, also from Baie Comeau, decided that they were tired of working for someone else and together planned a contracting business to build houses that they were certain would be in short supply after the war end. They decided to set up the business in Calgary where Wilson moved his family in 1945. Unfortunately, due to lack of an adequate supply of building materials and Rounding's desire to return to eastern Canada, the contracting partnership ended after they had built about twenty houses and Wilson was again looking for employment. This coincided exactly with Robert Mackay's decision to hire a replacement engineer for the deceased Jim Lightbody. Wilson happened to drop in to the Electric Light Department office looking for employment and was hired forthwith in late 1946.

Wilson's management style was the antithesis of that of his predecessor. The authoritarian management style was, of course, the order of the day before World

War II although certain individuals, like R.A. Brown, occasionally broke the pattern. Harvey Wilson, however, went far beyond the limits that even Brown would have considered appropriate. The initial shock of Wilson's succession as superintendent was devastating. Suddenly the management survivors from Mackay's regime were faced, under Wilson's role of delegating authority, with the problem of deciding for themselves what actions were necessary in the regular performance of their duties, and coordinating these decisions with their fellows. Under the leadership of this tolerant and friendly superintendent some of the "old-guard" supervisors were able to respond with varying degrees of success but the real opportunities provided by Wilson's openness were largely exploited by those who saw the advancement opportunities which would present themselves as the older employees retired.

When the author, fresh out of university, began permanent employment with the Electric Light Department in 1949, the "old guard" was still very much intact, except for Mackay. and H.J. (Bert) Tyler, the Meter Room supervisor, who had retired shortly after the war ended. His successor was D.S. (Don) Brown, brother of R.A. Brown. Joe Rudolph, who held the dual positions of assistant superintendent and supervisor of overhead lines under Mackay and during the early years of Wilson's regime, came to Calgary from Chicago shortly after the end of the First World War. In every respect "Joe" was a genuine "character." Tall, handsome and debonair, he could spend an hour carefully explaining to a female customer the reasons why it cost as much as estimated to extend electrical service to her rural address. If there were children to accommodate during the interview he would set them at his desk and open all the drawers for them to rummage through without a word of complaint after they left. He tried his best to display sternness to his subordinates but was always betrayed by his genuinely good nature. He would fire an employee one day to maintain his image and rehire him the next, without batting an eye. The throngs of friends who attended his retirement party in 1957 were living tribute to the high regard in which this unique man was held. He always said that he wanted to "die with his boots on" and that is exactly what happened while playing on his favourite Inglewood golf course.

E.D. (Ted) Guinn was the supervisor of underground lines. From his birth-place in Kitchener, Ontario, he had moved through Winnipeg, Melfort and Regina, before arriving in Calgary in 1913 as a qualified cable splicer, a trade he learned with Bell Telephones. A gregarious man with a booming voice, he could always be heard approaching from a great distance. One never mistook this fellow with his broad smile, set off by gold-capped teeth, his dark suit, always vested, complete with heavy watch chain and elk's-tooth fob. In the days before the city engineering department had devised strict procedures to be used before any street was opened for utility installations, Guinn would simply point out to his foreman where he was to excavate for manhole construction and their inter-connecting duct lines. To the author's knowledge, Guinn rarely damaged or hit the buried facilities of other utilities. How he managed to know where everything was located always remained a mystery. He also retired about the same time as Joe Rudolph.

E.R. (Roy) Malcolm, was supervisor of substations. He arrived in Calgary before any of his contemporaries and his first job was to fire coal into the boilers of the original city-owned Atlantic Avenue Power Plant. He apprenticed as an electrician and after World War I advanced to the position he held until his retirement. Roy Malcolm seemed to have the quality of never aging. The author first encountered him in 1939 when he was one of a group of electrical technology students who were visiting the Electric Light Department. Ten years later, as a new university graduate, I met him again and was amazed by the fact that he looked exactly the same. He remained that way to the day of his retirement in 1956.

A lesser known member of the "old guard" was Arthur Neiman, supervisor of trouble. His background is entirely obscure. A lineman by trade, he was a gentle, soft spoken man, who had been promoted into his supervisory position quite late in his working career. He retired in 1957.

John E. Maberly, office manager in charge of billing and collections, was, like Mackay, a stern disciplinarian. He guarded office pencils as if they were cash, and, in true military style, a new one could only be obtained by surrendering the old stub. He was a compulsive statistician. For every category of electrical consumption he would divide the monthly revenue by the monthly sales of kilowatt hours, carrying the resulting figure out to six decimals even though the last four places were insignificant. Somehow it gave him a great sense of satisfaction and no one dared suggest that the figures could be rounded off to two decimal places. A.W. (Bill) Northover, the department accountant, was a bachelor who believed in using a minimum number of words to describe any occasion. He would sit behind his desk puffing on his pipe getting up occasionally to push his pencil into some mysterious opening in the back of his electric calculator which would, from time to time, refuse to stop calculating. His desk drawers overflowed with papers from which he always seemed to be able to extract the answer to any question about the accounts. He was a delightful character who could have come right out of a Dickens novel. He retired in 1958 and died shortly thereafter.

A group photograph taken in March 1948 of the Western Zone delegates to the Canadian Electrical Association is included in the pictorial record of this book and contains the only remaining composite record of most of these unique supervisors. Harvey Wilson inherited all of them as his key management group during his initial years as superintendent.

Beginning in 1948 electricity usage in Calgary showed signs of moving to a higher plateau. The average demand of 2 percent per annum which had been

Group photo of delegates to Canadian Electrical Association Spring Meeting in Calgary 1948. Electric light department personnel identified as marked.
Source: Electric System Archives.

1. E. Guinn — Underground Supervisor 2. A. Nieman — Trouble Supervisor 3. J.H. Wilson — Electrical Engineer 4. R. Mackay — Superintendent 5. E. Malcolm — Substation Supervisor 6. J. Rudolph — Assistant Supervisor characteristic of 1923-48 increased slowly until by 1950 it was obvious that the trend was imbedded in the local economy. In fact, that new plateau was an average annual increase of 9 percent between 1948 and 1958. Such a level of electricity demand quickly translated into the urgent need for substantial new plant facilities and providing this in an orderly and efficient manner could no longer be left to the relatively static planning process of the two previous decades. Wilson reported to the commissioners in 1949 on an enlarged "in house" engineering activity with the addition of A.A. (Albert) Bishop, and the author, both having recently graduated from the University of Alberta: "Their time has been completely taken up with studying means for taking care of system growth. With their help a comprehensive five year program has been tentatively drawn up, so that expansion will take place in an orderly fashion."[1] Suddenly there was a demand for new housing and the city developed its first large post-war residential subdivision in southwest Calgary called Knob Hill.

It was the author's first major project to provide for the distribution facilities to service this newly developed area with electricity. The city also started to renovate its antiquated street railway system with the introduction of electric trolley buses which required either the replacement or relocation of old direct current conversion equipment. This project, as well as new additions required in

No. 1 Substation, 1952.
Source: Electric System Archives

the downtown secondary network area, was undertaken by Bishop. The engineers were joined by an extraordinary electrical tradesman who had arrived in the administrative office of the Electric Light Department near the end of the war, assisting both Wilson, while he was the department engineer, and Joe Rudolph in his capacity as the overhead line supervisor. Edward Walker became part of the "troika" which would play a large part in the future corporate structure of the utility as it expanded in size to become one of the largest municipally-owned electical utilities in Canada.

The Electric Light Department acquired a new name about this time. The author was responsible for producing his own engineering drawings as was the

Installing secondary network transformer in under-sidewalk vault c. 1956.
Source: Electric System Archives

practice in previous years. It is customary to have drawings checked and approved by others before they are accepted for construction purposes. This had been done in the past by sets of initials and dates placed at random locations on the drawings but the idea of using a standard title block to provide those required spaces had not caught on. The author decided that a standardized title block was representative of good engineering practice and set about to include one on all drawings. The existing title was long and awkward and did not seem to reflect the new dynamic of the enterprise. So the name "City of Calgary Electric System" was arbitrarily chosen for inclusion in the drawing title block. It gained instant acceptance but did not receive formal santion until 1971. On 26 July 1971 By-law 94-75 respecting the administration of the city electrical utility was passed by council and the name "Electric System" was officially adopted.

Postwar technology produced an exciting array of new materials and products. In particular, a new plastic insulation with the generic name of polyethylene provided electrical utilities with a whole range of new applications. Prior to 1940 most underground high voltage power cables were insulated with special paper wrappings which were then oil-impregnated and sheathed with a lead covering to provide a barrier against the loss of the oil, and for mechanical protection. These cables were expensive but were widely used from the earliest days of the industry. Low voltage wires of less than 600 volts were insulated with rubber compounds and, after 1939, with polyvinyl chloride (PVC) plastic but neither insulation was entirely adequate for high voltage application. Polyethylene plastic, however, could be modified to meet almost any desired electrical characteristic for insulation in addition to having excellent mechanical properties thus providing the potential for the development of low-cost underground residential distribution systems. It did not take long for Edward Walker to realize the potential. Using standard sections of concrete pipes in which to house ordinary distribution transformers and the terminal blocks from which houses could be serviced, a trial installation was designed and installed in late 1950 to service the homes in a small subdivision along Crestview Road in southwest Calgary. This installation became a prototype for postwar low-cost residential underground distribution systems and attracted national and international interest through the Canadian Electrical Association and the American Institute of Electrical Engineers.[2]

By 1953 the old 12,000 volt "ring main" which had been built around the perimeter of the city in 1911-12 had reached its capacity and while its usefulness was extended temporarily by breaking up the original "ring main" into several smaller "rings," it was merely an interim solution. The 4,000 volt grounded four-wire system which had served as the primary distribution system in the city since the 1930s was no longer suitable as the city expanded and distances became greater. After considerable study, Bishop recommended that all newly developed areas be serviced by a 13,200 volt grounded four-wire distribution system which, for the same area serviced, would provide for a four-fold increase in capability over that of the old 4,000 volt system. Its implementation required a new 66,000 volt "ring main" around the perimeter of the expanded limits of the city. Since the existing wholesale power contract with Calgary Power provided for delivery of electricity at 13,200 volts, it was necessary to solicit Calgary Power's cooperation in building the higher voltage "ring" and the required substations to reduce the voltage to 13,200 volts at the appropriate locations. The company concurred fully with the city plan on the understanding that at some future date the city would purchase the high voltage "ring" main and the associated substations.

The new Bearspaw hydro plant became the western terminus of the new 66,000 volt ring. The first section of the line ran from Bearspaw eastward along the southern foot of Nose Hill to 24th Street S.E. (Barlow Trail) and then south to finally terminate at Calgary Power's East Calgary Substation in Highfield. The first substation was located at 48th Avenue and 6th Street N.E., serving Thorncliffe

No. 1 Substation, 1985. All 138kV overhead lines have been replaced by 138kV underground cables.
Source: Bilodeau/Preston Commercial Photographers

subdivision with the new distribution voltage. By 1955 the 66,000 volt ring was extended around the southern half of the city so that nearly all new development could be serviced at the new distribution voltage, although some additional 4,000 volt facilities were added within the area defined by the original 12,000 volt ring main. Any expansion of the 4,000 volt area was virtually restricted after 1960.

Calgary's postwar growth was due in no small part to the developing Alberta petroleum industry. The 1947 discovery well, Leduc Number I, established the fact that major oil fields existed in areas other than Turner Valley. Despite the fact that the new oil fields were now favouring central and northern Alberta, Calgary remained the base for the head offices of all the major oil companies that poured into Alberta to exploit the newly-found petroleum resources. This activity placed even greater pressures upon Calgary to supply serviced land for housing and commercial and industrial facilities of all types. All of this activity translated into escalating electrical consumption. When Wilson succeeded Mackay in 1948 the total staff numbered about 170, of which approximately 60 percent were trades-men or trades-related employees. The remainder was involved in administration, billing and collections, and accounting. Over fifty administrative, wiring inspection and engineering staff were crowded into an area of 2,500 square feet on the second floor of the seventeen-year old Utilities Building. The Waterworks Department occupied the remaining half of the floor area and it too was expanding in response to Calgary's growth.

Victoria Park Power Plant being dismantled, 1953.
Source: Electric System Archives

Clearly some new space arrangements were urgently needed. The original plan in 1954 was to remodel the old Victoria Park Power Plant building vacated following the removal of all the machinery in 1953. The renovation plan proved to be too costly and the Calgary Exhibition and Stampede Board wanted the old building as part of its expansion plans. An entirely new office and service centre complex was decided upon as the best answer to the needs of the Electric Light Department and a site was chosen at the intersection of 25th Avenue and Spiller Road S.E., immediately north of the Burnsland Cemetery. The new complex would consolidate all of the City of Calgary's electric system for the first time since 1905. The Billing and Collection Division, also needing space, expanded into the space left vacant in the Utilities Building. This allowed room for the installation of new IBM data processing equipment and this made the Electric System the first commercial user in Calgary of this type of equipment for producing customer utility bills. The move from the Utilities Building on 6th Avenue W. to the new complex in Manchester took place in April, 1957.

From the beginning of the Depression in 1929, the Electric Light Department had done very little promotional work except for a brief period between 1937 and 1940 when the "Better Light, Better Sight" campaign was part of a national program to improve indoor lighting conditions. During World War II any advertising was related to support of the war effort. From the cessation of hostilities to 1950 the shortage of electrical generating capacity in the province was so acute that no one dreamed of promoting the use of electricity beyond the immediate needs of the consuming public. With the addition of the Spray Lakes hydro-electric plant in 1950, electricity was no longer in short supply and the Electric System commenced active promotion of the use of electricity by load-building programs. For the next twenty-five years electricity was marketed aggressively in ways hitherto unknown. The advent of television in 1954 provided the campaign with its most powerful tool. In Calgary it became an open battle between electricity and natural gas. It was in this emerging battle that Don Little found his permanent niche in the Electric System hierarchy.

Little had started as a clerk with the Electric Light Department in the days when R.A. Brown was general superintendent. He had many years of practical experience working under Brown and Mackay, and had always impressed his superiors with his quiet, commonsense approach to any task to which he was assigned. He had played a substantial role in the "Better Light, Better Sight" campaign, acquiring a broad knowledge of the principles and applications of good lighting design. Wilson quickly recognized the abilities of Don Little and without hesitation assigned him to the new role of supervising the promotional and sales programs of the Electric System. When he retired in 1970, Little was the Manager of Commercial Services for the Electric System and highly respected by his colleagues, both on local and national levels.

Administrative office block of Manchester Service Centre, 1957.
Source: Electric System Archives

The clothes dryer was the major new appliance to arrive on the postwar market and initially was available in the electric mode only. Gas-fired clothes dryers were introduced in the late 1950s and the promotional war began in earnest. The old standby electric range, which had been promoted successfully in the mid 1920s, was also targeted for saturation promotion in open competition with gas. The foundation upon which the promotion of these major appliances depended was a new house with sufficient electrical wiring capacity to accommodate the major appliances. To ensure that the new homes built in Calgary and throughout Alberta could accommodate these appliances the Electric Service League of Alberta was founded in 1954. It was a voluntary association of all Alberta electrical utilities, electrical manufacturers, distributors and contractors to promote an upgraded standard of wiring in all new homes, issuing "Red Seals" to all that qualified. Superintendent Wilson was the first president of the League and during the first year of its operation nearly 500 homes were certified. Later the League adopted the "Live Better Electrically" programme of the Edison Electric Institute, which remained the flagship of all North American electrical load-building promotional projects until the energy crunch of the mid 1970s. These programs were so successful that almost every new home built in Calgary after 1954 was wired to the standards recommended. Wilson, with his customary humour, coined his favourite quip of "Let's keep gas in the basement." Energy costs for both electricity and gas were at their lowest in the 1950s and 1960s and the frenzied activities of the competing utilities to out-promote each other often reached heights of rhetoric bordering on the ludicrous. However, they were successful and in keeping with the mood and optimism of the period. Between 1948 and 1961, during Wilson's superintendency, the average residential consumption of electricity increased from 1,000 to 3,300 kilowatt hours per annum, whereas the average monthly bill for that energy only increased from $3.00 to $5.04 because of the low-priced runoff block in the Combination Rate.[3]

Postwar annual capital budgets up to 1954 were in the order of $100,000 and could still be financed out of current revenue and accumulated reserves. By 1954 the financing of all the new capital extensions could not be generated out of revenue alone without increasing the price of electricity substantially and such an alternative was not yet considered acceptable. Therefore $500,000 of the 1954 capital budget was capitalized for the first time since 1922. This amount increased in 1955 to $1,000,000 with the difference between the two years made up by the capital costs associated with the new Manchester Service Centre. This sudden need to capitalize substantial portions of the annual capital budgets was a matter of great concern to A.F. (Alan) Womack. Womack joined the Electric System as the replacement for A.W. Northover, who retired early in 1958. He had immigrated to Canada from Britain where he had been a chartered accountant with a London-based consulting firm that had clientele involved in the public utility business, principally in Belgium. Womack was an investigative financial analyst who insisted on knowing what decisions and actions lay behind every figure which arrived at his accountants' desks and because of this he ruffled a few feathers. His major concern was for the financial health of the electric system and he prescribed the policies which he believed essential to maintain that condition. We shall return to this matter a little later.

Prior to the move to the new Manchester Service Centre from the 6th Avenue Utilities Building, Joe Rudolph had retired as assistant superintendent and Albert Bishop was appointed as his successor. In 1957 negotiations had commenced with Calgary Power for a new purchased power contract which, when coupled with the alternative consideration of a city-owned power plant, required that some technical personnel be separated from the normal duties of servicing the utility's own expanding economy to concentrate on these additional matters. George Cornish, who was spearheading the city's new comprehensive streetlighting program, was appointed as a technical assistant to Wilson and was joined by Womack. The efforts of this complementary pair were devoted to the new power contract and related issues. Both of these men advanced to top posts of the civic administration as city commissioners, with Cornish becoming chief commissioner in 1981. Coincidental with these events at the Electric System, a new head of the city administration had been appointed in Chief Commissioner Dudley Batchelor. Batchelor had started his civic career as a clerk in the Collections Division of the Electric Light Department in the late 1920s, transferring later to the city treasurer's department, where he worked his way up to the position of city treasurer. Over the years he had developed extraordinary abilities as a financial analyst and administrator. Batchelor took an immediate personal interest in the affairs of the growing Electric System. This interest was no doubt stimulated by copies of Womack's earlier financial analysis reports.

It was not long before Cornish and Womack found themselves in a direct working relationship with Batchelor. Young Cornish, in particular, was very impressed with the calibre of the chief commissioner and there is little doubt that he resolved to develop his own management style using Batchelor as an example. Cornish was also an early disciple of Womack's financial philosophy and he learned quickly and thoroughly. Womack firmly believed that financial planning for a publicly-owned utility should be no different than that used by privately-owned utilities. From the beginning he had been impressed with the quality of the planning and development of the utility: "These, coupled with long range and continuing studies of power supply and growth patterns, will stand the utility in good stead in the years to come."[4] He maintained that it was largely fortuitous that the Electric Light Department was debt free at the beginning of the 1950s. The main objective of a sound financial policy, Womack contended, must be to provide adequate cash resources for extensions while properly rewarding those who provided the capital funds. In a municipally-owned utility much of that capital was provided by the users who, in his mind, were no different from the investors of capital in a privately-owned utility. Womack's concerns with regard to the problems associated with a rapidly expanding and capital-intensive utility, were to play a substantial role when the policy was clearly defined in 1961.

Wilson was just the right man to lead the Electric System through its transition period from a prewar economy into a new period of growth and expansion. Why, at the peak of his latest career at the age of sixty-one, did he decide to resign? The question was often asked. The reasons were partially intrinsic to the nature of the man. His daughter, Mrs. Tom Pinder, said that her father rarely stayed at any of his posts for more than ten years because after that he would become restless and seek new challenges. In fact his period of leadership in the Electric System was the longest of his varied career. By 1959 Wilson shifted his interest to a new endeavour—a golf driving range. Like miniature golf during the Depression golf driving ranges became popular in the 1950s. Wilson, along with some other avid golfers, formed a syndicate to develop a golf driving range near the entrance to Calgary's new airport terminal and for one year before he decided to resign from the Electric System, the new enterprise was an unqualified success. However, the fad died as quickly as it had begun and by late 1961 Wilson found himself with an enterprise in which public interest had dwindled. During his last years in Calgary he personally managed and supervised the surviving interest in his golf driving range. Ed Walker and the author visited with him on many occasions, feeling a considerable sense of personal sorrow for the fortunes of a man who had contributed so much to our personal development.

There was, however, another reason for Wilson's early resignation. In 1959, a public hearing known as the Turcotte Inquiry followed from the notorious ''thirty-five bags of cement'' incident which caused the fall from grace of the popular Mayor Don Mackay. While the inquiry was unable to demonstrate conclusively any malfeasance on the part of most city officials, it did result in the election of Mayor Harry Hays, who ran on a civic reform platform. Chief Commissioner Batchelor's promotion to his powerful position was largely due to the Turcotte Inquiry, in which his impeccable public record had been applauded. These two crusaders set about to implement their reform policies without any delay and an early start was made when the mayor disbanded the Association of Civic Department Heads on the grounds that the Association had become nothing more than a bargaining agent for department head salaries. The mayor and commissioners summoned the department heads to a luncheon meeting to announce this decision and to further advise the heads of their expected response to the new reform administration. It was not an overly happy occasion and was made even less so when it was announced that each department head would be responsible for paying for his own lunch. Wilson, without any hesitation, let it be known that he objected to such treatment and that the commissioners should pay since they convened the special meeting. Wilson's objection was overruled and it was the beginning of a deteriorating relationship between him and Batchelor, climaxing in the latter's request for Wilson's resignation. Harvey Wilson resigned on 31 March 1960. After a few disappointing years with his golf driving range he fell

City of Calgary Electric System head offices, 1985.
Source: Bilodeau/Preston Commercial Photographers

on happier days with the sudden acquisition of real estate in Calgary's Elbow Park, which he managed until ill health overtook him during the mid 1960s. He died in Victoria in 1972. Wilson's open and relaxed management style, supported by an enormous amount of pertinent experience, was exactly the formula required for leading the Electric System into the postwar era. His legacy was a group of young upstarts who were eager and able to cope with any problem that the utility would encounter as it faced the most explosive expansion period in its entire history.

References

1. City of Calgary. Electric System Archives. Electric Light and Power Department. *Annual Report* 1949.

2. City of Calgary. Electric System Archives. Electric Light and Power Department. *Annual Report* 1951.

3. The residential rate in effect in 1961 was unchanged from its 1940 form when the city council ordered the "Combination Light and Heat Rate" to apply. It was a block rate. First 25 kilowatt hours 5 cents per kW.h Next 150 kilowatt hours 1.75 cents per kW.h All over 175 kilowatt hours 1.1 cents per kW.h The higher front-end blocks recovered the fixed costs of providing the service. The last or run-out block had no usage limitation and as more units of electricity were consumed, the average cost of each unit became less. Compare this rate with the comparable one in 1983: Basic charge $6.85 All kilowatt hours 4.85 cents per kW.h. It can be readily seen that with the unusually high costs now associated with electrical energy that promotion of load growth is neither applicable or desirable.

4. City of Calgary. Electric System Archives. Report dated 4 April 1960.

Chapter 10

BUILDING FOR THE FUTURE

Calgary's economic recovery from the Depression started with the end of the Second World War. Nobody at that time, relying on the experience of the inter-war period, would have been so bold as to forecast almost four decades of unrestrained economic growth. However, the imposition of province-wide petroleum and its related petro-chemical industry upon the traditional agricultural economy of Alberta had a tremendous stabilizing effect on the economies of both the province and the City of Calgary. Although the greater part of the oil and gas field activity was not centered in southern Alberta, Calgary, during the 1960s, emerged as the undisputed "head office" for all the major petroleum companies and those service industries which were needed to sustain the field operations. The effects were quickly felt by the city's electrical distribution system as the demand for electrical energy escalated at rates even higher than those experienced during the 1950s. The stage was being set for further major internal changes in the City of Calgary Electric System. Out of the ferment of the 1950s emerged a group of young, eager people who were more than capable of leading the Electric System into the 1960s and beyond. However, some dislocation and re-grouping of these people was needed in order to fit them into areas of responsibility where they could make their maximum contribution to the future.

When Albert Bishop was appointed assistant superintendent in 1956, the pattern being followed was simply an extension of an organizational practice which nearly all the various municipal departments had maintained from earliest times. It was a structure which, while perfectly adequate in the past, did not lend itself to the marshalling of all of the new talent that was available to cope successfully with the oncoming challenge of the second phase of postwar expansion. In 1958 Bishop was given the task of reorganizing the staff so they could become more responsive to the demands being placed upon them. His plan organized each clearly definable activity area into a group of autonomous mini-departments, each with a divisional head, who was responsible for the planning, engineering and field activity within each division. A technical administrative assistant to the superintendent was also appointed with responsibility for acting as a coordinating force between the various divisions. It was no surprise that this important staff position fell to Cornish who had already served as technical assistant to Superintendent Wilson.

When Wilson resigned as superintendent in March 1960, he was succeeded by Bishop but the position of assistant superintendent was eliminated in view of the recent departmental reorganization. Bishop was a very capable person, having graduated with distinction in 1949 from the University of Alberta. He was a very quiet, introverted person who was often misunderstood except by his closest associates. Cornish, on the other hand, was anything but introverted and as he observed his superior gradually becoming more and more isolated from his divisional heads, the opportunity to become a "shadow" superintendent quickly developed. In all fairness to Cornish, it was essential for someone to assume that role and apart from the general suspicion of the divisional heads regarding Cornish's motives, he never pursued his duties in a Machiavellian manner.

This situation persisted throughout 1960, coming to a head in early 1961 when Bishop had to defend the 1961 Electric System capital budget before the city council. Unfortunately he ran into a totally unexpected encounter with an alderman who took the opportunity to draw him into a debate regarding one of his constituents who had recently had his electricity supply terminated for reasons which the alderman held were very obscure. In 1957 all of the Electric System except the Billing and Collections Division had moved from the Utilities Building. If Bishop was isolated from his own immediate operational divisions then the isolation from the remote downtown operation was even greater. Many years later, Bishop remarked that of all the matters he could possibly have been unfamiliar with, the activities of the Billing and Collections Division were highest on the list. This became abundantly clear as he tried to defend the actions of the Electric System in the termination of the aggrieved customer's service. Chief Commissioner Batchelor was not impressed and decided that Bishop should be placed in the position where his superior talents could be used to better advantage.

It was in March 1961 that the author was summoned to the office of Mayor Harry Hays and informed that he had been selected to become the new Electric System superintendent with a new organizational plan in which all operational aspects of the utility would be combined into a single division with planning and engineering functions incorporated as a companion division, each with a divisional head. It was a simple but brilliant plan which eliminated most of the communication problems associated with the earlier organization while providing for the maximum use of available personnel resources. Bishop assumed the title of Chief Engineer and was made responsible for all the planning and engineering activities. With his concise and logical mind, Bishop's ability to come to grips with planning or engineering problems gained the support of his professional and technical staff. Edward Walker took charge of all field operations as operations superintendent. He had already distinguished himself as a proven administrator, and the choice was beyond dispute. The Electric System head would henceforth be called Manager, thus retiring the old title of Superintendent. In later years, as the Electric System grew, the title was changed to General Manager, with the divisional heads becoming managers. The smaller staff activity areas such as commercial services, accounting and electrical inspection came under the direct supervision of Cornish, who retained his position as technical assistant to the Manager, changing that title to Assistant Manager in 1963.

For the next decade this team guided the Electric System through a period of sustained expansion. Ironically, in the 1961 reorganization, the Billing and Collection Division become part of the Finance Department where it has remained until the present. In late 1961 Womack was moved to the Finance Department as the city's chief accounting officer. A year later he resigned to return to the private sector, only to return in 1972 as commissioner of finance, joining his earlier contemporary, Cornish, now commissioner of utilities and services.

Immediately prior to the 1961 reorganization, Cornish and Geoffry Daniel, the recently appointed supervisor of Safety and Training, became interested in the use of direct-hand contact working practices for use by linemen up to voltages of 15,000 (15kV). For the uninitiated, it should be noted that power linemen have traditionally worked on energized power lines up to 5 kV. While it may appear on the surface to be a risky business, sound working practices have made the work of a lineman extremely safe. This is achieved by using construction methods which provide adequate clearances within which linemen can work while wearing rubber gloves and using other protective devices as needed to cover live conductors. As long as the lineman remains clear of a second point of high voltage or ground contact, he remains in a safe working environment. However, for voltages above 5 kV, the traditional working practices were not dependable and these energized lines had to be manipulated with "hot line" tools which made even the simplest job very slow and cumbersome. In 1960 some American utilities, notably in Minnesota and Louisiana, had gone beyond the experimental stage in the development and application of fully insulated "man-lift" devices in which the lineman was lifted to the work level in an insulated basket rather than by climbing the pole. Since the man-lift device was fully insulated and the lineman was no longer attached to the pole, the possibility of a second point of contact was greatly reduced. In addition to rubber gloves the lineman wore rubber protective clothing, designed for higher voltages, over his upper arms and shoulders. By 1961, nearly all of Calgary's power extensions were being made at 15 kV and new work practices were urgently needed.

Cornish and Daniel went on a fact-finding tour of the northern and southern states and returned after a month with a favourable report recommending that the electric system adopt the new work methods immediately. Discussions were opened at once with the International Brotherhood of Electrical Workers, the union representing city electrical workers. Union approval to establish two experimental crews operating initially under strict supervision, was granted. Two 15 kV fully-articulated, insulated man-lift devices were ordered and placed in service in the spring of 1962. The new working practices were an instant success and the remainder of the utility fleet was converted as quickly as possible. The gain in productivity was so great that the capital cost of the new equipment would be recovered within one or two years. The Calgary experiment was the first serious one in Canada using direct-hand contact of energized conductors at 15 kV. This practice soon became standard throughout the North American industry.

A strike against the Calgary Transit System occurred in the early summer of 1961. The commissioner of public works, a recently-hired Scotsman by the name of John Steel, believed that the downtown traffic pattern could be substantially improved if traffic was reversed on the existing 6th Avenue and 9th Avenue one-way couplet. This required the relocation of much of the overhead trolley wiring and, not wishing to further aggravate the bargaining stance between the city and its bus drivers, the work forces of the Electric System were recruited to make the alterations which were accomplished in speedy fashion. Commissioner Steel was impressed by this demonstration of the capability of the Electric System crews and he proposed that Transit System crews, who would have done this work under normal conditions, be transferred to the Electric System with all future extensions and maintenance to the overhead trolley lines being carried out by the Electric System acting as a contractor. The transfer of personnel was made without incident but it rendered the position of the electrical engineer in the Transit System redundant. As a result, R.S. (Roy) Trussler, who during the 1950s had been responsible for the conversion of the transit system from the old street cars to modern trolley buses, became part of the Electric System. Trussler's happy combination of engineering and administrative ability became a great asset for the Electric System. He became chief engineer in 1971 and then assistant general manager, a position he held until he retired in 1977.

As the 1960s progressed, a major problem facing the electric system was that of financing, and new policies were required to deal with the financial pressures brought about by rapid expansion. Womack had devoted considerable time to this problem. In his 1959 annual report he had drawn attention to the fact that by the end of that year, the outstanding borrowings represented 44 percent of the net assets in use, compared with 39 percent in 1958 and only 9 percent in 1954, showing dramatically how the equity position of the utility was being eroded. The dust created by the March 1961 reorganization had barely settled when Chief Commissioner Batchelor moved to define a radical and unique financial policy for the Electric System. The essence of his policy was that the municipally-owned utility should finance itself much in the same manner as a privately-owned utility would. Batchelor was concerned that the provincial government would, at some future date, require all municipally-owned electrical utilities in Alberta to defend their rates before the Public Utilities Board and he wanted to be certain that when that time arrived the Electric System would be able to mount a successful defence. The policy differed from that of a privately owned utility only in respect to raising equity capital by the issue of shares or stock. The municipal utility was not required to pay federal income tax although the electric system did make substantial indirect contributions because it bought all of its wholesale power from a private company.[1] The financial policy decisions that were taken on 30 March 1961 formed the base by which Calgary's municipally-owned electrical utility became the most financially successful and profitable one in Canada. The policy, as recorded in the minutes of that meeting, is as follows:

> *Equity to Debenture Ratio*: the Utility's ratio of equity to debentures would in no case be allowed to fall below 50%, and that every effort should be made to improve this figure during slow growth periods.

> *Level of Rates Charged to Customers*: should be that necessary to provide a rate of return on net capital invested...equivalent to that allowed to be earned by an investor-owned utility.

> *Percentage Rate of Return*: the percentage rate of return to be applied to the net capital invested should be calculated to include as part of the return on investment an amount equivalent to the income taxes paid by an investor-owned utility.

> *Assessment of Return Obtained*: For purposes of assessing the amount of return obtained by the Utility, it was decided that:
> (1) Taxes on Revenue should be treated as an expense.
> (2) Depreciation should be calculated on the basis of a 30 year life for all capital assets.

> *Payments on Equity Investment*: the maximum payment to the City under normal circumstance will be 10% on equity investment in the utility.[2]

All of the criteria for the comprehensive financial policy advocated by Womack in his earlier financial treatises were at once realized and the results accruing from the newly established policy were phenomenal. The Electric System was now locked into a closed financial model where no part could be altered without a corresponding effect on the other parts. The cost-consciousness of the utility management team was raised several plateaus and the mentality of the management personnel began to parallel that which would be found in a privately-owned utility where financial responsibility to shareholders is a principle of major concern. No longer would the Electric System simply accumulate a surplus against its annual operation as a matter of some chance. The newly formulated financial policy immediately set the Electric System apart from other civic departments. It would be many years before the other capital-intensive utility operations of the city were gradually shifted to similar financial policies.

The effects of the financial policy were striking. For example, in 1961, administration costs accounted for 6.4 percent of total revenue, reducing to 4.6 percent in 1965, at which level it remained almost constant until the explosive growths of the late 1970s and early 1980s, when administration costs rose to just over 6 percent of gross revenue. Similarly, the costs relating to the operation and maintenance of the entire electrical network were 8.8 percent of total revenue in 1961, reducing to 6.0 percent in 1965, and reaching a low of 3.9 percent in 1981. The 1981 figure is undoubtedly lower than normal because of the extraordinary growth of the city during that period and this meant that most manpower resources were allocated to the capital budgets of the same period.

The expense item chargeable to the utility revenue called "Taxation of Revenue" had for its rationale the cost to the city of providing rights-of-way on streets to accommodate the electrical distribution facilities and it is also charged to the local natural gas utility. Alternatively the tax could be considered as the cost of a franchise granted by the city to the appropriate utility for the purpose of carrying on its business. It has always been a source of irritation to the city that the provincially-owned Alberta Government Telephones is exempt from such a tax by virtue of the provincial legislation under which it operates despite the fact that a significantly large part of the gross revenues of the telephone company are generated from the Calgary market. The "taxation of revenue" charge to the Electric System is, on occasion, viewed by civic administrators as a good place from which additional revenues can be derived in some years to subsidize the property tax rate. Consequently the rate of taxation has risen from its 1961 level of 5 percent to its present rate of 10 percent. The policy resulted in cash flows into the city coffers which were previously unknown, even without consideration of the fact that over 50 percent of the utility's annual asset requirement also came from that year's revenue.

Naturally, there was only one place where the money required to meet all of the requirements of the new financial policy could come from and that was the electricity consumer's pocketbook. At the same meeting at which the criteria for a new financial policy were established, it was recognized that a 4 percent increase in revenue was required to satisfy the demands of the policy.[3] This was accomplished by the elimination of the remaining 5 percent prompt-payment discount. Discriminatory higher rate schedules which had applied to all consumers outside the corporate limits of the city were eliminated. The argument for this move was that once the "rural" rate structures were brought into parity with those applicable within the city, electrical consumption would immediately increase and, in fact, this actually occurred as rural customers took advantage of the lowered rates. These minor adjustments to the rates prevailing prior to 1961 were quite adequate to maintain the new financial policy and while long-range studies were undertaken immediately to redesign all of the old rate structures, no further upward adjustments were required until 1968.

Another important policy decision was taken at the eventful meeting of 30 March 1961. This eliminated customer deposits with an undertaking to refund all old customer deposits with accrued interest. Over the entire history of the Electric Light Department, a customer deposit taken with all new customer service applications was standard policy. The reason for the policy was to ensure that at least one month's additional revenue beyond the time that a customer might default in the payment of his monthly bill would be available. However, the administration costs of maintaining these customer deposit accounts and records began to grow out of proportion to the deposit amount. These deposits were all refunded and, surprisingly, the ratio of bad debts to total revenue did not change thus confirming what most of us already knew: most people are basically honest.

It will be remembered that a 66,000 volt (66 kV) "ring" main system had been built around the perimeter of the city between 1953 and 1956. By 1961 Chief Engineer Bishop was forecasting that the usefulness of this "ring" was limited to a further fifteen years by which time it would be seriously overloaded. In 1960, Bishop had produced a planning report recommending a 66 kV ring located five miles outside the existing one.[4] In his 1962 report, however, Bishop abandoned this plan in favour of a 138,000 volt (138 kV) ring system.[5] It was becoming obvious that with the growth of the city and the 10 percent annual electrical growth pattern, the 66 kV system had no future role to play.

Bishop's 1962 planning report formed the base from which all future electricity sub-transmission systems would develop in Calgary. He considered going as high as 240 kV for this purpose but finally conceded that "it (138 kV) is the highest voltage presently practical for single-pole structures and hence suitable for construction on streets and lanes."[6] Bishop's observations were shrewdly appropriate and saved enormous amounts of money which otherwise would have been required to acquire the necessary rights-of-way. Most of the area projected for city expansion in 1962 was still farmland and the choice of 138 kV meant that as subdivision development proceeded, all that was necessary was that suitable alignment of some major roadways be maintained. As extensions of 138 kV into the core of the city were needed, it was achieved by underground pipetype or gas-filled 138 kV cable systems. In fact the downtown commercial core expanded so much in the 1970s that the existing electrical supply facilities required major extensions. Since land assembly for enlarging by conventional means was so costly, it was decided to use a new technology that had developed in the late 1960s— gas-insulated high voltage switchgear.

An order was placed with a West German manufacturer and the gear was installed in 1976, using the available space while increasing the available capacity threefold. It was a "first" for Western Canada and broke new ground for the electrical supplies in concentrated high density areas. Such far-reaching planning also accommodated the major bulk electricity supply points which were established by Calgary Power (TransAlta Utilities) outside of the city distribution area on the west and east sides. The plan and its implementation were as important for the future development of the city as had been the 1911 decision to surround the city by a 12 kV "ring" main.

Throughout the 1960s and 1970s the city expanded as new subdivisions, both residential and industrial, were added. The city developed very few of these subdivisions, having adopted a comprehensive policy in the early 1960s of having this work done by private land developers. The cost of the various utility installations was, for the large part, borne by those developers and recovered in the selling price of the land parcels. Underground electrical distribution was demanded in almost all land development projects after the mid 1960s since the elimination of poles and overhead wiring was deemed to be a strong selling point. Since residential underground electrical distribution systems initially cost about three times more than an equivalent overhead wiring system, it became a standard policy for the developer to pay the additional costs, or two-thirds of the total cost, with the city retaining full title to the asset and providing for the normal maintenance costs over the life of the asset. As fortune would have it, the costs of installing underground wiring fell dramatically as the utility geared itself to nearly total underground installations. Winter frost conditions which, in the past, would have shut down all such operations were overcome by the development of a ground-thawing system that utilized long strips of electric heating elements covered by non-combustible insulation. Up to a thousand feet of these electric elements could be installed and energized using a temporary overhead line to bring power to the site. After three days the ground would be frost-free to a depth of at least four feet and mechanical high-speed trenchers would quickly open up the common trench for the installation of electrical distribution, street lighting, telephone and television cables. The incremental winter costs incurred were of little significance to the developer who could now market his serviced land without regard to the long prairie winter.

By the early 1970s underground residential distribution (URD) systems were accounting for almost all of Calgary's installations and the methods developed and used by the Electric System became models for the industry. It was not uncommon in any year to service over 6,000 residential building sites with underground wiring as well as additional sites for multiple housing and commercial developments. These were unprecedented "boom" years and the work could never have been completed without highly standardized engineering procedures and efficient work methods in the field.

Growth rates in electricity usage continued unabated during the 1960s. Since the demand component of the purchased power rate was considerably more expensive than the energy cost, every effort was expended to encourage the building of "off-peak" electrical loads and to offer incentives to customers to reduce their electrical demands during the winter peak demand period. The success of this effort is proven by the fact that during the 1960s the average demand growth was 8 percent per annum while energy sales increased at almost 12 percent per annum. The domestic combination rate which had remained unchanged since 1940 was adjusted upwards for the first time in 1961 so that the average consumer paid $5.38 for his monthly usage of 273 kilowatt-hours of electrical energy instead of $4.96. The adjusted rate continued unchanged until 1972.

In 1961, when the new financial policy was inaugurated, it was also recognized that the existing commercial and industrial rates which had remained unchanged since the 1920s required radical restructuring to recognize both the new electricity usage patterns and the fact that electricity was being purchased on a demand-energy formula rather than by the straight energy charge in use prior to 1959. It required seven years of intensive study and analysis to finally produce an entirely new set of commercial and industrial electricity rates which were designed to allow any commercial user to make a smooth transition to an industrial rate as soon as his usage was sufficient to qualify.

In 1968 the Province of Alberta proposed legislation which would have incorporated the Alberta Power Commission and the Public Utilities Board into a single regulatory body. The Power Commission Act had been in existence for many years and while its main purpose over those years had been to regulate the development of the private utilities in Alberta, it also gave the province the right to engage in the electrical utility business, a right which was never exercised. The Public Utilities Board was responsible for regulating the financial rates of return which private utilities were permitted to earn from their operations. Since the proposed legislation did not appear to abrogate the right of the new authority to engage in the operation of an electrical utility, it was vehemently opposed by every electrical utility in Alberta, whether privately or publicly owned. The result of this opposition was a public hearing by a special advisory committee of the provincial government, chaired by Dr. Gordon Burton, a highly regarded agricultural economist from Claresholm.

Briefs were submitted by every electrical utility in Alberta, including Calgary, and the terms of reference set for the Advisory Committee were broad enough to allow each utility to speak to any matter in which it felt it had either a vested interest or a grievance with either the province and its proposed legislation or another operating utility. The hearing was a landmark event for the electrical utility industry in Alberta and ran for almost an entire year before all the evidence and cross-examination was completed. The cities of Calgary and Edmonton were the principle municipal intervenors, and both stressed the absolute right of municipalities to operate, with complete autonomy, any utility operation permitted under legislation governing municipalities. Edmonton further insisted upon the right to expand its electrical utility outside of its corporate limits in order to include the lucrative petro-chemical industries which had developed along its eastern border where electrical service was provided by Calgary Power. Calgary believed that any such sweeping annexation would raise the cost of power to the remaining customer groups of Calgary Power because they would be required to bear the extra cost of the investment made by the company to service the east Edmonton industrial complex. The matter became a contentious issue between the two cities and remnants of that issue remain to the present.

The final report of the Burton Commission was a massive document summed up in sixteen recommendations. The most important recommendation for Calgary and the other municipally-owned utilities in Alberta was that: "The municipalities should enjoy the exclusive right to generate, distribute and price power within their corporate limits." The Commission recommended that Edmonton should be permitted to apply to the Power Commission to expand its distribution area outside of its corporate city limits, but excluding the "defined industrial area." For Calgary Power Limited, it recommended that the rates it charged be "determined in the same manner as is now prescribed in the Public Utilities Board Act for other utilities." Before 1972 Calgary Power was not under the jurisdiction of the Public Utilities Board because of its federal charter. Surprisingly, the Commission did recommend the amalgamation of the Public Utilities Board and the Power Commission..."since there appear to be advantages to integrating the accounting and economic aspects of regulation on the one hand with the physical aspects on the other."

Although the proposed provincial government legislation which precipitated the inquiry received the approval of the Burton Commission, the government chose to ignore the recommendation. Instead it expanded the jurisdiction of the Oil and Gas Conservation Board to include all energy sources under a new agency called the Energy Resources Conservation Board (ERCB). One branch of that newly expanded board became responsible for the province-wide regulation of all electrical utility developments. The Public Utilities Board was left intact and Calgary Power placed itself under the jurisdiction of that board for rate regulation.

Prior to the publication of the final report of the Burton Commission the generating utilities in the province had formed a coordinating council to plan the orderly addition of new generating capacity and the operation of existing facilities to optimize load-sharing. In effect they voluntarily decided to operate their individual generating and transmission systems as if they were a single system serving all of the province. This coordinating council was soon expanded to include Calgary and other interested governmental agencies, and became the Electric Utility Planning Council (EUPC). Membership in the council is governed by a memorandum of agreement to which Alberta Power, TransAlta Utilities Corporation, the cities of Calgary, Edmonton, Lethbridge, Medicine Hat, and Red Deer are signatories and voting members. Non-voting advisory and observing members come from various provincial government agencies such as the Energy Resources Conservation Board, the Public Utilities Board, and the Alberta

Electric Energy Marketing Agency. Since 1971 the EUPC has determined all the planning of electrical generating and transmission facilities in Alberta and has allocated these extensions between the various voting members in an orderly fashion. All decisions made by the council are arbitrated before the Energy Resources Conservation Board at public hearings after which the ERCB may grant permissive orders to proceed with the projects. The arrangement has worked exceptionally well and has given non-generating electrical utilities, such as the City of Calgary Electric System, a voice in planning the future power developments in Alberta.

In December 1969 Donald Little retired from his position as commercial services manager. His forty-two years of continuous service has rarely been equaled and his retirement marked the last significant link with the predepression years of the 1930s. Little had always been an advocate for the customers of the Electric System and in a very real sense had become their unofficial ombudsman. His retirement was followed in 1974 by that of Chief Engineer Bishop, who had joined the Electric Light Department in 1935. Bishop's legacy to the Electric System was his acute planning concepts which moulded the electrical network into the new forms that could accommodate the electrical demands of a city which grew from a population of 100,000 in 1948 to over 600,000 three decades later. Bishop was also a conservationist and carefully preserved those facilities inherited from the earlier Brown/Mackay period wherever they could be refurbished to continue operating efficiently. Consequently, despite the enormous expansion of the distribution network from 1950 onward, there still remain small areas in Calgary serviced from remnants of the original 12 kV "ring main" system of 1911. The 1961 management team of Bishop, Walker and Hawkins was finally dismantled in 1972 when Walker was chosen director of the new civic Mechanical Services Department. Walker was succeeded by K. W. (Ken) Simpson who had been so well-groomed for the position that the transition was barely noticeable.

By the 1970s the two major divisions of the Electric System, engineering and operations, were no longer capable of servicing the demands of both the public and the regulatory bodies. Energy was no longer the cheap commodity that it had been. Large industrial and commercial enterprises were becoming commonplace and had their own staff specialists devoted entirely to controlling operating and energy costs. The utility was forced to respond in kind with its own staff of experts who could consult with and advise customers on the best use of their energy dollars. The enlarged Commercial Services Division, renamed Customer Services, became a corporate division in its own right. The energy crisis of 1972 further enhanced the importance of this division and now, rather than encouraging the unrestricted use of electrical energy as had been policy during the 1950s and 1960s, the new thrust was to foster the wise and efficient use of energy in every area from the housewife's kitchen to massive petro-chemical plants.

Forecasting and planning for the financing of the Electric System became a highly technical activity during the 1960s and 1970s. The addition of new regulatory authorities created demands hitherto unknown and the relatively small pre 1960 accounting function was enlarged into the Financial and Corporate Planning Division under which all matters relating to accounting, finance, rates and Public Utility Board hearings were amalgamated. These staff experts were further utilized by the city commissioners in conjunction with the Gas and Power Committee on matters related to the regulation of the natural gas and telephone utilities operating within Calgary when these companies made their regular applications to the Public Utilities Board for rate increases.

For a quarter century the growth of the Electric System had continued at a relentless pace. In 1950 the peak electrical demand had been 46,500 kilowatts with annual energy sales of 190 million kilowatt-hours. In 1977, when the author retired, the electrical demand had reached 653,000 kilowatts with annual energy sales of almost 3,500 million kilowatt-hours, an increase of fourteen and eighteen times on demand and energy respectively. But somehow, lurking behind this unabated growth, there was always the latent fear that it could not possibly last forever. The only question was whether the downturn would be a simple regression to a lower level of growth, or precipitous as it had been after the First World War and during the Great Depression. The imposition of Public Utility Board regulation on Calgary Power Limited in 1972, and in each subsequent year, had the immediate effect of lowering growth rates of energy consumption from an average of 11 percent to 7 percent throughout most of the remaining years of the 1970s, thanks to higher prices. From 1979 to 1981 Calgary surged forward in what can only be described as a frenzy of activity, with electrical demands reaching nearly 900,000 kilowatts and 5,000 million kilowatt-hours on energy sales. The prospect of petroleum megaproject developments in the Alberta oil sands and the frontier Arctic region inspired a frenzy as Calgary's downtown skyline mushroomed almost overnight with more skyscrapers to provide the commercial office space for the anticipated development. Unfortunately, the introduction of the National Energy Program in 1981 deflated all of these grandiose plans and the phenomenon ended as quickly as it began with the growth rate of the electric system dropping precipitously to 1 percent on both electrical demand and energy.

Calgary has always had the reputation of being a ''boom or bust'' city, but that observation is more correctly applied to the whole of the Canadian western prairies. If we can accept this cyclic view of western Canadian history as axiomatic, then Calgary will again overcome the economic doldrum. However, the world is a much smaller place than it was in the 1930s and Calgary's recovery is likely to hold many surprises as it becomes increasingly a piece of the international recovery puzzle. We can only hope for the best. The future of Calgary's electrical utility is unclear at the present time but whatever form it takes will be inexorably bound up in its relationship with TransAlta Utilities Corporation as it has been for the past seventy-five years. Certainly, Calgary has lost all of its pre 1970 negotiating advantage with TransAlta by virtue of the regulatory process begun in 1972. If that were not enough the more recent provincial Electric Energy Marketing Agency has succeeded in destroying any remnants of these old advantages by making the citizens and industries of Calgary subsidize the electricity costs of more remote user areas.

The past one hundred years of electrical power supply in Calgary has been a kaleidoscope of constantly changing political, economic and social factors which have run the entire gamut of corporate possibilities. But with these factors being the volatile ingredients that they are we can be certain that the story is still unfinished.

References

1. The federal income tax "problem" leading to the 1966 decision to refund 95 percent of the tax was discussed in Chapter 7.

2. City of Calgary. Electric System Archives. Minutes of meeting dated 30 March 1961 between City Commissioners and Electric System management.

3. Ibid.

4. City of Calgary. Electric System Archives. "Report on System Planning," February 1962.

5. City of Calgary. Electric System Archives. "Planning Report," February 1962.

6. Ibid.

INDEX